HAWAIIAN REBIRTH

HAWAIIAN REBIRTH

QUESTIONS, STORIES AND STRATEGIES TO GUIDE YOU TO YOUR LIFE'S PURPOSE

BY YVES NAGER

ISBN: 978-1-946697-93-6

Published by:
Lifestyle Entrepreneurs Press
Las Vegas, NV

If you are interested in publishing through Lifestyle Entrepreneurs Press, write to: *Publishing@LifestyleEntrepreneursPress.com*

To learn more about our publications or about foreign rights acquisitions of our catalogue books, please visit: *www.LifestyleEntrepreneursPress.com*

Printed in the USA

DISCLAIMER: The author of this book does not dispense medical advice or prescribe the use of any technique as a form of treatment for physical, emotional, or medical problems. The intent of the author is only to offer information of a general nature to help you in your quest for emotional and spiritual well-being. In the event you use any of the information in this book, which is your constitutional right, the author and the publisher assume no responsibility for your actions. Thank you.

Endorsements for *Hawaiian Rebirth*

Yves Nager is a wisdom teacher, navigator, and guide for meaning and purpose. Here he provides tools, stories, and maps for the most important journey of your life...home to the truth of who you really are and why you are here. This exquisite book, *Hawaiian Rebirth,* will inspire and awaken your heart and soul while showing you how to fulfill your heart's desires.

—Marcia Wieder, CEO, Dream University and Bestselling Author

Yves Nager, a truly passionate adventurer of life and a humble mystic, shows brilliantly in his new book, *Hawaiian Rebirth*, how following your heart and continuously choosing in favor of your passions leads you to a life filled with wonder, a sense of destiny, and unlimited possibilities of living your greatness.

—Janet Bray Attwood, NY Times Bestselling Author of *The Passion Test* and *Your Hidden Riches*

In this book, Yves Nager has expanded the principles of the Passion Test to help you clarify your passions and deepen your understanding of the reason you were born. *Hawaiian Rebirth* will take you on a journey that will serve as a map to use as you fulfill your unique contribution to the unfoldment of yourself to itself.

—Chris Attwood, President at the Beyul Club, Bestselling Author of *The Passion Test* and *Your Hidden Riches*

I have known Yves Nager for many years and joined with him and his wife, Eunjung, in some of their journeys of life. I am touched by their sincerity and their passion, their dedication to service, and their love for this Earth. I am touched by their fearlessness, their ability to move as the wind moves them, and to become the wind itself. Thank you, Yves, for demonstrating the 'passion way,' and for holding your candle through all the ups and downs of life, so that each of us might learn to trust the One Light that has always already been shining so brightly, even through the darkest of nights.

—Kiara Windrider, International Spiritual Teacher and
Author of Several Books, including
Gaia Luminous, Homo Luminous, and *Ilahinoor*

I have known Yves Nager for many years. Yves is one of those rare individuals who has the know-how to dive deep into his soul and create healing for himself and those around him. His journeys across the globe give him keen insight into human behavior, which adds to the depth of his storytelling. He makes a difference in this world because he is willing to do the hard work of personal transformation and he wants to share his knowledge. Yves' book, *Hawaiian Rebirth*, inspired me to examine my own journey and created many opportunities for me to look within.

—Shajen Joy Aziz, creator of *Discover the Gift*,
Award-Winning International Bestselling
Author, Educator, Filmmaker, and Entrepreneur

You will find Yves Nager's new book, *Hawaiian Rebirth*, intriguing and inspiring, yet practical. Yves offers guidance to what he calls "the most meaningful adventure of your life—the discovery of your gifts and passions." He is clearly here to be of service and he shares what he has learned through his own experiences and transformations. He is passionate in his desire to help you discover how to live your highest destiny. He offers a cornucopia of knowledge and wisdom and comes from the heart. I hope you will say yes!

—Sharlyn Hidalgo, Author of *Nazmy: Love is My Religion*

Each of us have four life realms we must attend to—mental, emotional, physical, and spiritual. Give too much attention to one and offer too little to one or more of the remaining realms and your life will be out of balance. All four realms are intimately linked and when one of them is lacking, all of them will suffer and the individual will suffer.

Far too many people simply exist, living out pointless, meaningless lives without passion or purpose, adrift and directionless from an unbalanced approach to living. I believe the realm most often ignored and responsible for those bereft of purpose is their spiritual realm.

If you believe your spiritual realm may be suffering and causing you to feel a lack of a sense of purpose, Yves Nager's new book, *Hawaiian Rebirth,* will offer you a reliable roadmap for discovering your true and intended purpose. Increasing self-awareness, goal-setting, what it means to be happy, and achieving your dreams are just some of the topics covered in this actionable step-packed book. If you are ready to get to work on changing your life for the better, releasing an unbridled passion for living by discovering your true life's purpose, and having a more meaningful and balanced existence, then I highly recommend this book.

Get it, read it, believe it, follow it, and live like you've never lived before.

—Dr. Clark Gaither, Medical Doctor, Bestselling
Author of *Reignite* and *Powerful Words*

The inspiring, intriguing stories from Yves Nager's mystical, worldwide adventures will open your heart wide and expand your visions. If you are looking to bring more passion, purpose, and meaning into your life, then *Hawaiian Rebirth* offers you an insightful array of tools and life strategies that will guide you toward achieving your most cherished dreams and aspirations.

—Geoff Affleck, Bestselling
Author of *Shine Your Light* and *Enlightened Bestseller*

I met Yves Nager through the Passion Test and found him and his work genuine, refreshing, and profound. His new book, *Hawaiian Rebirth*, is so full of nuggets of wisdom and inspiring, intriguing stories that you cannot but feel transformed by just reading it. Of course, if you actually put into practice the insightful steps and strategies Yves has mapped out in the book, your life will definitely turn around for the better, with you following your heart and living your highest purpose.

—Terry L. Sidford, Author of *One Hundred Hearts*, TEDx Speaker, Passion Test Facilitator, and Professional Coach

Yves Nager's book *Hawaiian Rebirth* is one of the most in-depth and detailed guides I've read on the transformational process involved with uncovering and pursuing one's life purpose. Yves' simple, straightforward, and passionate demeanor comes forth in this book which elaborates on some of the more challenging topics in transformational consciousness. You'll come away from reading *Hawaiian Rebirth* with the belief that transforming your life is a challenge worth taking on and that it is a healing journey you must embark upon immediately with his guidebook in your hands.

—Patrick Wyzorski, Principal WyzGuy Consulting

Dedicated to my parents, René and Suzanne Nager and my brother, Alain. I am blessed that I grew up with you as my family in Switzerland. Without you, I would not have become the man I am today.

And to my beloved Eunjung, thank you for being my magical co-navigator on this amazing journey of our lives. Thank you for your love, inspiration and encouragement and for sharing our purpose in this world.

I am forever grateful and I love you all.

"The meaning of life is to find your gift. The purpose of life is to give it away."

—Pablo Picasso

TABLE OF CONTENTS

HAWAIIAN
REBIRTH

ILLUSTRATIONS LIST

FOREWORD

By Chris Attwood

The illusion we call life is by its nature dual. There appear to be differences when in fact these differences are the interwoven threads of one fabric. However, it's in the appearance of differences that the play of life or *Veda Lila* unfolds, sequentially and in perfect order.

What upholds the flow of life in wholeness is dharma. Dharma is built into every person's body, mind, emotions and spirit. Everyone is born for a special and unique purpose only they can fulfill. And the common purpose we all share is to serve each other. When someone is connected to dharma, then their life feels rich and full. Nothing is missing, nothing needs to be added or taken away. Life feels meaningful, purposeful.

In these times, many people appear to struggle in their life. They struggle because they are disconnected from dharma, that path of action which will allow them to fulfill their unique and special role in the unfoldment of knowledge (for what we call life is actually the sequential unfoldment of consciousness coming to know itself).

As long as a person is disconnected from dharma, they are unhappy, they suffer, and they become miserable. We see this in every country in the world today. The statistics tell us that more than seventy percent of the population is unhappy with their work and their lives.

In the Bhagavad Gita, the sacred Vedic literature of India, Lord Krishna (the living expression of pure consciousness) says: "Whenever dharma declines and the purpose of life is forgotten, I manifest myself on earth. I am born in every age to protect the good, to destroy evil, and to reestablish dharma."

My personal feeling is that the Lord does not simply manifest in human form, but also in the form of tools like The Passion Test (which I developed with Janet Bray Atwood), to reestablish dharma.

For those who are not lucky enough to be spontaneously connected to dharma, the path to meaning in their life is through their passions. It's not an accident that a person loves the things they love or that they care about the things they care about. Even when one is immersed in the Self, neither repelled by nor attracted to one thing or another, the path of an individual life takes that person in some directions rather than in others.

The path to wholeness is through the vehicle we call love. Love connects. Love draws what appears to be separate together. When we fall in love with every aspect of life then life becomes one magical, connected whole.

Passion is one aspect of this love. When someone makes a list of the things they love most about their life, they are expressing elements of their unique nature, of their dharma, their purpose for being alive. Because our brains are designed to only be able to hold five to seven things at one time, it's almost impossible to give attention to twenty or thirty or more passions, or loves, at once.

So, the Passion Test provides a simple method to take this expression of one's dharma in the list of passions, and identifies which of these are the five that have greatest meaning, that are dearest. This doesn't mean everything else is not meaningful. The list of five passions that comes out of the Passion Test process is simply an indicator, right now (not forever), of the things that will bring the most fulfillment in life and lead one on to fulfill one's purpose, or dharma.

This list of five passions becomes a decision-making tool. As Janet and I say in *The Passion Test* book, "Whenever you're faced with a choice, a decision, or an opportunity, choose in favor of your passions." While this is a simple and perhaps obvious truth, so many people today do what they think they "should" do that this simple instruction changes their whole experience of life.

And our experience from sharing the Passion Test all over the world is that as people consistently choose in favor of their passions, they discover that their life begins to feel more and more meaningful. Of course, not everyone needs the Passion Test. Some people spontaneously follow their passions. Yet, most people in the world today are not in that boat.

In this book, Yves Nager has expanded the principles of the Passion Test to help you clarify your passions and deepen your understanding of the reason you were born. *Hawaiian Rebirth* will take you on a journey that will serve as a map to use as you fulfill your unique contribution to the unfoldment of yourself to itself.

AUTHOR NOTE:

Chris Attwood is co-author of the New York Times bestseller *The Passion Test – The Effortless Path to Discovering Your Life Purpose* and *Your Hidden Riches – Unleashing the Power of Rituals to Create a Life of Meaning and Purpose.*

Chris is an expert in the field of human consciousness and is also deeply grounded in the practical world of business. Chris is the founder and CEO of the Beyul Club, a company dedicated to personal and global transformation. *www.BeyulClub.com* I am honored and grateful that I was personally trained by Chris as I find his work truly inspiring and regard him as a great role model who is living his purpose to the fullest.

PREFACE

> *"The reason people find it so hard to be happy is that they always see the past better than it was, the present worse than it is, and the future less resolved than it will be."*
>
> —Marcel Pagnol

As long as I can remember, I've loved expressing myself through writing. Whenever I write, I feel happy, present and centered.

I've often had difficulty finding the appropriate words to describe how I feel. During my teenage years, I discovered that writing was a helpful way to reveal what I felt deep inside. It didn't matter if I was just journaling for myself, or writing an essay at school. When I reread my journals and essays some years later, it always helped me understand more about myself and others.

However, twenty years later, I had the courage, self-confidence and commitment to start publishing my writing for others. I started by creating content for my website and then began to write articles on various topics, sharing my insights and experiences through blogs, newsletters and social media. A door opened for me when I was asked to contribute my writing to two books, one a collection of chapters about following your passions and another focused on global awakening.

In the compilation book *Inspired by the Passion Test: The #1 Tool for Discovering Your Passion and Purpose,* I relate my initial awakening experience while in Hawaii. I also share ten practical steps to help you embark on your own journey of healing and transformation. I am one of sixteen passionate storytellers in the book, including *New York Times* bestselling authors Janet Bray Attwood and Geoff Affleck.

In the book *Ilahinoor - Awakening the Divine Human*, written by my friend Kiara Windrider, I contribute an extensive testimonial. It's an account of my transformative experiences across the globe teaching and working with Ilahinoor, a gift to help humanity experience multi-dimensional consciousness. You'll find a section called "Exploring the World with Ilahinoor" later in this book.

You hold in your hands my latest writing endeavor. If someone had told me five years ago that my name would be displayed in three books—and that they'd all be published within only two years—I'd have treated their words as fantasy.

However, as you've likely experienced on your own journey, life sometimes takes twists and turns, leading us to places beyond our wildest dreams in completely unexpected ways. *Hawaiian Rebirth*: *Questions, Stories and Strategies to Guide You to Your Life's Purpose* is the outcome of opening myself to something bigger and allowing myself to transcend the person I once believed I was.

I grew up in Switzerland, in a town called Spiez, located next to the beautiful Lake Thun and surrounded by forests and mountains. When I went to Hawaii for the first time in 2008 to improve my English skills, writing a book in English was far beyond my abilities—entirely out of reach. During that time, I studied for three months at Global Village Hawaii, an international language school in Honolulu. Somehow, it's still a miracle for me that I'm now allowing myself to express my gifts in this way. I'm deeply grateful because for many years I perceived my life's journey as being mostly challenging. When I was younger, I began to feel a mounting level of crisis and desperation. This feeling climaxed when a series of deaths occurred in my family in 2005. Within seven months, I lost my father and two grandparents and nearly lost my brother. Since then, my life has never been the same.

At first, I immersed myself in work by day during the week and partied by night on the weekends, all in a futile attempt to free myself from the uncomfortable feelings of loss and pain. Out of my element and disconnected from my purpose, in the following years, my inner life became increasingly chaotic. I kept searching for meaning, even as my personal relationships and career succumbed to more chaos and confusion. I was finally gripped by massive depression, to the point where I considered ending my life.

Around Christmas of 2007, I started to pray desperately for help and guidance, something I hadn't done in years. Only ten weeks later, through the grace of divine guidance and the loving support of my mother, I found myself in Hawaii, on the island of Oahu.

Within two weeks of arriving on Oahu in mid-March 2008, I had my first huge spiritual awakening. It happened through a mystical healing that turned my life around in an incredible way. I also started reading many self-help books, applying to the best of my ability the techniques I'd learned. Some of the tools and steps I encountered yielded fast and fantastic results, others prompted new questions.

Wikipedia defines a self-help book as a book written with the intention of instructing its readers about solving personal problems. Did you know that the history of self-help books goes as far back as the year 1859, to the bestseller *Self-Help* by Samuel Smiles, a Scottish author and government reformer?

And, did you know that now, almost 160 years later, there are more than a half-million products available on Amazon when you search for "self-help?" It's evidence that countless people are out there, seeking a deeper understanding and a more fulfilling life.

Over the past decade, I've read many self-help books, watched many transformational and spiritual movies and videos and attended numerous courses and workshops. Between 2008 and 2010, I literally became a "transformational workshop junkie."

All these authors and workshop leaders shine light on how we can improve our lives. Although each takes a slightly different approach, with his or her unique point of view based on their rich life experiences, I have discovered that the advice we receive from these authors is not as diverse as I had initially believed. There are certain common threads in self-help books. In essence, most self-help books assert that you'll have lasting positive changes in your life when you let go of old patterns and behaviors and continually replace them with positive habits.

Positive change happens when you let go of old patterns and behaviors and replace them with positive habits.

Author Simon Sinek states this principle wonderfully: "Optimists have a habit of seeing positive. Pessimists have a habit of seeing negative. All that is required to change a habit is practice."

Here are ten of my favorite books in the self-help and transformation category that have positively influenced and inspired me, helping me to improve my life over the past decade. Please refer to my Recommended Reading List at the end of the book for more information on these wonderful books:

- *Life's Golden Ticket: A Story About Second Chances* (Brendon Burchard)
- *Loving What Is: Four Questions That Can Change Your Life* (Byron Katie)
- *Supreme Influence: Change Your Life with the Power of the Language You Use* (Niurka)
- *The Five Love Languages: How to Express Heartfelt Commitment to Your Mate* (Gary Chapman)
- *The Four Agreements: A Practical Guide to Personal Freedom* (Don Miguel Ruiz)
- *The Four Desires: Creating a Life of Purpose, Happiness, Prosperity, and Freedom* (Rod Stryker)
- *The Grace Factor: Opening the Door to Infinite Love* (Alan Cohen)
- *The Power of Now: A Guide to Spiritual Enlightenment* (Eckhart Tolle)
- *Your Hidden Riches: Unleashing the Power of Ritual to Create a Life of Meaning and Purpose* (Janet Bray Attwood, Chris Attwood with Sylva Dvorak)
- *Zero Limits: The Secret Hawaiian System for Wealth, Health, Peace, and More* (Joe Vitale)

Why did these books positively impact my life? It was because the authors all had established some sort of relationship with me. I found each book's content easy to apply straightaway and, more importantly, I was committed to continue working with what I'd learned. On the other hand, I confess I also experienced times when I put other self-help books I read down and gave up altogether. What was the difference between the books I stuck with and the books I gave up on? The difference was that the books that taught me valuable lessons were written with clarity and focus, they were readable, and they provided clear guidance and useful information. In short, they mapped out a path for the reader to follow.

Since my early teenage years, I've been passionate about creating orienteering maps. When I work on such a project, the first step is to map what I believe will be useful to people trying to find their way through the same terrain in the future. For me as a mapper, out in the terrain, the main task is determining which features to put on the map and how to represent them.

The second task is creating a good design to enhance the readability of the map. I probably spend more time devising a clean and attractive design and layout than many other mappers do, because I always appreciate a readable map. It helps others trust my maps more. *Generalization* is the keyword here, meaning that I must focus on selection, simplification, displacement and exaggeration. You'll find a section called "Mapping Your Inner Landscape" later in this book.

This book was created in a similar fashion to how I create maps. I put together many questions, tools and exercises that will be helpful to you in finding your life's purpose. Then, I summarized them and compiled them into the 7 Questions, 12 Steps and 12 Stories you're about to engage with.

Of course, this book is not a direct representation of what your life's journey is all about—just as an orienteering map is not the territory itself. But it will serve as a guide to help you understand the territory you're in and how to move through it to enrich your life through self-development, self-empowerment and determination.

Since my wife Eunjung and I got together in 2011, we've been teaching and sharing a variety of workshops covering topics such as energy work and self-development and we've been working at sacred sites with groups. It's been essential for us to structure the contents of our teachings clearly and in a manner that's easy to understand. We've also found that by presenting the information we share interactively, and by including inspiring personal stories, we can maximize the benefits to our participants.

One of the challenges I face as a writer is that I don't get feedback right away from readers. Having spent the past decade working with many people from various countries and cultural backgrounds, all I can try to do is anticipate the feelings, thoughts and behaviors that will arise while readers work with this book. The only way for me to truly know your response, however—as well as any questions or results you may want to share—is if you leave me feedback on Amazon and through social media or email. I encourage you to do this and I welcome your honest comments. I hope you enjoy navigating this map to discovering your life's purpose!

This book is roadmap. You can use its questions, steps and strategies to discover your gifts and fulfill your destiny!

GIVING THANKS

First of all, I thank you, dear reader, for joining me on this journey. Thank you for allowing yourself to open up to and work with the many questions, steps, tools and techniques I have provided for you in this book. Thank you for making a positive difference on your own journey and for those who travel with you. Thank you for shining more light into the world.

I am grateful to all the people and other living beings that have loved, helped and supported me through the many different phases of this lifetime. I express my deep gratitude especially to those—whether in the visible or invisible realms—who were here for me and never gave up on me even during what I perceived as the darkest hours and most challenging moments of my journey.

I am also grateful for everyone who has celebrated with me the beauty, richness and abundance of life when I could share what emerged from the seeds I had planted along my path. To those who have been with me during my darkest and brightest times, I can't thank you enough for being there and sharing these precious moments with me.

I give thanks to *Ke Akua* for gifting me with this beautiful life beyond my wildest imagination and for being with me through periods of adversity and grace. Thank you so much for blessing me with the many gifts that have enabled me to write this book from my heart and to share it with others. I am forever grateful that you shower me with your grace and blessings whenever I think that all hope is gone and there is no way out.

I would like to acknowledge and express my gratitude to three people who supported me with the creation and editing of this book. Without them, the birth of this book would not have been possible. I am eternally grateful to my beautiful life partner and beloved wife, Eunjung Choi, for everything we have shared together through our amazing journey of life, for supporting me whole-heartedly on my book projects and for providing valuable initial editing.

I give my huge thanks and appreciation to my gifted editors Sarah Torribio and Michael K. Ireland who provided such thorough and excellent editing along with their valuable and constructive feedback. It was wonderful working with Sarah who helped edit my book throughout the three years when I was writing individual pieces that were to be masterfully put together as this book. And I am so grateful to Michael, who added such eloquent editing touches to the entire book and made my storylines more cohesive and clearer.

I'd like to express my deep gratitude to all the authors, teachers and friends who granted me permission to either quote or use some of their work for this book. Each of these gifted individuals has inspired me and helped me to change my life for the better. I hope the readers of this book will also learn valuable wisdom from the works mentioned.

My heart-felt gratitude goes also to Jesse Krieger, Kristen Wise and everyone from the awesome team of Lifestyle Entrepreneurs Press for the immense professional support I received during the entire process of getting this book published. I cannot recommend LEP enough to anyone who is looking for an amazing publisher to work with.

And thank you again, dear reader, for making this book part of your self-development library. I wish you happy travels on your road to self-empowerment and living your dreams.

Thanks to all...Aloha!

INTRODUCTION

The present moment is all that ever is, and in each new moment we die and are reborn. For example, people block love and close off their hearts out of fear of being hurt again. If they lived in the present moment, there would be no fear and they would walk forward in life with confidence and certainty that there is the joy of new experiences to be had.

—Alaric Hutchinson

I heard a soft voice say, "You look so beautiful now, and the color of your eyes has changed."

When I opened my eyes, I found that I had woken up in Paradise. I was reborn into the most beautiful world. I felt like I was waking up in another dimension or reality. There was no difference or separation anymore between how I felt deep within and what I perceived in the outside world. I felt "one with creation" and the Creator. All the pain, all the struggles, all the suffering, and all my feelings of separation and inadequacy were completely gone. All my senses were crystal clear as never before, and tears of gratitude flowed down my face.

I realized that the loving and caring voice I heard belonged to Paul, the man who had guided me to this magical place less than two hours earlier. With his help, I had found myself again, in a clearing in the tropical forest above Honolulu, Hawaii.

With a gentle smile in his eyes, Paul said, "Watch this now." He raised his right hand and snapped his fingers.

I looked up, amazed to see the clouds parting to reveal a patch of blue sky right above us. The clearing in the trees we were standing in was filled immediately with a huge, bright column of light.

Paul snapped his fingers again and we found ourselves in absolute silence.

Just moments earlier, the whole space had been full of the melodic chatter of singing birds. I was absolutely present and experienced the power of the moment more profoundly than ever before.

A few moments later, Paul snapped his fingers once more. Instantly, the birds started to sing again, the opening in the sky closed and the clouds returned. Paul said, "Yves, it is now your turn to try. You can do the same."

I was doubtful that I could create such a miracle, but I put my trust in my magical new friend. I snapped my fingers. I watched in awe as the same column of light came down to fill the clearing. The birds stopped singing until I snapped my fingers again. I was blown away. Was I dreaming? This was the biggest miracle I had experienced in my whole life.

How is all of this possible? Who is Paul? Why is this happening today? Will this beautiful dream last forever? These were some of the questions running through my head, and I asked them of Paul while we were driving back to Honolulu.

Paul smiled at me again and said, "It is possible because of *Aloha Ke Akua*."

"Paul, I just got here two weeks ago," I said. "I am not yet familiar with the Hawaiian language. Could you please explain what that means?"

"It means to recognize God as the Supreme Being, to acknowledge the divine spirit in all things, and to be grateful for its many blessings."

While Paul spoke these words, I felt as though the divine itself was speaking to me.

Paul continued, "We were brothers in another lifetime here in Hawaii. In that lifetime, you helped me, and now I am here to help you."

"I was struggling for thirty-two years," I said. "Why didn't we meet earlier?"

"Because you chose to have this experience today."

"I feel so wonderful now. Will it last forever?"

We had arrived near the ocean. It was almost sunset.

"Yves, look out at the ocean and the waves," Paul said. "It will be just like the waves—sometimes high and sometimes low. Sometimes you will feel as wonderful as you do right now, and then you will find yourself feeling disconnected again. However, even when you feel low, always remember that you are like a drop of water, part of the ocean, and will be carried through the low and high tides of life."

You are like a drop of water, part of the ocean, and will be carried through the low and high tides of life.

Paul had to hurry to catch his flight back home to the Big Island and our time together was running out.

"Paul, all I wish for is to do the same thing you just gifted me with. What do you recommend as my next step?"

"Learn and practice energy and healing work, and you will start to create and share the same experiences with others."

"When will I be ready?"

"Whenever you choose to be ready."

Paul smiled at me one last time, gave me a long, loving hug, and drove away. I sat by the ocean, gazing at the gorgeous, magical sunset. I felt more clarity, peace and inner calm than ever before, and I tried to recapture what I had just experienced. It had only been four days since Wendy, my host in Oahu's Manoa Valley, told me she had received a phone call with an important message for me. Paul, who had called her from the Big Island, told her he was having vivid dreams and visions about someone staying at her place and he needed to fly in to help this person as soon as possible.

The description of the person in his dreams fit me. Of course, I said yes to his offer of help. Four days later, on this magical afternoon, Paul had shown up at Wendy's door in a truck that even carried a massage table. I had wondered how he had managed to bring that table on the plane from the Big Island.

During my sunset contemplation, I wondered if I would ever see Paul again. Later, I tried many times to locate him, but without success—I never saw him again. It was up to me to make this dream last forever and to remember that I am a part of the ocean of love that surrounds me always.

The foregoing story has been excerpted and edited from a chapter I contributed to the Amazon bestselling book "Inspired by the Passion Test - The #1 Tool for Discovering Your Passion and Purpose." You can find more information at: www.InspiredByThePassionTest.com

This book is my way of sharing Paul's magical message with you. "You are ready when you choose to be ready," Paul told me. I am ready—and I hope this book helps you to realize that you are ready too!

Tropical Forest above Honolulu, Hawaii

The purpose of this book is to present you with a guide on how to use 7 questions and 12 steps to discover your gifts, find your life's purpose, and ultimately fulfill your destiny. I hope this book will make a lasting, positive impact on your life, and help you to inspire everyone you are connected with and everyone you meet.

I've written this book from my heart, with my best efforts and highest intentions. However, as with reading any other self-help book, to change your life you need to invest time and energy and really delve into the book's subject material. You must commit yourself to reading actively, not just skimming. To get the maximum benefit, ask yourself the 7 questions and follow the 12 practical steps—as well as the related tools and exercises provided—as you go along.

In 2014, I wrote a thirteen-page article about finding your life's purpose. During the summer of 2015, I presented the article in greater depth (and in a more digestible way) to my newsletter subscribers. I published the original contents in smaller excerpts over a period of two months and made it easier for readers to follow the steps and to start putting the steps into practice. I also incorporated further insights that I'd become aware of since I first wrote the article. I also encouraged readers to participate with one another—and with me—in an interactive dialogue. I asked them to send me an email with a brief question, whether they were seeking clarity on their current situation or simply wanted to know more about finding their life's purpose. Each week, I picked one of these questions and provided my response. *Hawaiian Rebirth* was in part inspired by the uplifting conversations and questions and answers that arose from the lively interaction of my readers and the subscribers to my newsletter.

I have divided this book into four parts:

Part I is focused on 7 questions—your answers will help you to live your dreams.

I've divided the questions in this book into seven main categories. If you want to move closer to your purpose and start living a life that fulfills your destiny, asking the right questions and finding your own answers is an important step. And, the language that you use in your answers must move you toward your desires and goals, rather than away from your vision.

A gifted, dynamic speaker and teacher in the United States, Niurka, states that the quality of our lives mirrors the quality of the questions we ask. Check out her website at: *www.Niurkainc.com* I learned from Niurka that our language patterns reveal our motivation, and indicate whether we're moving away from or toward what we're seeking. For example, when we use the language of necessity ("must" or "need to"), negation ("not") and comparison ("better" or "worse"), it signals that we're moving *away*—perhaps unconsciously—from what we seek. On the other hand, when we use the language of possibility or empowerment ("accomplishing" or "confident"), it signals that we are moving *toward* what we seek.

Part II – the 12 steps, provides you with tips, tactics and tools to help you gain clarity about your life's purpose.

Some of the concepts and techniques you'll read about in this book—and hopefully start to apply in your life—may be familiar to you. I hope you'll learn a few techniques to help you make strides in implementing changes in your life. I'll be delighted if this book helps you enjoy more confidence in your life, so that you can get clear about your life's purpose and move forward to realizing your dreams.

In Part III, you'll find twelve stories in which I share how I came to be living in alignment with my purpose.

Living your purpose comes in many different forms and paths. These stories provide examples of people—and even animals—who are living or have lived their purpose. I also tell you about some places that have helped me learn more about my own purpose. The people and animals featured in these tales are shining examples of living from the heart and being in touch with their own essence, qualities I believe are essential to fulfilling your destiny.

In Part IV, I introduce several exercises to help you take action and manifest your goals.

These exercises teach you, firstly, how you can start each day being centered, aware and inspired. There are numerous examples of successful people who emphasize how important it is to start each day with focus, awareness and gratitude. When you do this practice, you are establishing a foundation for attracting what is in alignment with your purpose. It is also important to fine-tune your perception about yourself and others.

Secondly, these exercises show you how you can learn more about yourself and others. When you have a clear understanding of yourself and others, it will help you to find those who have visions or purposes that are in resonance with yours. Together you can help each other create something far more powerful and valuable than what you are capable of creating individually.

Finally, in this section, you will also receive valuable tips on how to use social media consciously, how to set goals, how to get motivated and how to take action to achieve your dreams and visions.

When we follow any self-development system or read any self-empowerment book, after our initial high, we often face limitations when it comes to putting what we've just learned into practice. Jack Canfield, an American author known for creating the uplifting *Chicken Soup for the Soul* book series, says that it takes at least thirty days to create new habits that will help you overcome the limiting beliefs that have kept you from living your purpose and fulfilling your destiny.

Over the years, I've taken and taught many self-awareness courses. I've witnessed many people who were at first extremely inspired by what they learned, either in group settings or individual sessions. But sadly, many failed to implement the teachings they'd just experienced. After my initial awakening in Hawaii, I started attending workshops and seminars and had similar experiences—I was excited while I was with the group but my inspiration and excitement slipped away a few days after the workshop adjourned.

So, just know that as you move through this book and work with the questions, steps and strategies provided, you may feel inspired at times. At other moments, you may encounter resistance. Some days, you may leaf through the pages of this book and find a passage that speaks to you exactly where you are right now. Other days, my words may not resonate with you. Or, sometimes an idea will resonate so profoundly, you might want to run away. When you are reading, you might feel fully engaged, or you may feel uncomfortable or notice you're tired and yawning. You might suddenly remember something else you should be doing. Don't worry—it's all part of the process. It's something I've experienced many times while reading self-help books, attending transformational seminars or watching spiritual movies. All of these kinds of resistance may signal that you need more time to process an idea, or it may mean that unconsciously, you want to put off implementing life changes.

While it's interesting to hear about different ways of living in or looking at the world, real transformation involves effort and commitment. I've often returned to material that initially caused me to feel resistance, only to discover that it is exactly the message I need to hear. The only way to find out what works for you is through direct experience, by putting what you've learned into practice.

What you learn—and how—is up to you. The questions, steps and strategies in this book have enhanced the quality of my life in many ways. They've also been useful to many others I've shared them with. They are available here as a roadmap for you—but remember, your journey will be unique. Each of us starts from our own point of departure. And while each of us has the same goal of finding our life's purpose and ultimately fulfilling our destiny, we're all headed to different places. Luckily, this "roadmap" has the potential to help you however you use it.

You may benefit from reading the book straight through, following the exercises religiously. Or you might want to focus on a portion of the material, leaving the rest of the ideas for another time. If you fall into the latter category, I invite you to start reading Parts III and IV first. Embedded in my personal stories in Part III are several valuable questions and tools—and Part IV presents several useful steps that can help lead you to your life's purpose.

There are so many ways you can start living your life's purpose and fulfilling your destiny! This book offers you a number of options and I'm confident that however you implement the ideas in this book, it will help you on your path to finding your true passion and manifesting your heart's desires.

On my life's journey, I've been gifted with answers to some of the questions that have nagged at me for many years—among them: "Why is humanity suffering?" "How can I help others release some of that suffering?" I'm a Yoga Nidra and meditation teacher. Yoga stands for union and Nidra stands for sleep. Yoga Nidra is a powerful and ancient technique through which you can learn to relax consciously. It consists of a series of relaxation techniques and visualizations to eliminate the layers of conflict that exist within the mind and body. Ultimately, Yoga Nidra guides you back to your most natural state of inner peace. When you practice it regularly, the nature of the mind can be changed, diseases can be cured, and your creative genius can be restored. For more information, check out: *http://YvesNager.com/energy-healing/yoga-nidra/*

According to the precepts of yoga, there are four main reasons suffering arises:

- We don't perceive things as they are and act based on our misunderstanding.
- We don't get what we want.
- We want to repeat a desirable experience.
- We no longer have what we once had.

Yoga defines clouded perception (*Avidya*) as the source of suffering. The clouded perception is expressed as identification (*Asmita*), desire (*Raga*), refusing (*Dvesa*) and fear (*Abhinivesa*). Having experienced all of these forms of suffering myself—and having truly believed at one point that there was no way out—I want to offer you encouragement. Don't give up on your hopes and dreams, even when you feel like you're at the end of your rope. If you commit yourself to moving in the direction of your desires despite challenges and obstacles, miracles happen, and new paths are revealed. My own story is a testament to that.

In his great book *The Four Desires: Creating a Life of Purpose, Happiness, Prosperity, and Freedom*, Para Yoga founder Rod Stryker *www.parayoga.com*—widely considered one of the preeminent yoga and meditation teachers in the United States—shares some wisdom from the Vedas. According to these ancient yogic scriptures, our soul has four distinct desires:

- The desire for purpose; the drive to become who we're meant to be.
- The desire for the means (money, security and health) to prosper in this world.
- The desire for pleasures like intimacy, beauty and love.
- The desire for spiritual fulfillment and lasting freedom.

I feel honored and blessed to study with Rod, and I highly recommend his book. My book, by contrast, is only focused on the first of these four desires. The same steps you take toward finding purpose, though, can enhance any life area and any goal you choose to act upon. The more commitment and self-responsibility you bring to the process, the greater the effect.

Near Waikiki Aquarium, Hawaii

And now, it's time to read what you'll soon start practicing. As Pilipo, a wise and charismatic Hawaiian wisdom keeper (you'll meet him later in this book) shared with me one day: "To know something and not act accordingly is like not knowing anything at all. Wisdom is always revealed when you act upon what you know to be true."

The Wheel of Life

To lead a happy, healthy and fulfilled life, it is important to look at all areas of our lives. Before we move on and start working with the questions in the first part of this book (the answers to which will

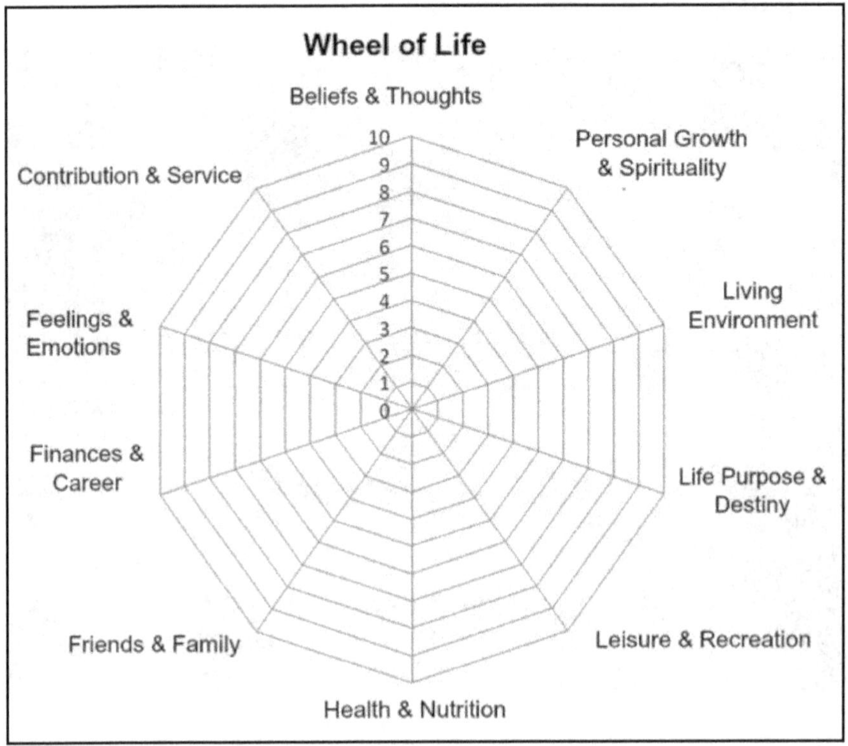

help you move closer to your life's purpose), please take a moment to fill out the Wheel of Life below. The ten sections represent different aspects of your life. Rank each category on the wheel from 1-10 (1 is least satisfactory and 10 is most satisfactory) based on how well you are currently doing for each of these categories. Place a dot where it corresponds to the number. Once ranked, connect the dots to see how "balanced" your wheel is. My thanks to the creator of the rendering of Wheel of Life below—you can find many versions online and choose the one that resonates best for you. You might want to make several copies of the Wheel of Life, and keep them in a file so you can reference them over time. At the end of this book, you'll be comparing your first wheel with your last—so keep them handy for easy reference. And above all, have fun!

***To lead a happy, healthy and fulfilled life,
it is important to look at all areas of your life.***

After you draw your wheel of life, ask yourself these questions:

- If this were a real wheel, how bumpy or smooth would my ride be?
- What causes a lack of balance (if anything) in my health and happiness?
- What could I do to achieve more balance?
- What contributed to higher scores in certain areas of my life?
- One month from now, which life areas do I want to have progressed in the most?
- What am I grateful for? In which life areas do I feel the deepest gratitude?

- What are my next steps to create a higher score in the areas with lower numbers?
- What concrete steps will I take in the next seven days?
- Where do I want to be thirty days from now?
- Where would I like to be in three months from now? (please draw with another color)

Hanging Lake, Glenwood Canyon, Colorado

PART I
THE 7 QUESTIONS

Asking Life's Deepest Questions

"What is our life's purpose? How do we fulfill our destiny?" Human beings have been asking these questions since time immemorial. In this book, I expound on 7 questions and 12 steps and provide 12 inspirational stories from my personal journey of growth and empowerment. These questions have been asked by students and answered by teachers—and in each instance the questions and answers bring clarity and inspiration. In this journey toward enlightenment, none of us are merely students or teachers. We're both—we're here to teach each other, to learn from each other, to grow together in community and to co-create. Embracing a communal spirit is a precious tool that both teachers and students can use to venture ever closer to fulfilling our life's purpose.

Achieving our goals in this world takes time, and the process can be slower than we think it should be. It needs continuous practice, including working with the subconscious and unconscious levels of your being. It's crucial that you recognize and honor each milestone you have achieved. It's important to notice how much you've changed, even since the beginning of the current year, and to be grateful for each step in your progress. I hope to bring you further clarity about your life's purpose through these words. By asking you these 7 questions and by guiding you to find the answers deep within yourself, I hope to inspire you to take responsibility and start aligning your life with the things that *really* matter to you.

In 2008 and 2010 I went through some difficult experiences and ultimately experienced a burnout twice. During these times, I frequently asked myself, "Who am I?" "Where am I going?" "What is my life's purpose?" and "How do I fulfill my destiny?" When I look back, I realize that it was during these tough but valuable times that I learned the most. Through my work and travels, I've learned I'm not the only one to grapple with these two important questions. Many people around the world are searching for their life's purpose and ways to fulfill their destiny.

Your life's purpose is based on the language of your heart, mind and soul. Living your life's purpose can gift you with focus, life force and direction. Your heart can guide you to important places and people with a magnetic force that's difficult to obtain through intention and goals alone. When you have a mission, listen to your heart—it hears the voice of your soul. When you let your heart guide your mind to make the right choices, it becomes easier to overcome obstacles, attract the right people into your life, and change the world!

To help you hone in on your mission, I encourage you to spend some time working with these 7 questions and their accompanying exercises. Many of us have a tendency, when presented with material aimed at improving our mindset and lives, to skip the exercises. Our eyes wander over the words and we nod our heads, thinking, "Yes, that's right. That's the way it is." But we fail to follow the steps. We may feel we've done something positive for ourselves just by reading the text. Perhaps that's true for some people.

However, it will serve you better if you allow yourself time to contemplate your life's purpose, perhaps by journaling or taking a walk in nature. I've found that I make remarkable progress when I take a few moments to work with these insight-provoking exercises and questions.

Before we jump in, I should clarify some details. I chose these 7 questions for this book because many seekers on the journey of life have asked them. As always, I share my own perspective and the insights I've received in my life's journey to help you to find clarity as you seek your own answers. Remember, there are no right or wrong answers to these questions—I respect everyone's beliefs and principles, so I invite you to take from this book only the ideas and concepts that resonate with you personally.

For your convenience, you'll find some empty pages for you to journal in at the end of this book. *Here we go....*

Notes on Questions #1 - #4

Question 1, *What continually attracts your attention?* is self-evident and profound in its simplicity. The other Questions, 2-7, need some introduction. My newsletter readers frequently asked these questions so they are, in a sense, universal questions which many self-empowerment seekers ask. If these questions resonate with you, I hope this section brings you clarity.

"Isn't it true that I need to ask and wait for divine guidance from spirit or God regarding my purpose in life? I don't think it's up to me to decide."

Many of us feel that guidance must come from the spirit, originating from somewhere "higher up." As a result, we decide it's not our place to make important decisions. This mindset originates from a deep-seated belief that we are somehow separate from the divine. There's a fine line between following the spirit we are at our essence and following the spirit we think lies somewhere outside of us.

I believe that here on the physical plane we are spiritual beings having a human experience. We are here co-creating with the spiritual world. Of course, some of us hear what we consider to be the voice of God or spirit loud and clear and being tuned into this voice can lead to great transformation. More often than not, however, the voice of the divine is subtle and comes from within. Messages from the divine can also arise from ordinary things you encounter in everyday life: a road sign, something a friend says to you, a song you hear on the radio, a message on a t-shirt someone wears, a specific number sequence you keep noticing, an experience in nature, etc.

Tapping into the voice of the divine is really about listening to your own heart—and having the courage to follow it. By going deep into your heart, you connect with your soul and communicate with the gentle but powerful voice of the divine. As you do this, I encourage you to trust yourself and to act without second-guessing yourself.

Often, I see people paralyzed, unable to make decisions because they keep ignoring the gentle voice within. They want to hear a loud, clear voice from spirit. But spirit does not shout, it whispers. Not recognizing these inner whispers as divine guidance, these people let go of their dreams, they become resigned to believing that what matters most to them is not important or worth pursuing. After all, they reason, they haven't heard or seen a clear sign telling them what to do. That was my own attitude for most of my adult life, and it took me a long time to change this pattern and start to create new habits.

It takes practice to build self-trust, and to believe that we are indeed spirit in a human body. But when we see ourselves as one with the divine voice, when we follow our heart and tap into our joy, we find that no matter what decision we make, it creates a beautiful stepping-stone for us in our lives and ripple effects for others.

When I went to Hawaii in 2008, I started to realize that I am an essential part of this divine co-creation, and that the spiritual realm needs me as much as I need help from the spiritual world.

Until I had this epiphany, I avoided taking full responsibility for my own life. Instead, I allowed others to make decisions for me. I have since realized that this was one of many tactics used by my mind and ego to keep procrastinating on what really mattered to me. I am so grateful that I live a different life now, and that I can share what I have learned with people around the world.

Notes on Questions #5 - #7

"I've done a lot of positive thinking, visualization, affirmations and meditation and really worked on my goals and dreams. However, nothing really seems to work and I'm really frustrated. What's wrong with me?"

I chose to answer this question because I too sometimes find myself in a space where nothing seems to move forward, despite my best efforts. It can be annoying and frustrating. I still occasionally complain about how slow I *think* my progress is. However, when I compare my life now with how it was ten years ago, I'm amazed at how much I've achieved. I've changed so much since 2008, when I came here to Hawaii for the first time.

While I studied on Kaua'i in 2011, I found my beautiful life partner, Eunjung, and we've made wonderful friendships with like-hearted people around the world. Since 2012, I've travelled with Eunjung to thirty-five countries, teaching and leading workshops in almost half of them. I've worked with people and animals from across the globe, from widely different backgrounds, and I now live on the beautiful garden island of Kaua'i. I could not have imagined, even seven years ago, that I'd be living this wonderful life of my dreams.

So, when you say, "Nothing seems to be working for me, I don't seem to be moving forward," I invite you to really examine your life. Is there any area in which you find progress? We tend to overlook our progress. Instead of taking a moment to acknowledge what we've accomplished, we continuously create new goals. We keep chasing the goal in front of us, so it seems like we're never where we intend to be.

We overlook our progress. Instead of acknowledging our accomplishments, we continuously create new goals.

When we talk about life's purpose, one of our most fundamental aims is to be a creator. Through the act of creation, we discover our gifts, we embark on a life aligned with the things that matter most to us. But sometimes, what we intend to create doesn't show up for us so we wonder if we really do have the ability to manifest our dreams. But remember, just because something doesn't show up right away doesn't mean it will never show up. In this three-dimensional world, it can take much longer than we'd like for our intentions and actions (the cause) to yield the desired results (the effect).

We need practice, persistence, focused attention—and patience! It can be overwhelming to dedicate yourself to your goals only to have them feel elusive. So, start small. Put a concrete action plan in place. Cut down the number of goals you pursue every day and adopt an attitude of gratitude for everything you have. Then, achieving even the highest aim becomes much more manageable and realistic. And remember—believing in yourself is an important part of the process.

When you're on a transformational path, it's common for doubts and fears to arise. When I undertook my own journey, one of the first things I noticed was that the biggest obstacle in my way was myself.

It requires a lot of determination to stay focused on what we choose to create. It's important that we recognize—and celebrate—the subtle shifts, changes and small achievements we experience along the way. It's important to congratulate ourselves for our triumphs. So, instead of ignoring minor victories and moving onto your next goal, create a new habit. Be aware of what you're grateful for. Write down at least five things you're grateful for every day. Then, slow down and reflect on what you've attained so far. Celebrate!

If you find yourself saying, "I've been making a lot of effort but nothing is happening," ask yourself, "Am I fully aware of what I'm paying attention to?" So many people become frustrated and unhappy because they aren't present, centered and aware of the slight shifts occurring every single day. Instead, they chase after a never-ending array of new goals. They do their affirmations and then look for results. But doing affirmations fifteen minutes a day is not enough to bring about a desired shift. Manifesting your desires requires continued practice, focus and positive energy.

For many years, I caught myself—after engaging in some sort of meditation, visualization or affirmation—going back and saying, "Oh, it didn't work." Sound familiar? We do something to move toward our desired outcome, then we negate what we've just focused on. That's one of the reasons many people get stuck and don't move forward. So, be honest with yourself: How do you feel after you've meditated, fixed your mind on a goal, or affirmed your ability to achieve it? Are you maintaining a state of gratitude and appreciation, or are you going back to the belief that it doesn't work?

Another reason many people get stuck is because they do their visualizations and affirmations in the Beta or Alpha state of the brainwave instead of going deeper—into a Theta or even a Delta state. There are many layers of consciousness in our human psyche, and we can experience more profound changes in our lives when we engage with the deeper vibrational frequencies. You will read more about these various forms of brainwaves later in the section "Blessing of Relaxation."

If you feel you've already done everything and you're still not moving forward, there may be a core belief that is holding you back. Although you're trying hard with the conscious part of your mind, there can be huge subconscious and unconscious blockages that can keep you from moving forward.

If you're consumed with doubt, you'll fail to achieve your desired transformation. You can sit in meditation for several hours a day and it still won't work if you have a deep-seated part of you saying, "It's no use." Answering the questions and doing the exercises in this section will help you to bust through that barrier and get back on the path to realizing your dreams. Ready? Here we go, with Questions 1 – 7!

Question 1 - What continually attracts your attention?

When you're walking down the street, working, watching TV, surfing the internet or travelling, what are you continuously aware of? What attracts your attention over and over again? In what ways do you see, hear or feel better or more intensely than other people? For example, do you notice advertisements? How display windows are decorated? How customer service professionals perform for their companies? How politicians present their speeches and arguments? What do you notice about the service you receive from a restaurant, hotel, airline or car rental agency? If you are especially sensitive, perhaps you notice how and to what degree people are honoring (or not honoring) their souls or physical bodies. Or perhaps you notice the ways, lovingly or carelessly, that parents engage with their children.

Once you establish what it is that attracts your attention regularly, check in with yourself. What are you thinking and feeling in those moments of awareness?

Perhaps you've asked yourself why others are less aware or less conscious of certain situations, statements or behaviors than you are. But being aware of *what you notice* can provide you with hints that can guide you to your life's purpose. I encourage you to work with this question for the next few days, and become deeply aware of what attracts your attention. Journal about your awareness and take notes about what you observe and how you *feel* about it over a few days. See if you can find some common themes—you could find a clue to your heart's desires!

Question 2 - What do you do with love and joy? What matters to your heart?

What do you most like to do in your free time? What gives you the most happiness in these moments? What would you most like to share with others? What would you like to share with animals and with nature?

If you were to volunteer (if you are not yet doing so), in what ways and where would you help? What activities make you feel as if time is flying by? What pursuits gift you with energy and joy? In which area would you like to be number one on this planet? (You can mention several options!)

Again, jot down your answers to these questions in your journal. Write a few paragraphs about the salient points and expand upon them. How does it *feel* when you think about doing something you love and that you are passionate about?

Question 3 - What fields would you like to know more about?

Is there something you feel you don't know enough about? Is there a subject that interests you so much you feel compelled to learn more about it? Is there a subject that fills your mind and your heart with joy and appreciation?

Do you find yourself reading certain books and magazines over and over again? Do you like to watch movies or DVDs on certain topics or fields of study? Is there any subject you enjoy discussing, hoping to learn more about it from others? If you were trapped for several hours in a library, in which part of the library would you spend time?

Once again, find some quiet space and some time to reflect on your answers to these questions—and journal about them. Maybe you'll find that a poem or a story about your life arises from your subconscious mind—write it down!

Question 4 - When do you feel inspired and creative?

Are there certain activities in which creativity, inspiration and ideas seem to "bubble out of you?" What do you feel in those moments? Where in your body or in your being do you feel it the most strongly?

Have you experienced a sense of expansion within you while doing something in particular? Has something you've created become more powerful than you expected?

What signs and synchronicities are revealed to you during times of creativity and inspiration? (I will address this topic in depth later.)

Have you ever felt like something you've worked on created itself...like you hardly had to think as the perfect words, pictures, colors and ideas presented themselves at just the right moment? Write it down—or express it in art using your favorite colors, patterns and textures!

I invite you to work with these questions for the next few days, and become even more aware of what matters to your heart. Delve into the things you want to know more about and start to recognize the moments in which you feel inspired, creative and engaged.

Question 5 - When others compliment you, what do they say?

Our first four questions are focused on *internal* subjects, looking within to discover your passions and what you like to do. This question, on the other hand, focuses on an *external* subject that can provide hints about your life's purpose. For many, it may be easy to believe even the slightest criticism from others, but difficult to accept compliments. However, others' compliments can point out talents you may not be aware of and can show you that something big is awakening within you.

So, ask yourself, "What compliments do I receive repeatedly from others?" "What compliments have guided me for a long time?" "Are there talents slumbering within me that I have been denying?"

Have you caught yourself thinking things like, "Oh, everyone can do that," or "I didn't really do anything special?"

Your life's purpose always unites the following three aspects: inspiration, passion and ability. It's not enough to have a vision or to really like doing something. Consider, for example, a talent show contestant who longs for a career as a singer and who has studied voice for many years. But after much training, they still are not a virtuoso artist. They might be a good performer but might just not have "the pipes." Perhaps they are in the right field but on the wrong path—perhaps for this person, success would come when he or she composes a song, writes song lyrics or jumps into a role in musical theater. There's always a "right path" for everyone—but finding it can be tricky!

To find the path that is meant for you, it helps to have good guidance from others who are on your team. In my work as a life coach, I work with a tool that reveals how we perceive ourselves and how others perceive us. You'll find this tool later, in Part IV of this book. Have you worked with such a tool? What were the results? What were your insights? Write them in your journal!

Question 6 - What would you do if you knew you couldn't fail?

This question is often attributed to American Pastor Robert Schuller. Whether you succeed or fail can often depend on your mindset. Did you know that your mind can be either your best friend—or your enemy? Your mind serves as a friend when it alerts you to opportunities that can benefit you—and when it keeps you from acting on plans that could be detrimental or even dangerous. But the mind can also be your enemy, if you're unaware of its unconscious programs or if it estimates a risk incorrectly. When that happens, you can miss out on an opportunity that may help you grow while also inspiring others.

If you were absolutely certain that you could rely on your mind to be your friend, a friend who could show you ways to move forward in your life that were fail-proof, what would you do? Where, how and with whom would you do it? What would the results look like?

You always know when your mind is being your friend when you feel inspired and expanded by ideas that light you up. You feel it emotionally, spiritually and physically—deep within your heart.

As you are working with this question, find some quiet time alone with your journal and try this exercise. It comes from ceremonialist Andrew Soliz, who is one of my favorite speakers in the movie *Discover the Gift*. Soliz advises that when you have a question to ask, place your hand over your heart. Then, listen. You'll hear the subtle, quiet voice of the heart telling you the answer. Journal about what you hear.

Question 7 - What would you like to do in your next life?

Asking this question allows you to bypass your critical mind, which is pre-programmed with statements like, "It doesn't work," "I'm not allowed to," or "I shouldn't do this." It can reveal your mission in this life because it bypasses those limiting programs. The mind doesn't need to step in with all the reasons you can't do something, thereby holding you back from implementing your ideas and dreams in this lifetime.

So, close your eyes and imagine your next existence: How, where and with whom would you like to spend your life? How would you feel? Who would you like to be? What kind of difference would you like to make in the world?

Take some time alone with your journal, get quiet and write about the dreams and visions of your ideal "next lifetime" that are possible for you to achieve in *this lifetime*. Can you feel the inspiration?

These seven questions will support you in the process of finding clarity about your individual purpose in life. Here is an overview/cap-up of the questions:

Question 1: What continually attracts your attention?

Question 2: What do you do with love and joy? What matters to your heart?

Question 3: What fields would you like to know more about?

Question 4: When do you feel inspired and creative?

Question 5: When others compliment you, what do they say?

Question 6: What would you do if you knew you couldn't fail?

Question 7: What would you like to do in your next life?

I encourage you to take time to work deeply with these seven questions over the coming days and weeks. The more you engage with the process, the better your results will be. Check in with yourself often as you move forward in this work. Do you feel elevated, enriched and empowered?

In the next section, we will work with 12 steps to help you discover your unique purpose. At the beginning of each step, you will find a question or comment I have selected from input I have received from clients over the years.

Point Lobos State Natural Reserve, California

PART II
THE 12 STEPS

When I travelled to Hawaii in 2008, I was seeking my life's purpose. Through a series of events that I can only attribute to the Law of Attraction, I learned about inspirational author Alan Cohen, a psychotherapist and author of many inspirational books who also lives in Hawaii. One of the topics he touches on in his teachings is life's purpose. He talks about how important it is to "follow your blessing." Alan developed a wonderful system that can support seekers in discovering their life's mission. Alan's system has inspired me for a long time and it is my pleasure to share it with you in this book, complemented by my reflections on the material and supplemented with questions and tools.

I'd like to express my heartfelt gratitude to Alan, who has given me his permission and blessings to share these 12 steps with you. Please check out www.*AlanCohen.com* for more information on Alan's amazing work. Please note that I have taken the liberty of changing the titles of the original steps slightly.

As you can imagine, Alan's philosophy has touched me deeply and has profoundly affected my decision to work as a life coach. I am sure these 12 Steps will influence and inspire you as well. I invite you to open your awareness, discover your inner power and start your journey toward self-discovery now.

NOTES ON THE STEPS

Notes on Steps #1 - #4

In Step 1, we examine what it means to be fully present and honest with yourself, then we move on to Step 2, getting started on changing your life. These two steps will help you "begin-at-the-beginning," first getting in touch with your authentic self and then moving forward, empowered and committed to reaching your fullest potential and becoming who you came here to be.

In Steps 3 and 4, we look at procrastination and motivation. A client once asked the following question, which is a great teaching tool for everyone. "*Although I know what changes I need to make in my life, I keep putting things off. Do you have suggestions on how to stop procrastinating and start acting?*"

Procrastination

I sometimes procrastinate, we all do. The following section summarizes what I've learned while studying habits of avoidance that plague countless people.

Procrastination is the act of intentionally and habitually putting off something that should probably be done right away. The word *procrastination* generally has a negative connotation. Believe it or not, though, procrastination can be constructive. Engaging in an activity like going to a yoga class or cleaning out your closet can mentally and creatively prepare you for an important task. However, if putting things off until the last minute seriously hampers your career, educational pursuits, family or other important areas of your life, it's time to look honestly at why you're procrastinating and find strategies to beat this destructive pattern. Usually, when we procrastinate we are consciously or unconsciously experiencing confusion, uncertainty, self-doubt or fear.

When you catch yourself putting something off, write down what you're uncertain about. Keep it brief; don't spend too much time on your list, or you'll just add another source of procrastination. Next, list all the reasons you're not taking action. Then determine if these reasons are valid. Probably they won't be, but some may ring true.

The next step is to write down a couple of small strategies to help resolve your hesitation. Then take action on these strategies. In this process, trust your intuition, connect with your wisdom and develop strategies such as time-management and self-motivation. It will be helpful as well to connect with someone who holds you accountable and to check in with them from time to time on your progress.

Below, I'll discuss three common causes of procrastination. I'll also share some simple strategies for taking action and moving forward toward your goals.

Fear of Failure

You're afraid that you'll fail in your efforts and you wait until the last minute before taking action. By doing so, you can say you failed because you didn't have enough time.

If fear is holding you back, just imagine the worst possible scenario that could happen if you failed. Maybe you could lose your job by missing a deadline on a critical assignment, or become tongue-tied at an important meeting. You might let a life-changing career opportunity slip through your fingers by failing to follow up with a resume or lose a meaningful relationship by neglecting to respond to a call.

Of course, our attempts—even the unsuccessful ones—rarely yield disaster. But for some people, placing their fear of failure in an absurd light can help put the task at hand into proper perspective. Another thing you can do is remember a time you succeeded at something in the past. You've had success before, and you can repeat it.

Fear of Success

Are you afraid of your own success? Perhaps you fear that if you accomplish a task successfully, you may be given even more tasks or responsibility. That can be an unpleasant thought, but why borrow trouble, worrying about something that may or may not happen? Spiritual teacher Marianne Williamson says, "Our deepest fear is not that we are inadequate. Our deepest fear is that we are powerful beyond measure. It is our light, not our darkness that most frightens us."

To manage fear and uncertainty, focus only on the task at hand. Stay in the present moment. You never really know what the future will bring, and you can always say "no" to future assignments later and set boundaries accordingly.

Perfectionism

How do you know if you're a perfectionist? You put too much pressure on yourself to complete tasks perfectly. Perfectionists are never satisfied—nothing ever seems to be good enough. Since it's impossible to fulfill the standards you've created for yourself, it's easy to lose motivation before you even get started. The French philosopher Voltaire spoke to this problem when he said, *"Perfection is the enemy of good."*

If you suspect perfectionism is sabotaging your progress, review your standards. Are your expectations realistic? If they cause you unnecessary stress, anxiety or pressure, adjust any lofty expectations. Also, remember that what we perceive as an error can yield valuable insights. Mistakes always provide you with another opportunity to learn and evolve.

Notes on Steps #5 and #6

"How can I communicate what I am going through more clearly? How can I discuss my new perspectives on life with family members or friends who don't necessarily share the same path?"

I still sometimes find myself in a space where it's hard to share with others the profound transformative journey I'm undergoing. When I look back, I had a particularly difficult time expressing myself at the beginning of my journey in 2008, when I returned to Switzerland after an almost four-month stay in Hawaii.

My life had changed profoundly during my time in Hawaii, and I literally returned home to Switzerland as a different person. I was changed but the circumstances and people in my life in Switzerland were unchanged. It was difficult for me to reconcile the business-as-usual atmosphere with my drastically altered worldview.

When I look back at this transitional period, it was a valuable experience I wouldn't miss for many reasons. My difficulties motivated me. I committed to keep working on and practicing daily the things I'd learned in Hawaii. I was inspired to study new healing modalities and to attend yoga classes, workshops and seminars about spirituality. And, I realized it was crucial to not only talk with others about my experiences in Hawaii, but also to listen actively to what others wanted to share with me. I needed to learn how to communicate to others the person I had become and reconcile that with the person I had been.

I'd like to take this opportunity to summarize a few points I feel are essential and relevant about learning how to communicate well. Of course, the topic of communication is broad. Countless books have been written on the subject, and there are many workshops and seminars you can attend to improve your communication skills, both in the business world and in private situations. Based on my own experience, I've come to realize that most of us believe that in order to be good communicators, we must first learn how to express our thoughts, ideas and emotions in a more effective way. On the contrary, to become a really good communicator we must first learn how to *listen*—actively—to others. Active communication requires that one person talk while the other listens. Let's look at four of the most common obstacles to active listening: filtering, advising, being judgmental and pleasing. The first step is to recognize these obstacles while you communicate with others. The second step is to find simple and effective strategies to overcome them.

Filtering

Do you often catch yourself filtering out part of what someone is saying to you? When we're listening to another person speak, we can't hear everything they are trying to tell us. Filtering is so natural, we do it unconsciously. But it can be helpful to use filtering consciously, especially to lessen the impact of addressing a topic you'd like to avoid or when you don't have a lot of time to talk to someone. However, if you catch yourself filtering a lot of what someone says over a sustained period of time, I suggest you honestly examine the reason and work toward resolving it. Also, try to gift yourself and your partner with more time when you communicate with one another—when you slow down, you'll find your exchanges with others much richer and more engaging.

Advising

You don't have to fix every problem someone else talks about. If you tell someone how to think, feel and even how to behave, you might unconsciously belittle them. Some people like to give advice instead of actively listening, because it makes them feel needed. On the other hand, advising can also be a way of distancing ourselves from hearing someone's true feelings. Whenever possible, ask the other person for permission before offering your advice, counseling or coaching.

There are differences I would like to highlight between coaching and counseling. Counseling is often conducted to heal past wounds and traumas and involves giving advice (once your client gives permission). On the other hand, coaching is future-oriented, helping people to make positive changes and achieve their goals in their lives—mostly by asking the right questions. When I coach clients, I focus on asking the right questions, helping them to keep track of their progress and holding them accountable to their action plans. When I take the role of a counselor, which usually happens when I do healing work, I am more focused on helping them to be in the present moment, giving advice only once the client has given me permission to do so.

Being Judgmental

Everything we view as our "truth" or "reality" is based on how we perceive things. When you have a negative perception about someone, you immediately stop listening openly to what they have to say. You start to gather evidence supporting your negative assumptions. As a result, you are likely to become more firmly convinced of your opinion and unable to listen authentically to what the other person is trying to say. In Part IV of this book, you will find a section which will help you fine-tune how you perceive yourself and others.

Pleasing

The opposite of being judgmental is pleasing others. Because we like to be loved and appreciated, many of us have a hard time saying "no" to requests and interactions that are misaligned with our passions. Because of your desire to please someone else, do you prevent yourself from actively listening to what the other person wants to communicate? If you are concerned about keeping the peace and keeping everyone happy, it might be helpful to start looking deeper into the basis of your relationships and to explore why you feel compelled to please certain people.

Listening Strategies

How can you overcome the obstacles we just looked at and improve your communication skills through active and effective listening? If you are facing challenges in learning to listen, what are some simple and effective strategies to overcome those obstacles?

If you truly and honestly intend to communicate effectively with someone, it's helpful first to become aware of why listening is important for you. Next, I suggest you work every day with the following four strategies:

Clarify

Ask questions about what the other person says, making sure you come from a place of curiosity, empathy and support. Clarifying does not involve manipulating, coercing or belittling the other person in any way. Instead, make sure the other person understands that you are fully engaged in listening and that you want to learn more about what they have to say. So, practically, you can ask questions like "How do you mean?" or "What did you think when I said (…)?" or "How did you feel when I just interrupted you?"

Paraphrase

Paraphrasing helps you correct misperceptions the moment they occur. Paraphrasing keeps you and the other person from feeling misunderstood, staving off defensiveness. Use statements like "If I understand correctly, you're telling me…" or "What I just heard you say is (…)." You're not only showing genuine interest in the other person, it also helps you to remember more effectively what the other person just talked about.

Give Feedback

When you give constructive feedback, you express your ideas and insights to the other person. Whenever you give feedback, state your thoughts, feelings and opinions in a calm, gentle and constructive way. Keep your sentences short and concise. And keep in mind that your feedback is a chance for your partner to learn if you got the message they're trying to convey.

Be Responsive

Give verbal and nonverbal responses to the other person. For example, you can nod your head, smile or frown when it's appropriate or say something like "Yes, I see," or "That's a very interesting point." Most importantly, don't interrupt as long the other person is speaking. Let your partner complete their thoughts. Maintain eye contact while the other person is speaking and keep your posture open; leave your arms and legs uncrossed. Also, eliminate distractions when you speak with someone—start by turning off your digital devices, radio and television!

In Steps 5 - 8, I share many questions, steps, tools and techniques about how to interact more effectively with others. When you start working with these steps and become more conscious, you will start to perceive yourself, others and situations differently. This may feel uncomfortable in the beginning, because you can become acutely aware of how others may have perceived your ideas, emotions and actions so far. You may even cringe at the thought of your past behavior, attitudes or interactions. The happy news: you are on a new path to creating a new you! But remember: It takes at least thirty days to create a new habit. So, why not get started now?

One of the first things that happens to many people when they embark on a transformational journey is that they realize the biggest obstacles to their progress lies within them. They realize it's time to stop blaming others for their experience. In fact, there are three main signs that you are stuck in your own story: blame, shame and justification. You might *blame* someone else for whatever you're unhappy with. You might feel *ashamed* or guilty about something you may have done to create a situation. Or you might *justify* your actions, making excuses for why things are the way they are and why you aren't prepared to make a change. But you are reading this book, so you are prepared to change! That's the first step in solving this type of problem.

Every problem has a solution, but I've never promised to provide foolproof solutions to anyone for the challenges they face in their lives. The solutions are—and always will be—yours to discover. However, I guarantee that when you commit yourself to using the tools and techniques you learn in this book regularly, both you and the situations in which you find yourself will start to change. Sometimes, these changes can be subtle, at others they can be obvious.

So, now that you've realized the changes you need to make and where the obstacles are in your life, it's time to meet them head on. It's time for a paradigm shift!

Shifting your life to a place of greatness and fulfillment takes commitment. It takes inspired and focused action as well as patience and perseverance. Are you ready?

Shifting takes commitment, focus, patience and perseverance. Are you ready?

Notes on Steps #7 and #8

After you have read Step 6, you'll have become aware of how to engage in the art of active listening. You will likely find yourself paying more attention to how the people in your life communicate with you and others. In Steps 7 and 8, we examine how to further improve communication with others. A class participant's question once again provides a foundation for seeking clarity in this area. The student asked, *"What should I do when others change the subject in the middle of a conversation, interrupt me while I am still talking, or turn away as soon as they're done talking?"*

My answer: be present and authentic in every communication with others. Ask them if you could share with them some of the valuable communication tools you have learned and let them know that you are committed to communicating with them differently in future—invite them to be genuine in their exchanges with you as well.

Riegelsee, Switzerland

But what if those you are interacting with are unwilling to change, even after you've offered compassionate input? At that point, your best option may be to accept them as they are, perhaps allowing for more space between your interactions. If continuing an association with someone is painful or not worth the trouble, you may need to consider letting go of that person. Be grateful for their friendship and welcome the opportunity to cultivate new relationships in which you can communicate as your true, genuine self. Remember, when you shift, some relationships fall away naturally over time and create space for new friendships.

Notes on Steps #9 and #10

"Yves, I understand that creation is a dance between being active and being passive. For example, when I listen to your recorded meditation, I'm open, receptive. I absorb it, then let it go. However, there seems to be a fine line between taking action and receiving. How can I master that fine line between the active and the passive?"

My life coaching clients often ask me this type of question. How can they be both receptive and flexible while simultaneously being creative? How can they balance their longing to see their dreams and hopes come to fruition with the responsibilities of providing for themselves and their families in everyday life? They've asked me for tools and tips on how to adopt the ideal mindset to manage their thoughts, maintain confidence that their goals are attainable and take creative action to manifest their dreams.

I had some profound discussions on this subject with Eunjung in the summer of 2015 while hiking and meditating in beautiful Rocky Mountain National Park in Colorado. I'll summarize the insights we gained from our discussions and meditations below.

These insights were based on the messages Eunjung received from her guides during one of our meditations.

Nine Principles for Creation and Manifestation

Merge with what you seek.

What you seek to create and experience is already within you. Ultimately, there's no gap between you and what you want; you are one with your goal. Your creation is not separate from you, rather, you are birthing it. Everything, whether it's material, mental, emotional or spiritual, is within you.

Stop. Take some deep breaths, focus on your heart, and visualize something you really want right now. It's essential to imagine that you're already one with what you seek to create and that you're not separate from it. Once you understand and fully trust that you aren't separate from what you seek to create, there is no limitation.

When you realize that you're one with what you're seeking, there's no longer any doubt, anxiety or disappointment. Feel the peace and harmony arising from this knowledge. There's nothing lacking and there's nothing that needs to be added in your life, because ultimately, you're already All That Is.

When we create with the knowledge that we're one with everything—and trust that we're the directors of our own creations—we manifest from a place of joy and excitement. If doubts arise in you, do the best you can to release your attachment to outcome. Merge with and bless what you seek.

Remember – perception determines creation.

The desire to manifest something that matches your intention and vibration arises out of your vast library of creative energy. You're the ultimate director of your life movie, the virtuoso conductor in the orchestra of creation, joined in the act of manifestation by your higher self, your multi-dimensional selves and many helpers or guides from other realms.

Feel the emotions of fulfillment, joy and satisfaction during the process of creation and manifestation. Another way to practice being one with what you seek is to see yourself living your most heartfelt intentions and greatest visions in a movie of your life.

Know when to be active and when to be passive.

There is a deep synergy between being active and being passive. Even when you are receiving and being passive, other parts of you are being active, and vice versa.

If you feel like you want to act, act. When you want to be passive and listen, do that. If you want to act but feel you can't, that's fine too. We can assume any role, that of listener or communicator, that of passive receiver or active respondent. If you are helping others, let go of the conviction that you need to change someone.

Even when we seem to have faltered—to have taken the wrong path (or to have taken no path at all)—there are other parts of us moving automatically, working with spirit to arrange the infinite elements of creation into the reality we hope to manifest. And, there are infinite ways of creating. With this deeper understanding, you release the stress of worrying about whether something is right or wrong. It just is.

Flow like a river.

To understand the concept of creation and manifestation more deeply, we can use the metaphor of a river. The essence of a river is that its water flows down. If you throw a rock into the river, the water flows around or over it. Water always flows.

In the same way, creation always finds a way to create. We are the creators, the re-creators and the experiencers of creation itself.

There is nothing wrong with anything we create or do not create. Whatever we create is always perfect, just as a river is always perfect.

Acknowledge and honor your emotions.

Just as a river is an expression of flowing water, our emotions are an expression of the creative energy that flows through us. It is important to acknowledge and honor our emotions, because their degree of intensity indicates the strength or weakness of our desire to create and to manifest.

Pay close attention to how your emotions *feel*. For example, when you are feeling angry or disappointed, you are focusing upon the opposite of what you seek. Creativity arises so much more easily from joy! So, when you feel happy and content, that indicates that you are aligned with what you are seeking.

Envision your goals.

An essential part of manifesting your dreams is knowing exactly what you are seeking. As a creator, it's vital to know what you are creating, down to the finest detail. You should be conscious of what specifically you're drawing from the universal pool of limitless potential.

So, instead of focusing on what you *don't* want to experience in your life, set your intention for what you *do* want to create and experience. Write it down. Be specific. Once you've achieved clarity, you're ready to merge with what is to be created, what goal is to be manifested.

Transform negative experiences.

Perhaps you have a deep-rooted belief that you can't have what you really want. That's why doing affirmations sometimes doesn't work. You might repeat over and over, "I'm a successful (*fill in this space…*)." But no amount of repetition can change your attitude if there's another part of you saying, "No, I'm not at all successful in (*fill in this space...*)."

Perhaps you've had negative experiences with the manifestation process. Maybe you've visualized and affirmed something repeatedly but still haven't created something you really wanted and you feel discouraged. Maybe you tried something a hundred times and had one positive experience, whereas the outcome for the other ninety-nine tries was negative.

Instead of getting bogged down by adding new affirmations or new visualizations, this is a good situation in which to try asking some different questions. Things like: "What evidence is there that I was successful in (....)?" "What evidence is there that I was successful as a (....)?" "What evidence is there that I did get some of what I wanted?" What you might discover by asking these questions is that you reframe your negative perceptions and find the positive aspects. Then, you can use the positive results as building blocks to move forward in manifesting your desires.

Seek evidence that supports your new belief.

Keep seeking and noticing evidence, however small or significant, that you are moving closer to your goal. If you take the time to collect just three examples, you can often easily find more.

Sometimes we're too hard on ourselves, minimizing our accomplishments or overlooking them altogether. If this is the case, shift your focus to the things that have worked in the past and the things that are working right now. Ask yourself, "What evidence is there that the thing I want to create is achievable?" "What proves it can be done?" Write down whatever comes to mind.

Complete the following statement: "What I really want is (....)." After completing the statement, pay close attention to any doubts that arise. Transform your doubts from "I can't" to "I can." Feel that spark of inspiration—and run with it!

Observe others' life examples.

When you are looking for evidence that your goal is attainable, you don't have to just look at your own life—examine other people's lives too. For instance, if you think you're too old or don't have enough money to start something new, seek examples where others have achieved great things at a later stage of their life despite financial hardship. You'll realize that there are many people who came from poor families or who grew up under difficult circumstances. And out of their trials and tribulations, they created something amazing. Other successful people hit roadblocks when they were older. In some cases, they faced external obstacles. In still others, they nearly succumbed to negativity, depression, cynicism or a victim mentality. Yet they managed to move through the dark times to thrive.

Remember, nothing is impossible. We are re-creating what has already been created, and we are finding new expressions of the creations that have occurred.

Here is an overview of the nine principles for creation and manifestation:

- Merge with what you seek.
- Remember – perception determines creation.
- Know when to be active and when to be passive.
- Flow like a river.
- Acknowledge and honor your emotions.
- Envision your goals.
- Transform negative experiences.
- Seek evidence that supports your new belief.
- Observe others' life examples.

Notes on Steps #11 and #12

"Your sharing about life's purpose has really inspired me. I've gained more clarity by putting what you've shared into practice, and things have started to change positively in my life in many areas. Sometimes I still struggle with negative emotions, though. Sometimes they take over and seem to get out of control. What can I do when this happens?"

Embracing Your Emotions

When it comes to emotions, what we first perceive as negative can have a lot of value, and can help us to move closer to our life's purpose.

I read an article in *Psychology Today* asserting that there is an upside to negative emotions. I wholeheartedly agree, and I'd like to share the gist of the article with you. The article's author explains that emotions we perceive as being negative can be beneficial, motivating us to change. In recent years, so much attention has been paid to the pursuit of happiness that negative emotions have been identified as unhealthy. In a religious context, in some circles they may even be viewed as sinful.

Emotions are not, however, inherently negative or positive. They're just a part of human existence. And it's true, sometimes uncomfortable feelings can serve as the catalyst for important change. If we feel envious of someone, for example, we may be moved to change our perception—cultivating gratitude for what we do have instead of bemoaning what we don't have. Or, we may realize that a person whose life looks perfect to us may in fact be struggling. Feeling angry may result in us thinking, "Well...I'll show them"—but instead, we can choose to change our point of view and cultivate compassion for the person we feel angry with. As you will see, any negative emotion can prompt us to move toward our goals—if we are mindful and embrace our emotions in a positive way.

Let's explore some emotions that we commonly perceive as "negative." As you will see, we'll find evidence that they can serve us in beneficial ways.

Anger and Frustration

Anger and frustration often arise when we feel undervalued or underestimated. When we're besieged by these emotions, we can feel out of control. If we let ourselves progress to rage, it may exacerbate the situation at hand. And yet, swallowing our pain for too long is also a mistake, for it can contribute to depression and health problems.

Anger and frustration can sometimes be experienced as pent-up energy. When you feel angry or frustrated, you may take risks, which in turn may fuel further anger and frustration. But allowing yourself to act when you feel angry or frustrated can sometimes be necessary—especially if the alternative is losing something that really matters to you. There is, however, a positive way to view these so-called "hot emotions." While many "negative" situations can encourage avoidance, anger and frustration, typically stimulating us to confront a problem head-on—that can be a healthy, empowering way to resolve a challenge and reach a positive solution.

Confusion and Boredom

Confusion, frustration and anger all produce a furrowed brow, a physical indicator that emotionally, we feel blocked in manifesting our goals. When confusion persists, you can become frustrated or angry. But the ongoing discomfort and chaos of frustration and anger—and the uncertainty they cause—can force you to take action. So, even confusion can be productive!

If you do not act when you feel confused, you may keep repeating the same action and ultimately get nowhere. After a while, boredom can ensue. But boredom too can nudge you to take action and start looking for solutions as to how to bring more inspiration and passion into your life. While stuck in the doldrums of boredom, you might be inspired to create new dreams or to embrace new challenges—and from the resulting insights, great ideas and solutions may emerge unexpectedly.

Envy and Jealousy

Our success often depends upon our status within a group and the resources we have access to. Our happiness and contentment are greatly influenced by how we compare ourselves to others. In that sense, when we long for what another person has, we may feel envious. Similarly, when we believe a third party has threatened a valued relationship, feelings of jealousy may arise. But these emotions have their benefits too. Envy and jealousy can motivate us to reverse what we perceive as inferiority through one of two paths: increasing our own standing in a group or decreasing the standing of others.

When we act to make our lives something we're proud of, we increase our standing in our community. By turning inward and shifting our focus from an external comparison to an intrinsic one, we no longer permit what other people think of us to affect our own self-esteem.

Fear and Anxiety

Fear and anxiety are our defenders. In some circumstances, they're an ideal, appropriate and natural response when we feel threatened. They heighten our awareness and prepare us to escape from dangerous situations. Fear stimulates in our minds vivid pictures of what might go wrong, and alerts us to impending danger so that we can remove ourselves from a dangerous situation before it manifests.

Without anxiety and fear to guide us, we might become indiscriminate risk-takers. So, feeling anxious and fearful about how we're living our lives can alert us to ways in which we are not being true to ourselves. They can highlight ways in which our actions don't align with our deepest values.

Regret and Disappointment

Regret emerges when we think about what could have been, if only we had done something differently. On the positive side, regret and disappointment point to lessons we can learn from our mistakes. Learning by doing is an important part of our soul's education.

Disappointment and regret can also work as positive factors in our lives, motivating us to fix difficult situations we may have caused, whether that means apologizing to a friend or returning an impulse purchase to the store.

It can be healing in such a circumstance to distinguish feelings of regret from feelings of disappointment. If, for example, we regret a choice we have made in our lives, we can become motivated to *abandon* a goal rather than persist in pursuing it. While disappointment might be the result of letting go of a dream, disappointment can serve a purpose. Sometimes quitting should be perceived not as failure but rather as an opportunity to change tack and get closer to your true path.

Sadness and Grief

Sadness and grief come in response to real or potential loss. We can become especially sad, for example, after the loss of a beloved person or a cherished pet. Whatever the source of our sadness, it signals that restoration, retreat and time for ourselves is needed.

When sadness and grief affect our lives, we may find it necessary to make significant changes in order to return to happiness and joy. It may be time for us to reach out to the people in our lives, letting them know we need their support. Or, it may be time for a change in lifestyle or time for us to adopt a new philosophy or engage in new pursuits.

But like the many other emotions we have covered, sadness and grief can have positive effects in our lives. For example, experiencing sadness and grief can make us more empathetic to others' struggles. When we accept and embrace sadness and grief in the "now" moment—instead of blocking these emotions—we sidestep the risk that over the longer term, we could be fighting an even bigger battle: with depression.

Shame and Guilt

To ensure that we live in community successfully, everyone must agree to adhere to social and moral norms. When we violate these norms, the emotions of shame and guilt signal the need to pull ourselves back toward more appropriate behavior. Without these emotions, we wouldn't be able to trust each other—or ourselves.

When we act out of character and do something we are ashamed of or that we feel guilty about, the discomforts of guilt and shame serve as a sort of compass, turning us inward to examine what led us to behave in the manner we did. But while it is advantageous to us to examine our own behavior, we ought not to blame or shame others or try to make them feel guilty for their behavior. It can be detrimental to us if we judge others or try to "fix" them. As the late, legendary author Dr. Wayne Dyer once said: "When you judge another, you do not define them, you define yourself."

Rather than finding fault in others, we'd be better off taking a note from a Michael Jackson song and take a look at "The Man in the Mirror." Moments of self-examination, which can range from painful to beautiful, can help us gain more clarity about what we need to fix in ourselves. If, however, you find yourself overwhelmed by shame or guilt (or any other strong emotion), there may be a deeper problem. Perhaps you are judging yourself harshly; perhaps you feel that you are inherently flawed; or maybe you have set unrealistic standards for yourself. If this is the case, you may be called to do some inner work, perhaps with the help of a psychologist, therapist or life coach.

When it comes to being able to relate more consciously to emotions, I highly recommend the movie, *Inside Out*. It's set in the mind of a young girl, where five personified emotions—joy, sadness, fear, anger and disgust—try to control her life. After watching this movie, you'll gain a new perspective on the emotions you and others around you experience.

In Steps 11 & 12, I use some examples to show that there are different ways we can deal with our emotions. These examples are not intended to be comprehensive or to analyze the whole spectrum of this topic, but they will give you some tips and tactics to help you navigate life's challenges on an emotional level.

So, when you're ready, find a peaceful space where you won't be disturbed. Get quiet. Have your journal and a pen handy to make notes. Then, get ready to tap into your power, embrace your creativity and use these twelve steps to reach your fullest potential and transform your life.

THE STEPS

STEP #1 - BE TRUTHFUL.

When we are unaware and unconscious, we go through life with closed eyes and we stumble repeatedly over obstacles on the way. With this outlook, it's more difficult to find the direction in which our life's purpose lies.

As long as our eyes are closed, we walk through life blindly. We go from one graduation to another and from one office building to another, or we bounce from one partner to another. Later, we wonder why we feel dissatisfied with how we have spent our lives.

We finally start asking ourselves what is missing, even if we've found the family we always wanted, furnished the perfect home, and have a great car outside the door. Although we are occupied with our work and have taken on more responsibility year after year, a deep emptiness grows inside us.

To forget their inner emptiness,
most people work more or withdraw.
Others awaken.

In an effort to forget their inner emptiness, most people choose one of the following options: they work more or they withdraw. Others come to a point of awakening; they open their eyes and reflect deeply upon themselves and their environment.

In my own journey, two burnout experiences guided me to important crossroads, where I had no choice but to open my eyes, look at my life, and reflect deeply within. During these tough periods, I was led to Hawaii. Of course, a "side benefit" of Hawaii is that there is so much beauty around you. But even if you are not surrounded by sand and surf and tropical blue waters, you can engage with the beauty in your life with all your passion and joy. That is a key step in self-awakening and finding your own, deepest truth.

This is the first step in the 12-step process. Alan Cohen recommends this easy exercise: Take an empty piece of paper and draw a vertical line in the middle, top to bottom. On one side, write down everything you love to do with passion, joy and whole-heartedness. Then, on the other side of the paper, write down the things you do in your work and private life that you like doing less.

Please be honest with yourself when you do this exercise. Hold back self-criticism and doubt as much as possible. No one but you will read this piece of paper—not your boss or the people in your private life. Just become aware and be honest. What do you like? What do you dislike?

Labyrinthe Vert, Nébias, France

STEP #2 - START SLOWLY. START NOW.

The second step can help bring passion and liveliness back into your life. It can help you move in your desired direction—not by plunging in but instead by taking small steps, starting today. I suggest you take action immediately after you've finished reading this section.

For example, you could allow yourself to do something you've wanted to do for a long time. Maybe you've wanted to go to a movie or enjoy a concert. Maybe you've longed to go to a certain restaurant with a friend to share a delicious meal. Maybe you want to book a journey you've dreamed of for a long time. Perhaps you've wanted to buy a book or a perfume and have held it in your hands several times, only to put it back again. Treat yourself!

Of course, the thing you want to have or do doesn't need to be something material. There are other questions you can ask yourself: When was the last time you really took time for yourself—not in front of a television or a computer, but perhaps at a spa or in a bathtub? When did you last relax and meditate? When was the last time you took a walk in a beautiful, natural setting? How long has it been since you painted, wrote a poem or created something?

Another thing you can do is get rid of negative thoughts and begin spreading positive energy. Maybe you've already heard about the law of attraction. It dictates that you attract to yourself whatever you think about most. There are basically two scenarios: either you create a positive life through positive thoughts, or you allow negative thoughts to bring you troubles.

We all radiate positive or negative vibrations. We put out higher or lower energy in every moment which others receive without realizing it. If you have a negative perception of particular situations, people or experiences, you will attract negativity. To prevent this unhealthy cycle, you need to change your thought patterns. Start to identify negative thoughts through a heightened awareness and presence. When you experience them, say "Get out of my head right now!" or something similar that feels right to you. In the beginning this might feel silly, but it's a simple and effective tool—and it works!

I encourage you to work with these first two steps for the next few days. Be honest with yourself, don't procrastinate and start taking the first small steps *today*.

STEP #3 - SLOW DOWN. STOP.

You must allow yourself to let go of the past so that something new and beautiful can emerge in the still, empty space you've created.

In my experience, it can be difficult to separate ourselves from familiar things. But it's not just situational changes—like moving into a new apartment—that call for us to evolve. If we hope to progress, it's crucial that we also transcend old thoughts, behavioral patterns and outdated subconscious programming. When we examine programs that no longer serve us, we often discover that we have adopted conditioning from our parents, from the society we were born into or from the collective consciousness.

Rituals or ceremonies can be an effective and powerful way to leave behind what no longer serves you. You don't have to work with a shaman. You can create a ritual or ceremony yourself by connecting with nature and its various elements. A ceremony might be as simple as clearing your space with sage, "sweating out" beliefs you don't need in a sauna, or picturing a healing light flowing through your body. Or, if you're having trouble disconnecting from an obsolete relationship, you can visualize yourself cutting the energetic lines that tie you to that person.

If you're someone for whom shamanic rituals or spiritual ceremonies do not resonate, there are many other "practical" applications you can implement in your daily life. Maybe you're part of a business or organization that is no longer meaningful to you. Perhaps you're pursuing an educational path that doesn't interest you anymore, or you're fulfilling a duty that's no longer your responsibility. When you're engaged in an activity and time seems to take forever, it may be a clue that the pursuit is no longer connected to your passion.

Letting go of things that no longer serve you in all areas of your life can clear your energy field to invite new, fresh, creative vibrations in. For example, do you go to parties, concerts or other gatherings simply to avoid "missing anything," or just so you can "be a part of it?" Can you let those types of social outings go and free up space to expand your circle to include people who are more in line with your passions? Similarly, do you hold onto expensive belongings you have for the sole purpose of impressing others? Can you let those things go and keep only things you truly love and that speak to your heart?

After we stop and disconnect—from our work, our social circles, our belongings—we often realize that letting go is much easier than we had feared. Again, you don't need to take a huge first step. Start with something small—but start today!

STEP #4 - DISCOVER AND DEVELOP YOUR TALENTS.

The term "talent development" is common in the business world. While studying human resources management many years ago, I realized that goal-oriented training, staff development and employee relations are crucial if a company wants to thrive.

One tool in talent development involves creating a personalized plan for an employee, one devised to capitalize on their strengths and to bolster any weaknesses. Many companies retain managers longer by setting up career models and options, giving workers a glimpse of how they can grow along with the business. Perhaps you've had the experience of this type of appraisal interview at your workplace.

Of course, we can apply talent development to more than business. We can apply it to life in general. Maybe you're asking yourself, "Do I even have any talents and gifts?" You might entertain doubts about your abilities, even as others gift you with appreciation and positive feedback for certain things you do. We're taught to be humble. If you want to develop your abilities, though, you need to celebrate them. So, ask yourself, "In what aspects of life am I truly gifted?" What might your best friends say if you asked them what distinguishes you from others? When you answered the questions and did the exercises I shared earlier, it's likely you found talents you hadn't been fully aware of.

None of us are exceptional at everything we like to do, but we are all talented in many ways. Your small passions, talents and gifts can be hints about your huge potential, and these gifts may be slumbering within you.

So, what are *your* gifts? When you think about it, everything in your life is a gift. So, take a look at your life, be grateful for everything you have. Then, having grounded yourself in gratitude, take time to reveal the hidden talents that are not yet awakened within you. Use the exercises in this section to empower yourself to step forward with these gifts. These exercises will help you learn to prevail in the face of apprehension and to step through your fears. When you conquer your fears, it unlocks unforeseen possibilities—you become free to be who you truly are!

I encourage you to work with Steps #3 and #4 for a few days. Create a meaningful ritual or ceremony. Gift yourself with time to connect with nature and its elements. Keep asking yourself and your friends:

"What do I do well?" Then, pay close attention to the answers—and the aspects of life in which you are really gifted will be revealed to you.

STEP #5 - DISCERN. THEN, CHOOSE.

When something no longer serves you or when your life choices and pursuits no longer feel right and a new option presents itself, it's time to make a decision and choose.

After my first powerful, transformative experiences with healing and energy work in 2008 in Hawaii, I pursued further personal development when I returned to Europe. In 2009, I decided to work with a life coach. As a result, I experienced systemic coaching from the perspective of a client before embarking on my own life coaching education. Systemic coaching assesses human relationship dynamics to help people change unhealthy aspects of their relationships. It postulates that if one representative of a human system can recognize and change dysfunctional patterns, other members of that human system can also change. At the end of the coaching process, I was clear—I wanted to work as a certified life coach!

But even though I felt called to this new line of work, I wasn't yet ready to become self-employed. It was only after my burnout experience in 2010 that I was finally able to move forward on my coaching path. In that time of crisis, I had many valuable experiences—the most important of which was that I learned which kind of support, tools and strategies worked for me and which did not.

I'd like to share with you an exercise and decision-making tool that I was introduced to during my training in life coaching. I have used it with several clients and you can use this tool for yourself:

> *First, write down the problem. Then, write down two options for a particular scenario (solution A or B, or*

'certain' or 'uncertain') on two pieces of paper. Then, put the sheets on the ground. Next, stand with both feet on one of the two sheets, and then move your feet to step on the other. Close your eyes and become aware on a 'feeling' level what each choice will bring to you.

This simple exercise cultivates a gut feeling that is stronger than your thoughts. It encourages you to find a holistic, grounded solution that feels right, both in your mind and in your heart.

After I had some positive experiences with this tool, I started to share it with others. Many clients reported that the two (or more) pieces of paper they stood on prompted them to admit their feelings. Once clarity arrived, they didn't need the papers anymore.

When you stand at a crossroads and feel uncertain about which path to follow, it is helpful to close your eyes and focus on your breath. Imagine the outcome of each possible decision. Let your feelings determine your path. Which path feels most alive, exciting and truthful? That is always the right path.

Many people describe this as letting their "belly" decide. Each time you do this, you learn more about what you really want. Keep it up and your gut feelings will become stronger and more reliable over time.

STEP #6 - LET YOUR PASSIONS GUIDE YOU.

Money is one of the main reasons many people believe they can't improve their situation and start living a passionate, purposeful life. They say, "If I had more money, I'd start pursuing my dreams and stop procrastinating," "If I had more money, I'd start traveling around the world," or "If I had more money, I'd quit this terrible job and pursue something better."

Below are three statements you can complete for yourself:

- When I experience total abundance, I feel…
- When I have abundance, where I love to contribute is…
- When I'm living in abundance, I can contribute more by….

After all, money alone does not bring long-lasting happiness. If someone is trying to achieve actualization only through material means, it means something is missing in their life. Of course, there's no harm in seeking abundance for yourself and your family. Having enough money can provide you with many opportunities and options—and free you from worrying about paying bills.

However, I invite you to ask yourself, "How would I feel if, one day, I lost everything I owned?" Would you decide you're worthless because you've lost everything? Would you worry that you're not yourself anymore?

When you look at the world, you see that economic crises or natural disasters can turn people's lives upside down. No matter how well you do in life and how much insurance you buy, there are always financial risks.

Although having money can bring temporary happiness, many people who have the best houses, cars or toys don't stop desiring more. They are discontent and, rather than expressing gratitude for what they already have, they keep buying, hoping they'll find peace through acquiring material things. Even if such a person got all the money in the world, it could never fill the void inside of them because it is important to first find meaning and purpose before undertaking any materialistic pursuit.

For many people, the first criteria in any decision they make is to weigh which option will yield the most money. For example, you might have to choose between quitting a well-paying job and, despite your limited income, instead enjoying a life filled with activities you love. Or maybe you need to choose between a field of study that gives you joy and inspires you, and one that is in a more revenue-generating field, like medicine, law or business. Or, maybe you have to choose between life partners: do you choose the financially established, conservative businessperson or the artist with less financial resources who is inspiring and loving?

All of these are examples of difficult decisions. Many of us may still believe, in our core, that money rules the world. But when you put things in perspective, your life's purpose can't be expressed through monetary amounts or numbers. Most self-made, successful people have followed their own path, not the path where the most money can be found. So, we need to stop looking outside of ourselves to find our life's purpose. We need to stop focusing on what others—be they people or companies—are telling us we should do and be. Look within—that is where you will find your own insights and answers!

I encourage you to work with Steps #5 and #6 for the next several days and become aware of the areas of your life in which you've been procrastinating. Start making choices! Complete the three statements about money, and ask yourself, every day, "How can I best contribute to the world with my talents and passions?"

Hwapo Cheon Wetland and Nakdong Estuary, South Korea

STEP #7 - FOLLOW YOUR INTUITION.

Do you hear a silent voice deep within you, whispering to you? Does that voice tell you where, when and with whom you should do something specific? Are you listening? Are you keenly aware of a particular development in society? Are you acting on your ideas? What significance do you give to your daydreams—and to your nighttime dreams?

One great tool you can use to follow your intuition is to write a diary about your dreams. The father of logic, René Descartes, created his groundbreaking method of philosophic inquiry based on a dream he had. I encourage you to learn more about techniques like dream work, hypnosis, energy work, meditation and intuition. Check out my services at: *www.YvesNager.com* It's important to create some space and time every day to become more aware of your natural, intuitive nature. The fastest way to get in touch with your intuition is to meditate regularly, in the morning or in the evening, for at least twenty minutes. Conscious breathing throughout the day can also be a great support in strengthening your intuition (in my own experience, the most powerful moments for meditation and conscious breathing—and to hear your inner voices—are during sunrise and sunset).

A big misconception among people who don't practice meditation is that those who meditate do so in an attempt to escape the present moment. In fact, meditation is about expanding your consciousness while becoming fully present and fully grounded in the present moment. When you get quiet and become aware of the here and now, that is when you can tap into your inner being and allow your intuitive senses to emerge. Just get still—and listen.

STEP #8 - STAY OPEN, RECEPTIVE AND FLEXIBLE.

If your longstanding dreams have faded over the years and bring you less joy, the time has come to create new dreams and new goals. It doesn't matter if this is in business or in private life. When your situation and experiences no longer fulfill you, the time has come to shift your focus.

Many people tend to balk at change because the unknown feels scary. Others believe that if they change course after many years, it will appear to others as though they've failed in their previous path. They're afraid to lose face in front of others.

When you become receptive and open yourself up to new possibilities, opportunities arise, giving you a great opportunity to proactively, consciously create new experiences and grow.

When they first contact me, many people seeking coaching or healing are stuck in the drama of their life situation. One of the first things I tell them is that engaging in the drama closes them off from attracting meaningful experiences. When you step away from the drama and focus on staying receptive and flexible, suddenly, new opportunities to share your gifts, talents and purpose begin to show up.

Demian Lichtenstein and Shajen Joy Aziz, the creators of *Discover the Gift, www.DiscoverTheGift.com* share with us that receptivity is about openness, and flexibility is about being fluid. When you become receptive, you may find things opening up quickly. Two things can happen: the things that arrive may seem mundane, or they may feel like more than you can handle. There is no need to analyze any of this in the beginning. Just be aware of it—receive it with flexibility and with gratitude—and let it go. Be mindful of what happens next—life is filled with surprises and synchronicities when you commit to being open, receptive and flexible!

I encourage you to work with Steps #7 and #8 for the next few days. Create some space and time every day to become increasingly aware of your intuition. Listen—can you hear the still, small voice within?

Limahuli Garden and Preserve, Kaua'i

STEP #9 - LEARN HOW AND WHEN TO REST.

Even when we begin to follow the right path toward our life's purpose, we are not immune to burning out if we work too much. For example, consider doctors and therapists who are on call seven days a week, musicians who play around the clock, writers who refuse to desert their computer keyboards, and painters who eat their meals with a paintbrush under one arm—sooner or later, all are forced to stop and rest.

Overwork can manifest in unpleasant symptoms of the body, mind and emotions, problems that require people to cancel appointments, drop their instruments, close their laptops, or put away their brushes. Obviously, it's better if we don't let things come to this burnout point!

Sometimes, burnout feels like a blazing inner fire has been suddenly extinguished. At other times, the sense of depletion is gradual, as though the flames are dwindling, getting smaller and smaller. Your inner fire needs new oxygen to keep burning. Maybe you've already noticed that when you allow time for rest, relaxation and rejuvenation, new inspiration, visions and ideas emerge from your subconscious. Don't forget to take periodic breaks during work, and set aside one day a week when you don't work at all.

It's important to take good care of yourself so you can renew your life force. In fact, it's a precondition of fulfilling your life's purpose. This can pose a huge challenge, especially for many self-employed people. Happily, there are many practical ways you can care for yourself: take regular walks in nature, meet with friends (without cell phones and laptops, please!), spend time with animals, engage in yoga or sports (and here, I don't mean competitive sports), journal, or—and this one is a must-do—meditate regularly.

There are both active and passive forms of meditation. Active meditation might include walking, combing the beach for shells, gardening or playing an instrument. Passive meditation can include sitting in silence, pondering a spiritual word or phrase, chanting a mantra, or other quiet forms of self-reflection.

As noted, journaling is also a good way to relax—and expand. Writing about your life can help you assimilate your impressions and experiences. You might focus on the good in your life by writing down a list of what you are grateful for. Or you could set out to answer some questions, shedding light on your life's purpose. And, of course, the helpful exercises in this book will be a great addition to your journal!

As you spend more time taking care of yourself and finding time to rest and recuperate, you'll discover many other forms of relaxation. You might choose to gift yourself with a massage, visit a spa, or go for a hike in the wilderness. Any experience that can bring stillness to your life is perfect. Of course, getting enough sleep at night is a good idea too. Whatever you choose to do to renew your life force will help you immensely as you prepare to manifest your next dream!

STEP #10 - NOTICE LIFE'S GIFTS.

Have you exerted yourself over a long period of time, and yet somehow your goal seems to move farther and farther away? Maybe it's time to adjust your course.

As Ken Robinson, an internationally renowned author and speaker, shares with us in *Discover the Gift*: "Life is not linear but organic. We create our lives symbiotically as we explore our talents in relation to the circumstances they helped to create for us." However, in the western world, our conventional educational system is built in a linear way. Whether we're pursuing vocational training, a university degree or a promising career, we spend an enormous amount of time, energy and money working toward goals that we or others set for us at a particular point in time. Hence, instead of being fully present in the moment and cultivating ourselves to the best of our ability in each moment, our lives are often put on hold until a next goal or next milestone has been achieved.

Amassing degrees, licenses, certificates and other signs of achievement can be attractive; all those letters after our names prove that we haven't been wasting our time. The problem is that we change and transform. If you're striving toward goals that no longer feel meaningful, there may be other places where you could better invest your time and energy. Are you really on the right path? When you look at the lives of many highly successful people, you'll often discover that they originally followed a completely different career. Then something—or someone—inspired them to jump off the linear path and allow their lives to unfold 'organically.' The result: dreams realized, life's purpose discovered!

My own career has been anything but linear. I've worked in many different fields and gained education in various areas of life. No matter what I've done, however, I've always followed an "organic" way. It started with my wish to become an elementary school teacher. I later pursued an education in business, specializing in social security. I held different positions in the fields of health insurance and retirement funds and worked as a volunteer for the transportation department at the Swiss Red Cross. I also served as an animal welfare and administration specialist for an animal welfare association. Later, I started to study socio-cultural presentations and got a technical diploma in human resources management. And now I'm self-employed and offer my services in the realms of life coaching, energy work, wellbeing and spirituality.

Intuition and serendipity can give you hints as to the best path to follow.

On my own journey of transformation, I've found myself at many crossroads. It's always been my gut feelings and intuition—as well as serendipitous experiences and encounters—that have given me hints as to the best path to follow.

With greater awareness, you can gain more clarity as to how you actually create. You can also discover—perhaps with the guidance of a life coach, therapist or good friend—whether the path you're currently on still feels right for you.

I encourage you to work with Steps #9 and #10 for the next several days. Learn how and when to rest. Pay close attention to the new inspirations, visions and ideas emerging from your subconscious. Stop trying so hard—instead, allow yourself to enjoy a calm and relaxed space. Become more aware of your gut feelings, and when you make decisions, ask your intuition!

Hanalei Bay

STEP #11 - READ SIGNS, SEE SYNCHRONICITIES.

Another important step toward finding your life's purpose is to notice *signs*. Start to take notice of what is happening around you—events, synchronicities, things people say and do. You'll soon discover that life is constantly giving you clues that can guide you to the right path to take on your journey toward your goals.

The renowned novelist Paulo Coelho is a follower of signs. For many years, he relied on the Chinese masterpiece, *The I Ching*, an ancient book of divination, to help him decipher the signs and symbols that appeared in his life. If you are interested in the topic of signs, Coelho's book *The Alchemist* will inspire you. Or, you may find insights in the Bible, the Koran, the Bhagavad-Gita, or in the spiritual poetry of celebrated writers such as Rumi, Rabindranath Tagore, or Kahlil Gibran. Even the words of dramatist William Shakespeare can be deeply inspirational for many people. You may, for example, select a passage in one of these authors' books, seemingly at random, and find the exact answers you're looking for! Now that's synchronicity at work!

The eminent Swiss psychiatrist and psychoanalyst Carl Gustav Jung described *synchronicity* as incidents that are connected to each other—events that are perceived and interpreted as related. Some people believe these "cosmic clues" appear via the intervention of a higher power or spiritual allies. Others feel that they are simply beneficial mediation points that can lead to great insights.

Synchronicities occur when an outer physical event reflects a manifestation of an inner condition: a dream, a vision, an emotion or an idea. To effectively define an incident as *synchronistic*, the inner incident must happen before or simultaneously ("synchronous") with an outer incident.

If you open yourself up, notice these meaningful clues and use them to guide your actions, you'll begin to recognize synchronicity everywhere in your daily life. For example, maybe you've had an experience where a person calls you at the same time you're thinking about them. Similarly, you might find yourself in a situation and are suddenly struck by the feeling that you have already experienced it (called "déjà vu"). Or, you might have a dream and then something from the dream actually happens (the next day or even several years later). Or, someone tells you about something, and then the next day, you hear someone else talk about the same topic. Or, you might become aware that particular combinations of numbers keep showing up and after a time you discern the significance of those numbers in your life. When you start looking for it, you'll find synchronicity everywhere!

STEP #12 - BE COURAGEOUS. TAKE RISKS!

To reach our goals and realize our fullest potential, often we have to make a change in our lives. Achieving what matters to us always involves a certain amount of risk. For example, after you quit an unpleasant job, a phase of unemployment may follow. During this time, you may find more clarity regarding what kind of environment you would like to work in and you may discover the most efficient approach to applying for your ideal job.

Daring to dream can make you vulnerable. When you share your greatest visions and dearest hopes with others, they might (if you choose to confide in the wrong person) characterize you as unrealistic and suggest that you make viable plans instead of focusing on "pipe dreams." But remember—their dreams for you are not your dreams for you. So, choose your friends, lovers and confidantes carefully. Dream your dreams—then take action to attain them!

The search for genuine love and friendship can expose us to potential hurt. But in this area of your life, you must be willing to take risks. On one hand, for example, it's true that a person you feel attracted to may reject you. But on the other hand, they may also be happy about your overtures...so much so that you may find yourself building a family together. So, it's true what they say: you never know until you try! When we are open, receptive and aware, new opportunities tend to pop up out of nowhere. So, take a deep breath and take risks with things that really matter to you!

Achieving your life's purpose is so important and valuable that it's inevitably linked to taking a risk and abandoning the need to feel secure—no matter how strong that need might be.

By sharing this book with you, I hope to support you in discovering your gifts, getting closer to your own life's purpose, and sharing your passion with others and the world. I'll be happy if you gain a bit more clarity and confidence about finding your life's purpose by reading this book. Even though some of the questions, tools and steps you've read and applied so far may be familiar, I hope this book supplies you with a few new tools, innovative techniques and concrete steps to help you implement effective, efficient changes in your life.

I encourage you to work with these final steps for a few days. Become aware of synchronicities and learn to read the signs life presents to you every day. Be more courageous and take some risks. Ask yourself, "What matters to me?" "What has value for me?" And then let the inspiration you feel move you forward!

Here is an overview of the 12 STEPS:

1. Be truthful.

2. Start slowly. Start now.

3. Slow down. Stop.

4. Discover and develop your talents.

5. Discern. Then, choose.

6. Let your passions guide you.
7. Follow your intuition.
8. Stay open, receptive and flexible.
9. Learn how and when to rest.
10. Notice life's gifts.
11. Read signs, see synchronicities.
12. Be courageous. Take risks!

Hanalei Bay

PART III
STORIES WITH PURPOSE

Part III consists of 12 stories I've written over the past three years, providing examples of people—and even animals—who are living (or have lived) their purpose. In some stories, we'll travel to parts of the world I've visited in pursuit of my own life's purpose. In some other stories, you'll accompany me on journeys that brought me my greatest blessings (as well as my toughest challenges!) and helped me to live from the heart and keep evolving. I hope these stories will inspire you to follow your heart, find your purpose, and fulfill your destiny!

Blessings from Hawaii

Hawaii has been a source of inspiration and a place of spiritual rebirth for me, so I'll start by sharing five powerful stories from this beautiful group of islands. They highlight what I feel are valuable qualities of the Aloha spirit that blessed me on my journey:

- Blessing of Gratitude,
- Blessing of Clarity,
- Blessing of Forgiveness,

- Blessing of Relaxation, and
- Blessing of Healing.

I believe these stories will encourage and empower you to live your life on purpose.

Blessing of Gratitude

On April 28, 2015, I celebrated my thirty-ninth birthday alone; Eunjung was on the East Coast for a work trip. She joined me on Oahu two days later. Before heading to Honolulu airport to pick her up, I decided to take a short walk—it was a decision that prompted an unforgettable Aha! moment.

While walking along the ocean from my hotel to the Waikiki Aquarium, I saw a concrete structure stretching out to sea. I was hit with a flash of memory. I'd visited this same beach often seven years earlier, after an ill-fated relationship fell apart. I remember that at the time, I believed I may have found the woman of my dreams. I was heartbroken when, after a month of dating, we both realized we couldn't have a committed relationship.

During this difficult time, I tried my best to release the pain. I craved a less crowded retreat than Waikiki Beach, so I found a smaller, calmer, quieter beach about ten minutes away, in front of a nice hotel—*this beach*. After my English classes, I went there to study, and as I leaned against the concrete structure, I read the books *The Mastery of Love* and *The Four Agreements* by Mexican author Don Miguel Ruiz. I also journaled, writing about what I was learning from the spiritual wisdom in Ruiz's books and in that phase of my life.

The first insight I received was how beneficial moments of solitude are. For me, sitting in solitude, meditating and accepting the circumstances of this challenging period was a first step in overcoming my fear of being alone. For the first time in my life, I let my sense of pain and sadness surface fully. As I embraced my true self and allowed myself to be in the moment, I felt my feelings transform. I discovered then that miracles reveal themselves to us once we overcome our fears and become willing to stay open and receptive. Later, I learned that there is a word for that experience—synchronicity!

Many people are afraid of solitude. How often recently have you spent time by yourself? Are you ready? I invite you to take some quiet time alone. Allow yourself to rest, relax and allow the grace of silence to enfold and empower you.

The second insight I received was the power of gratitude.
At that time, I liked to sit in the same place every day, leaning against the concrete wall and looking at the ocean. (The picture below shows me sitting at the same spot during my more recent visit.) I would sometimes daydream about what a wonderful time my prospective partner and I could have shared, right there at the beach.

As time passed, however, my pain at losing my relationship began to subside. It was replaced by feelings of gratefulness that I'd met someone who'd opened my heart again to love and, ultimately, to self-love. I was thankful I'd been able to experience this love, however briefly, about a year after my last relationship of seven years had broken down in Switzerland. I know now—though I didn't know at that time how things would turn out—that feeling gratitude in even the most difficult situations brings opportunities and synchronicities, which guide us closer to our life's purpose.

My initial reveries at this peaceful beach took place in June 2008. On that April morning in 2015, I suddenly realized that I was back at the same beach. I was staying in the very hotel I had been admiring while sitting on the beach seven years earlier! And, I knew I would see my beloved Eunjung soon and bring her here to this spot. This amazing realization touched me deeply and moved me to tears. This time, though, I wasn't crying because of grief but because of deep gratitude. My return to this familiar place was marked by an entirely new perspective and clarity about my path and my purpose in life.

When I look back on the difficult time I had ten years ago, I understand that the heartbreak was hugely beneficial for my journey. As painful as it was, the experience helped me become clear about what my ideal relationship would look like. Even more importantly, I was able to begin finding peace, self-love and harmony within myself again.

The third insight I received was the value of taking action toward what I consciously choose to experience next.

After the difficult breakup in Honolulu in mid-June of 2008, I was heartbroken and felt paralyzed, unable to let go and move forward. I like running, however my sadness manifested in such a way that the soles of my feet started to hurt so much that it became impossible for me to run. I knew something had to change. Finally, three weeks later, the first action I took to get myself out of my miserable mental and emotional state was skydiving. One of the most effective ways to get unstuck is to do something you've never done before. As I sat in the small airplane rising to the sky, I felt numb and emotionless. Surprised, my instructor wondered why I wasn't more excited about the jump and asked if I was afraid. I'll never forget the moment when we stepped out of the plane in mid-air, about 14,000 feet (4,200 meters) above the ground.

To get unstuck, do something you've never done before.

Upon seeing the magnificent beauty of the entire landscape of the North Shore of Oahu and the turquoise-blue Pacific Ocean from high above, a rush of adrenaline flooded through my body. From this extreme vantage point, I was finally able to feel the emotions that had been stuck inside me, completely suppressed by feelings of grief and loss. I'd been tense for about three weeks, and the freefall experience of skydiving offered a much-needed release.

Kaimana Beach, Honolulu

Blessing of Clarity

At the end of June 2011, as I was finishing a six-month long program at the Pacific Center for Awareness and Bodywork (PCAB), I felt a strong inner pull to go on a vision quest and travel to all of the Hawaiian Islands. One of several intentions I had was to meet a *kahuna* or *kupuna* during my journey. These two words are shrouded by myths and ancient legends. Briefly speaking, *kahuna* refers to a

Hawaiian priest or healer, whereas *kupuna* means a Hawaiian elder or wisdom keeper. When I embarked on my vision quest on June 30, 2011, I was clear about the "what," but I had no idea about "how" I would be able to find such a wisdom keeper or healer.

I first travelled to the Big Island of Hawaii and then to Maui. I visited many *heiau* (ancient Hawaiian temples) to pay respect and offer prayers of harmony and peace for the Hawaiian Islands and for the world. While I encountered many magical moments, and received profound insights during this first part of my journey, I didn't meet anyone who could lead me to a true kahuna or kupuna.

When I flew to Moloka'i, which is known as "The Friendly Island," I was unaware that I would soon find what I was looking for. On the second day after arriving, through a series of synchronicities I was guided to the Halawa Valley—located at the eastern end of Moloka'i. During my first dinner at a local restaurant, after learning about my deep interest in Hawaiian culture, the musician who was playing there told me to look for a master teacher of Hawaiian culture, Pilipo Solatorio (aka Anakala "Uncle" Pilipo) in the Halawa Valley.

When I drove down to this remote, sacred valley, I was struck by its awe-inspiring beauty and heart-opening energy. Upon arriving, I saw a few local Hawaiian families enjoying themselves at the beach. I asked an older man if he knew where I could find Pilipo. He was friendly and asked why I wanted to meet Pilipo. After I told him my intention of meeting a Hawaiian wisdom keeper, he said, "Just walk into the valley and you will meet him if that is the will of *Ke Akua Mana Mau*" (which can be translated as "eternal, mighty god").

As I followed the trail into the valley, I noticed several signs saying "no trespassing" and "private property." This made me doubt it was a good idea to walk in by myself—and wonder if it would be better for me to leave. Having learned to listen to my heart, however, I felt I needed to keep trusting and keep walking. After about fifteen minutes of treading along the path, I saw a house on the left-hand side. An older, dignified-looking man with a powerful presence emerged from the home. He walked straight toward me and asked what I was looking for, what brought me to the island, what my relationship with my family members was like, and what my intention in visiting him was. Elated that I was led to the right person, I answered as best I could.

That was how I connected with Pilipo. He told me that on Sundays he usually leaves the valley to visit family members on another part of the island, but said that he'd had a vision the night before that someone would come to visit him. He asked several more questions and I answered them honestly, with an open heart and much respect. Through this initial conversation, we connected in such a profound way that we sat down and shared our stories with one another for more than five hours.

During our precious time together, I learned about Pilipo's life, his Hawaiian culture and history and the way he grew up in the valley as a child. The most profound moment was when Pilipo started to cry as he told me about how the lands were taken away from the Hawaiians illegally. It was so touching that I started to cry too. We hugged for a long time.

Afterwards, Pilipo shared the following wisdom with me:

> *Many Hawaiian people suffer from what happened in the past. Some respond with anger and rage, while others choose a more peaceful way. However, no matter what happens on a personal, collective or global level, we always have a choice in every moment regarding where we want to focus and whether or not we let our thoughts and beliefs run our lives.*

I was deeply touched by everything Pilipo had shared with me. When I left in the evening to drive back to my hotel, my heart was wide open. Since that initial meeting with Pilipo during my vision quest, I've returned to this sacred valley and visited him three more times.

Pilipo's words about letting our thoughts run our lives resonated with me deeply. So, when I discovered a process called "The Work," *www.TheWork.com* developed by renowned author and speaker Byron Katie, I embraced it enthusiastically. "The Work" is a simple yet life-changing system of inquiry that teaches you to identify and question the thoughts that cause all the suffering in your world.

The main problem with all the stories you continuously tell yourself, and the deep core beliefs you hold onto, is that they refer to something that happened in the past or something which may happen in the future. If you believe and hold onto your stories as truth when they are no longer relevant to your life, you disempower yourself. This makes it difficult for you to consciously choose what matters most to you in the present moment.

I started to apply "The Work" regularly on my own transformational journey several years ago, and experienced a huge sense of freedom. I'd like to invite you to consider exploring "The Work." You can find information online about this powerful process of self-inquiry.

Royal Coconut Coast, Kaua'i

Blessing of Forgiveness

In the following story, I'll share another simple yet dynamic tool to help you unleash the power of forgiveness.

Pilipo was seventy-one when I met him seven years ago on Moloka'i but his face was nearly unlined. Maybe it's living in the remote and pristine Halawa Valley, where he grew up and raised his six children. Or maybe he draws strength from the boar's tusk pendant he wears suspended from a *kukui nut lei*. The history of the Kukui nut lei dates back to the arrival of the early Polynesians to the Hawaiian Islands. They brought the kukui trees and nuts with them from southeast Asia and cultivated them on the Hawaiian Islands. The nut from these trees has spiritual significance because of its many uses. The kukui nut lei was only worn by royalty in ancient times, and the reigning chiefs and kings treasured them and wore them proudly.

During our first meeting, Pilipo talked about an ancient Hawaiian forgiveness ritual. Many books have been written about this meaningful act, and people around the world have become aware of the practice in recent years. Have you heard of *Ho'oponopono*? It can be a little difficult to pronounce, but it's a simple and easy process to apply.

The principle behind Ho'oponopono is that many people suffer because of their thoughts and feelings about the past. We cling to old labels we've attached to events and experiences, even though they lost their true impact long ago. Our suffering originates from an unwillingness to let go of the stories we've created about the past. Along with "The Work" from Byron Katie, Ho'oponopono is a great tool to apply when we feel like "our story" is holding us back.

When I first met Pilipo, he asked me about my relationship with my family. He explained later why this question matters. Pilipo told me that when just one family member has a problem, the entire family—in fact, the whole generation—is influenced, far more than most people are aware of. The good news is that we can forgive ourselves and others. This act of forgiveness not only benefits our immediate family members, but also impacts our ancestors in a hugely positive way. Ho'oponopono is a key element of this forgiveness practice. The essence of Ho'oponopono is this: Your thoughts and emotions manifest as health or illness in your body. Ho'oponopono is a simple tool for peacemaking and spiritual cleansing, through which you can free yourself from sorrow and fears, destructive habits, old belief systems and any other negativity.

After learning about Ho'oponopono, I've applied it regularly on my own journey, with results that have exceeded my expectations. Ho'oponopono can guide us back to unity, inner peace and harmony. Here are the four simple statements of Ho'oponopono: "*I am sorry. Please forgive me. Thank you. I love you.*"

The origin of Ho'oponopono is ancient. It's an essential part of a system of Hawaiian wisdom called "Huna." The group of eight Hawaiian Islands is described as "The Land of Aloha" which, loosely translated, means "The Land of Love." Aloha is the essence of Huna, and provides the basis of this age-old ritual.

Neither Ho'oponopono nor Huna is a fixed system. You can use Ho'oponopono as one of many ways to release inner blockages and unhealthy programs that sabotage you, preventing you from being in the flow of life and receiving the gifts of the universe.

Another application is the "family conference," a Hawaiian tradition that can be beneficial in youth and social work. During my first visit to the Halawa Valley, Pilipo shared with me six steps that are an essential part of the great Hawaiian foregiveness ritual:

- Connection with the source of origin (*Akua*), the light beings and ancestors.
- Contemplation (*Hala*) and acceptance (*Hihia*) of the problem within the heart-space.
- Taking full responsibility (*Kuleana*) for the existence of the problem in your life.
- Willingness to act differently (*Ho'o*) after forgiving yourself and everyone else involved.

- Mutual forgiveness and pardon (*Mihi*).
- Gratitude and closing prayer (*Pule Ho'opau*).

On Moloka'i, islanders have often followed Ho'oponopono with the presentation of a lei made from the fruit of the hawa tree. You can give your loved one a small but meaningful gift if you want to. The best present you can give, however, is a greater understanding fostered by Ho'oponopono.

I've read several books about Ho'oponopono. There are two books in particular that you may find helpful. If you want a concise overview and summary, I recommend Ulrich Emil Dupreé's *Ho'oponopono: The Hawaiian Forgiveness Ritual as the Key to Your Life's Fulfillment* (Findhorn Press). If you feel inspired and want to go more in-depth, I recommend Joe Vitale's *Zero Limits: The Secret Hawaiian System for Wealth, Health, Peace and More*" (John Wiley and Sons).

I read Joe Vitale's book during a long flight back to Hawaii from Switzerland in October 2011. I took many notes. The last thing I wrote in my notebook was: "From here on, I choose to apply everything I just learned through this book to any difficult situation presented to me." This was about an hour before I landed at an airport on the U.S. West Coast. I'd already stayed in the United States for seven months to study, and afterwards had left the country for only eleven weeks. As a result, I faced unexpected problems with immigration, facing four hours of scrutiny. Of course, I missed my connecting flight to Hawaii.

I consciously chose not to go into fear mode, however, but to instead do the best I could in this unpleasant situation. I opted to stay solution-oriented and to look for the blessing in it. I decided to keep repeating the four Ho'oponopono statements as long as I faced this adversity, and to apply the six steps Pilipo had shared with me. It transformed the energy of the situation in such a way that, after the investigation concluded, the immigration officer apologized for what I had gone through and said, "*Welcome back to the U.S. We are glad you came back for another visit."* Before I left, she even gifted me with a hug and a big smile.

Although I missed my connecting flight and was tired after a long journey, I left with a big smile on my face. I was proud that I'd effectively applied the concepts I'd just learned. And I was exhilarated by this incredible, powerful confirmation of how amazing the Ho'oponopono process is.

This is just one of many uplifting experiences I've had since starting to apply the four statements and six steps of Ho'oponopono. I invite you to apply this ritual yourself whenever you face a situation that requires forgiveness and peacemaking.

Halawa Valley, Moloka'i

Blessing of Relaxation

After visiting the Big Island, Maui and Moloka'i, my next stop was Lana'i. It's wonderful to fly from one Hawaiian island to another. On the morning of July 12, 2011, I took a twenty-minute journey from Moloka'i to Lana'i. I want to share with you the amazing events I experienced on Lana'i, to underscore the power of synchronicity, the deep connection we share with animals and the lessons they can teach us if we keep an open heart. I'll also share another great practice to help you vanquish tension and act from a place of peace and calm.

While the flight to Lana'i was the shortest of my flights, I was awed by the magnificent beauty unfolding below me. I wondered what new experiences, connections and insights this next part of my journey would gift me with.

After I picked up my luggage, a friendly shuttle-bus driver welcomed me. While we drove to a car rental place in the downtown area, he told me about his home, sometimes called Pineapple Island because of its agricultural past. In the 1870s, a man named Walter M. Gibson acquired most of the land for ranching. In 1922, James Dole bought the island, with its rich volcanic soil, and turned it into the world's largest pineapple plantation.

At the time of my visit, David H. Murdock owned 98 percent of Lana'i. He acquired the property when he bought the Dole fruit company in 1985. The remaining two percent consists of government property and privately-owned homes. A year after my visit, Murdock sold his interest in the island to another billionaire, Oracle cofounder Larry Ellison.

I'd just spent time with Pilipo, and felt connected as never before with the ancient culture of Hawaii. I was heartbroken as the friendly bus driver talked about the huge gap between the past—when native Hawaiians lived off this lush expanse of land by ranching and fishing—and life on the island today. However, what I'd experienced on Moloka'i reminded me that whenever our heart breaks, it creates a sacred space for healing, miracles and blessings to occur. So again, I consciously chose to remain open, receptive and focused on the purpose of my quest.

Whenever our heart breaks,
it creates a sacred space for healing, miracles and blessings.

After the driver dropped me off in front of the car rental office, I was welcomed by an affectionate older dog. He seemed magnetically drawn to the palms of my hands. As soon as I started to touch him, he lay down on his back and enjoyed the little massage he was getting from me. The lady working there told me she'd never seen the dog, who's usually shy and wary of people, trust someone so quickly.

I checked into my room at the historic Hotel Lana'i. Built in 1923 by James Dole as lodgings for Dole plantation executives, it was the only hotel on Lana'i until 1990. Even though the hotel is located downtown, it felt peaceful and calm. The relaxed ambiance comes partly from the fact that there are almost no cars on Lana'i. Instead, there's an abundance of greenery and pine trees that perfume the air.

Once settled in my hotel room, I checked my cell phone and saw that my mom had called during my flight. When I called her back, she said my former partner had called, asking her to let me know that Cleo, a lovely and loving Siamese cat with whom I'd lived for more than six years, was very sick. She asked if I could do some distance healing on her.

Feeling it was urgent, I decided to seek a sacred site somewhere in nature. When I asked the hotel receptionist where I could find such a place on Lana'i, she directed me to a cultural heritage center close to the hotel, saying it would be best to ask there. Shortly after my arrival there, three older ladies entered and asked what brought me to Lana'i and what my intention was for visiting the center. I told them what I'd learned about Cleo, and shared that I was passionate about doing healing work for animals and visiting sacred sites. They told me to call Kathy Carroll, the wife of a gallery owner who has created a cat sanctuary on the island.

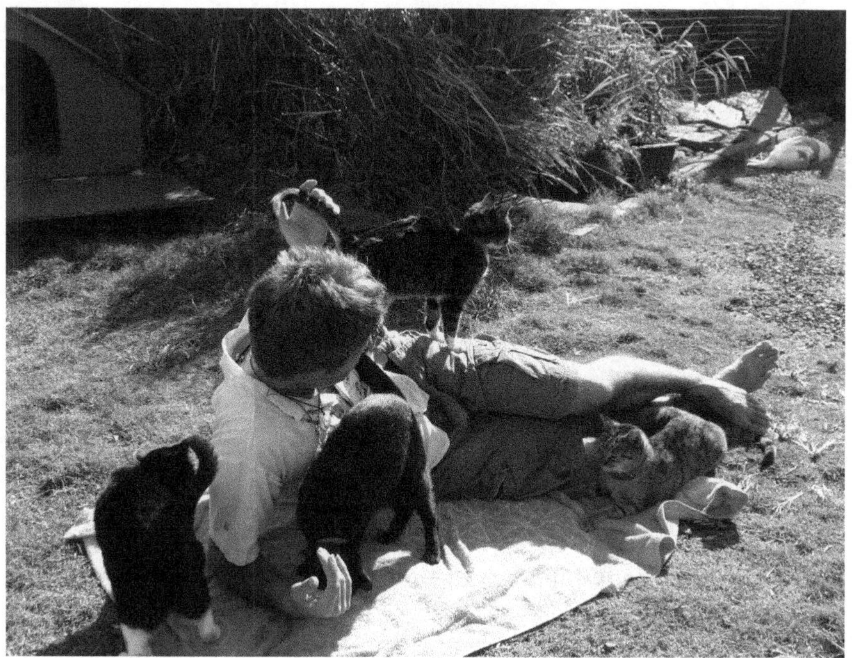

Lanai Cat Sanctuary, Lana'i

At first, I thought I was in some kind of dream! I expressed my deep gratitude to them, and to the divine spirit orchestrating this remarkable synchronicity. I drove immediately to the Lana'i Cat Sanctuary (*www.lanaicatsanctuary.org*), which is about a mile from the airport. As I arrived I met Kathy, who was just about to head back to town. I told her how I was guided there, and she introduced me to another person working at the sanctuary. I'd volunteered at various animal rescue places, but what I saw in front of me was completely different.

The sanctuary is a spacious, open-air, 15,000-square-foot enclosure complete with cubicles for sleeping, "pallet palaces" for hiding, eight-foot-long irrigation pipes for playing, and kitty-climbing jungle gyms. The enclosure contains a selection of bushes, long grasses and trees where the cats can play, nap and climb. Some of these trees also provide sleeping perches for the more adventurous felines.

I lay down on the grass and spotted cats swaying in the breeze in the crooks of tree branches. Almost immediately, ten cats approached me. Some surrounded me, while others plopped right on top of me. There are no words to describe the feeling of that moment. It was the perfect time to connect with Cleo and start working on her.

Usually I do this kind of healing work alone, but this time I had ten kitties supporting me. They not only helped me send healing energies to Cleo, they also helped assuage my sadness about the way Lana'i had been lost to the native islanders. I stayed for about two hours and left feeling calm, relaxed and rejuvenated. If you ever find yourself on Lana'i, you should make a point of stopping by this scenic sanctuary, which invites cat-lovers to a daily "Pet-n-Purr" open house. On the day of my visit there were 261 cats in residence. Now there are more than 500 cats, and they live in what I can only describe as cat heaven!

When it comes to living and acting from a place of peace and calm, cats are master teachers. We can learn so much from them. Adult cats spend up to fifty percent of their waking hours grooming. They relax through the ritual of self-cleaning and they groom each other as a sign of affection and friendship. They sometimes like to express their love to people through this act as well.

Research shows that cats typically sleep anywhere from sixteen to twenty hours a day. While cats spend at least two-thirds of their lives asleep, they're not "asleep" in quite the same way humans are. They spend a lot of this time in a hypnagogic state. This is the threshold between sleep and wakefulness, where contact with the subconscious and unconscious dimensions occurs simultaneously. As I mentioned earlier, there's an effective way in which you can connect with this cat-like state yourself—the practice of *Yoga Nidra*. Doing Yoga Nidra is about as close as you can get to having a cat nap!

After I returned from my latest journey to Hawaii in mid-May 2015, I took an eight-day training course in Denver, Colorado to become a Yoga Nidra teacher. My friend Jeremy had sent me the invitation shortly before I left for Hawaii. The training was in perfect alignment with my schedule, starting the day after my return. One year later, I took another Yoga Nidra training seminar with Rod Stryker, founder of Para Yoga and the author of *The Four Desires: Creating a Life of Purpose, Happiness, Prosperity, and Freedom*. Rod says:

> *Yoga Nidra is an ancient practice of deep conscious relaxation that aims to heal and bring balance into the body and mind at the deepest levels. It consists of a series of relaxation techniques and visualizations that eliminate layers of conflict within the mind and body, directing us back to our most natural state of inner peace.*

In addition to learning many theoretical and practical steps to incorporate into my own Yoga Nidra sessions, I experienced firsthand the profound healing and restorative effects of Yoga Nidra.

I struggled with exhaustion during the early parts of the training I took with my friend Jeremy. We were studying two levels of Yoga Nidra, focusing on each for four days. Despite those moments of feeling drained, I always left completely refreshed, clear and energized after the training weekends. Since then, Yoga Nidra has become a daily and beneficial practice for me.

Because Yoga Nidra is practiced in a lying-down position and is a gentle form of yoga, it's also ideal for people with physical restrictions. I highly recommend trying Yoga Nidra for yourself.

In the state of Yoga Nidra, remarkable healing can occur at the deepest levels of the self, where the roots of illness and imbalance lie. In a deep state of Yoga Nidra, you can access the innermost layers of the mind to replace or remove previous conditioning. You can also imprint new ideas on the mind at the level at which programming happens. For example, you can work with affirmations while you are in the Yoga Nidra state. That said, however, if you want to make your visualizations or affirmations most effective, I recommend doing them *after* engaging in meditation or Yoga Nidra. Learning to move between different states of frequency can help you greatly with your affirmations, visualizations and meditations on your life's purpose. If you want to know more about Yoga Nidra, I'm happy to offer my services to help you navigate the unconscious realms!

Yoga Nidra is also effective to help you move between brainwave states. Through a sequence of progressive, guided meditations and relaxation steps, a Yoga Nidra teacher can lead practitioners to a state of complete physical, mental and emotional relaxation. Your consciousness shifts to function at a deeper level of inner awareness. Through this relaxation, your mind is taken into the hypnagogic state, the threshold between sleep and wakefulness. In this state, you can simultaneously connect with the subconscious and unconscious dimensions.

Clients often ask me about how to focus more effectively by altering their brainwaves. For example, one client wrote: "*Yves, you wrote that many people get stuck because they are doing visualizations and affirmations in the Beta or Alpha state of the brainwave instead of going deeper. Can you can explain this topic in more depth?*"

To answer this question effectively, it will be helpful to tell you a little more about the powerful ancient Hawaiian healing tradition known as Huna. As I mentioned earlier, the priests and wisdom keepers of this tradition are called Kahunas. They believe that we human beings are a composite of three selves:

- High Self = super-conscious aspects of the mind.
- Middle Self = conscious aspects of the mind.
- Low Self = subconscious and unconscious aspects of the mind.

Similarly, shamans from the Amazon speak about three worlds that are constantly interacting with one another:

- Hanan Pacha = Upper World. Residence of higher selves. Angelic World. Realm of the Condor.

- Kay Pacha = Middle World. The world of the human selves. Animal World. Realm of the Jaguar.
- Ukhu Pacha = Lower World. World of subconscious instinct. Reptilian Brain. Realm of the Anaconda.

Both the Kahunas and the shamans say that the middle self can't directly access the higher planes of existence. However, there are various links between the low self (the subconscious and unconscious aspects of the mind) and the high self (the super-conscious aspects of the mind). The latest scientific research shows that ninety-five percent of our experiences are recorded on the subconscious mind and also imprinted on the unconscious mind.

What we each individually perceive as our "truth" or "reality" is really just a reflection of the storehouse of our unconscious minds. All of our past conditioning exists in the "inner library" of our unconscious minds—all of the fears, annoyances, insecurities and self-limiting beliefs we have acquired from our personal life experiences have been filtered, analyzed, compared and stored in this archive.

During my Yoga Nidra teacher training, I was reminded of another notion which is helpful to elucidate the concept of the unconscious mind and brainwave states. The brain is made up of billions of brain cells called neurons, which use electricity to communicate with each other. The combination of millions of neurons sending signals at once produces an enormous amount of electrical activity in the brain. With the discovery of brainwaves came the discovery that electrical activity in the brain will change depending on what a person is doing.

For example, the brainwaves of a sleeping person are vastly different than those of someone who is wide awake. Science has moved closer to figuring out exactly what brainwaves represent and what they mean about a person's health and state of mind. Researchers have found that not only are brainwaves representative of our mental state, they can be stimulated to change a person's mental state. That, in turn, can help a variety of mental issues—and it can help us to tap into our fullest potential when we are meditating and visualizing. As someone once wrote, "Everything is energy and that is all there is to it. Match the frequency of the reality you want and you cannot help but get that reality. It can be no other way. This is not philosophy, this is physics."

Remember we talked about Beta and Alpha states being less ideal than Theta and Delta states for creating effective affirmations? Beta brain wave frequencies are between 13 and 38 Hz. This is where you are wide-awake, alert and focused. If we try to sustain this state for too long, exhaustion, anxiety and tension can result. Alpha brain waves are between 8 and 13 Hz. This is the place of centeredness and mental stability. Here, you're relaxed, yet awake. There are many benefits of the Alpha state. For example, headaches get reduced and clarity is increased through the release of serotonin.

Theta brain waves are between 4 and 8 Hz. This induces relaxation and deeper sleep. In the Theta state, you experience profound inner peace and deep meditation, and your memory, focus and creativity are increased. Delta brain waves are between 0.5 and 4 Hz. Here, you experience deep sleep and there's no muscle movement. You experience a feeling of unity with everything, and it helps you achieve restful sleep and pain relief.

Meditation is a great way to move from a Beta state into a Theta state. When practiced on a regular basis, meditation can bring many benefits, including better focus, enhanced creativity and deeper compassion as well as less anxiety, stress and tension. There are many different ways to meditate and, since it's a personal practice, there are probably far more ways than any of us know about! But for me, the Yoga Nidra practice is ideal.

If you're inspired to learn Yoga Nidra and to use it as a tool in your daily life, I am more than happy to support you in your process.

Blessing of Healing

One can't really talk about the wonders and blessings of Hawaii without discussing its healing magic. Just being on the island makes you feel connected with its loving, Aloha spirit.

As you may know, when you deplane in a Hawaiian airport, the friendly Hawaiian people greet you with a flowery lei and a friendly "Aloha." But Aloha is more than a greeting or salutation. It's a condition, a way of life, a mindset and an attitude. I recently found a beautiful description of the deeper meaning of Aloha at the main airport of Maui and I'm inspired to share it here.

In this description, I read that a revered "keeper of the secrets of Hawaii," Auntie Pilahi Paki, tasked several of her students to be prepared for the future when the world would be in collapse. She spoke of the time when Hawaii would have the remedy to save the world, and the remedy was "Aloha." At a governor's conference in 1970, she introduced modern Hawaii to a deeper understanding of "Aloha."

A: Akahai – meaning kindness (grace), to be expressed with tenderness

L: Lokahi – meaning unity (unbroken), to be expressed with harmony

O: Olu'olu – meaning agreeable (gentle), to be expressed with pleasantness

H: Ha'aha'a – meaning humility (empty), to be expressed with modesty

A: Ahonui – meaning patience (waiting for the moment), to be expressed with perseverance.

An even deeper meaning of Aloha can be found in a quote from Queen Lili'uokalani from 1917: *"To gain the kingdom of heaven is to hear what is not said, to see what cannot be seen, and to know the unknowable—that is Aloha. All things in this world are two; in heaven, there is but one."*

This quote is more than 100 years old, yet we can still relate to Queen Lili'uokalani's message. We are indeed living at a time when the world increasingly seems to be spinning out of control and edging on collapse, just as Auntie Pilahi Paki forewarned. Many people feel that the systems and structures they were once familiar with seem to be breaking down. They realize that a huge shift is inevitable, both internally and externally. We truly are stepping into the unknown.

This is a crucial time on our planet, Earth. In order to live a life of purpose and manifest our heart's desires, we are all asked to do our inner work instead of hoping that others will fix our problems for us. I believe that ancient wisdom from indigenous cultures can assist us during this massive time of transformation.

I'm blessed to call Kaua'i home. I've always felt a deep resonance with the Hawaiian culture and the wisdom that can still be found all over the islands. *Aloha* means to be in the presence of life and to share the essence of one's being with openness, honesty and humility. It's a way of being, a way of behaving, a way of life. It's also a commitment to being real. It's a commitment to accepting others, giving dignity to who they are and what they have to offer.

I shared earlier that one of my intentions during my vision quest in 2011 was to meet a *kahuna* or *kupuna*. My friend Joy, whom I'd met on Maui earlier that year, guided me to a special heiau right before I flew to Moloka'i. It's called Kukuipuka Heiau and is a place of refuge and healing. "Kukui" means light and "puka" means doorway, signifying that this special place is a doorway of light.

All of these heiau have caretakers or guardians, whether they take the form of a human being, an animal or a spirit. During my vision quest, I didn't know who the caretaker of Kukuipuka Heiau was. Recall that after my initial, profound healing miracle in 2008 with the Hawaiian healer Paul, I asked him why I had to wait so long before I finally met him for the healing session. He told me that I had chosen this day at a soul level before I was born, and that now the timing was right.

It was the same with the caretaker of the Kukuipuka Heiau. The right time to meet her arrived when Eunjung and I returned to Maui for a week in May 2017. A powerful process of clearing had begun on the day of my 41st birthday on April 28, and I wanted to receive Hawaiian blessings and healing for what I was going through at the time.

Once we arrived on Maui, Eunjung remembered that Lei'ohu Ryder, from whom we'd bought a healing music CD a few years back, lived on Maui. Eunjung told me we should contact her and to my relief, she had an opening in her schedule the following day. So, we drove to her place in Kula, a beautiful town near Maui's Kula Forest. As soon as she welcomed us with "Aloha" and a big smile, I knew I was at the right place. Through Lei'ohu's gentle sharing of the powerful teaching of Aloha, its healing energies were transmitted palpably to all the cells of my being.

As a part of the healing ceremony, Lei'ohu led us to the sacred Hawaiian altar in her garden. She worked on me there; it was incredibly beautiful and powerful. I felt reconnected with the initial healing miracle I'd experienced with Paul because I was again on sacred Hawaiian land under the open sky, with trees and birds all around us. I also learned from Lei'ohu how we can use the leaves of the ti plant, a sacred Hawaiian plant with large leaves, in healing ceremonies. Afterward, she told us to return to the Kukuipuka Heiau several times to receive more healing, and mentioned that she, along with her partner, Maydeen, was the caretaker of this special heiau.

Eunjung and I both realized that our meeting with Lei'ohu was much more than just a healing session. It was another initiation welcoming us home as we moved our residence to Kaua'i to walk the path of Aloha with deeper awareness and to practice the ancient teachings of love and wisdom. I feel incredibly blessed to have met and learned from this wise teacher, kahuna and kupuna—who carries the true meaning of Aloha. Here is an excerpt of what Lei'ohu wrote in an article for *Wisdom Magazine* a few years ago. *Mahalo* (thank you) to Lei'ohu for giving me permission to quote her words in this book:

> *We humans have struggled with the self-imposed illusion that we are less than or we lack something. When we allow the heart to lead in a natural and gentle way, without expectations or judgment, it opens like a flower and allows us to be all that we are in the dance of freedom. We heal by recognizing and living the experience that the land and the sea are sacred. They connect us to the source of all that is.*
>
> *Hawaiian traditions teach us to honor all life and all traditions as sacred truths that embrace and unify us. They help us to understand that each one is a wise one, filled with the sacred streams of knowledge awakening within. Hawaiian traditions teach us to understand that what is you is me. And in this way, we offer each one a beautiful rainbow of Aloha.*

To Eunjung and me, Lei'ohu truly embodies the spirit of Aloha. She is also the founder of Aloha in Action. *www.AlohainAction.com* This organization serves love. It's about sharing Aloha with the Hawaiian community and the world by providing help wherever it's needed, however one can. They have undertaken many worthy projects to help and support humanity, not only in Hawaii but around the world.

As Eunjung and I now call this beautiful Aloha State home, we feel more dedicated than ever to serving the community we belong to—and our friends all around the world—as best we can. We're committed to helping as many people as possible to awaken their own sacred truth and to live a life of joy, purpose and freedom.

Kukuipuka Heiau, Maui

A Love Story with Destiny

When it comes to the topic of life's purpose, it's not uncommon to find people wanting to find a life partner, someone they can share their passions with. So many of us crave a relationship where we have the capacity and willingness to support each other's dreams and build a purposeful life together.

In our work together, Eunjung and I are often asked to provide support regarding relationships. We have encountered dozens of individuals over the years seeking just such a partnership—based on shared dreams and purpose—and asking for advice on how to create a relationship like the one we share. Many people spend a lot of time imagining the ways the "perfect" relationship will provide what's missing in their life. They visualize how their imaginary partner will look, what they will do and how this person will make them happy.

Below, we pose a few questions for you to reflect upon. You can contemplate these questions when you're in the process of finding a new life partner, or ask them of person you're dating. Or, if you already have a partner, you can ask each other these questions—they'll help you make a more intimate connection.

- What do you intend to bring to the relationship?
- What are you willing to share wholeheartedly, unconditionally and with joy in the relationship?
- What do you want your partner to bring to the relationship?
- What do you want your partner to share with you—wholeheartedly, unconditionally and with joy?
- What do you want to co-create with your partner?
- What do you want to contribute to others, with your partner?
- What do you want to experience with your partner in the world?
- What do you want others to contribute to you and your partner on your journey?

When you have clarity on the above questions, it will help attract the right partner or deepen the relationship you're in.

In any relationship, it's important to give before asking to receive.

In any relationship, it's important to be willing to give first before asking for what you want to receive. We're all growing, and we're helping each other to grow. Don't lose yourself in another person, but always focus on the essence and core of yourself and your partner. Also, don't try to change your partner. Allow them instead to discover and strengthen their gifts and talents, and to share those talents with you and everyone else.

After Eunjung and I came together in Kaua'i at the end of October 2011, we found out that both of us had experienced several heartbreaks and challenging relationships before we were led to each other. We'd been working on ourselves to bring more awareness and clarity to the relationship we had envisioned and, at our cores, we were pondering similar questions.

Without Eunjung's immense and precious support, it would not have been possible for me to finish writing this book. Hence, this book would not be complete without her sharing about our purpose-driven partnership.

Eunjung's Story ...

Yves and I didn't really date in a conventional sense before we became partners. Our first day of spending time with each other was for a meditation and ceremony at the Rosslyn Chapel in Edinburgh, Scotland on the autumnal equinox of September 21, 2011 and then one week later for another ceremony and channeling in a pristine Swiss mountain forest near Interlaken.

The next time we met and solidified our relationship was in the Blue Room, a large sacred cave on the North Shore of Kaua'i. So, our relationship literally started at sacred sites with meditations. We've continued to walk this path of remembering who we truly are, with our hearts committed to self-love as well as love for each other, the planet and our collective evolutionary path.

Yves and I journeyed back to the Rosslyn Chapel (which is prominently featured in Dan Brown's bestselling novel, "The Da Vinci Code," and its 2006 film adaptation) on September 23, 2014. There, on the third anniversary of our fateful meeting at that sacred site, we renewed our commitment to each other and to our purpose.

So far, Yves and I have traveled to thirty-five countries and worked with the land, people and nature, both by ourselves and with groups. We've led ceremonies, meditations and life-changing journeys in sacred places around the world, including Egypt, Hawaii, France, Cyprus and England. This has definitely been an intense but rewarding time.

Throughout our journeys, we've undergone the entire spectrum of emotions and frequencies together, from the highest bliss to the lowest despair. We've experienced profound, out-of-this-world encounters, deep soul connections, miraculous discoveries with many beautiful beings—people, animals, plants, trees, angels, magical unicorns and fairies—and traveled through portals, parallel time lines and multiple dimensions.

Yves and I have talked about writing several books together about our journeys, and I feel my contribution to this section may be the starting point of something much greater.

It often felt like we spent a lifetime in many places we visited. Traveling around the world and doing this work is not all glorious and magical. Going to powerful energetic sites brings up a lot to clear and transform, both personally and collectively, especially in these cosmically transformative times.

In January 2012 I got a message from Mary Magdalene that I needed to take a trip to the south of France, following in the footsteps of this powerful teacher of divine love. Yves and I travelled to the south of France the following June to visit and connect with Mary Magdalene sites. The first day I arrived at Rennes-le-Château, I started to break out in hives on my face and this condition became worse the longer we travelled in the region.

We had powerful meditations and energetic transmissions, but physically I was getting uncomfortable and miserable. After a few days, my face became red and swollen all over. And it got so hot that, while driving, I had to constantly put slices of cucumber on my face to cool it down. On the third day, Yves did a regression on me in an attempt to find the cause of my strange condition.

During the session, I saw an image of many people being burnt and dying at the stake. I realized I was re-experiencing the massacre of the Cathars during the Catholic inquisition in the twelfth century. No wonder I was telling Yves that my head felt like it was on fire! Regardless of whether I personally experienced being burnt during this historic timeframe, I was somehow tuned into the field of this tragic event for healing.

Once we realized this, we offered prayers of healing and transformation in the dark, sacred caves of the Cathar Mountains in Ussat-les-Bains—for all that had occurred in this land and for all the unjust suffering endured by Cathars. My symptoms started to disappear almost immediately.

Since our initial trip to the south of France I've been back to the region, leading a small group on a sacred journey, but this strange condition has never returned. This was just one of the many profound stories of transformation we've experienced in our journeys around the world.

This is an intense time that requires each of us to take a quantum leap of consciousness in order to usher in an age of peace, harmony and co-creation in the truest sense. We're asked to unite and embrace all aspects of ourselves—all shades of light and darkness within us and in the collective—to heal the division and embody divine wholeness and sacred union with all.

Although our constant traveling was challenging on multiple levels, after each journey Yves and I felt so grateful and inspired by the transformation and profound shifts we witnessed, not just in ourselves but in everyone we shared the journeys with. We know that this shift in vibration ripples around the world and the cosmos.

Each of us has a sacred purpose. Yves and I do what we do not because we're extra-special, but because we choose to serve and share together in this particular way. Everyone has a unique contribution, purpose and gifts to share, no matter what their circumstances are. That is what we learned through our journeys. Every being we met was our teacher, and we are so honored to continue this path of remembrance that we are truly one.

Love is the thread that weaves through all creations, and we're free to create the realities we wish to live in. I feel so blessed to have a partner who chooses to walk this path of awakening together for the planetary ascension in consciousness. We are fortunate to be able to create a life of shared purpose and passion in helping others find magic, sacredness and meaning in life.

After five years of traveling around the world, Yves and I once again returned on April 2017 to where we first met, Kaua'i, this time to call this magical island our home. Our heart's intention is to serve and live our purpose in more grounded ways from Kaua'i.

We will continue to organize workshops and trips and lead sacred journeys and retreats in other parts of the world, but on a less frequent basis. And we are excited and inspired to invite others to visit this extraordinarily beautiful and magical island for a deep soul journey of healing, transformation and new creations.

I'm deeply grateful to everyone who was, has been and will be a part of our journeys, however big or small. Each of you added to the magic, illuminations and transformation, and I thank you from the bottom of my heart.

Special thanks go out to our friend Bianca Basak Dikturk, whom Eunjung and I met in 2014 in Thailand. You can find the full story of how Eunjung and I were brought together through the interplay of our intentions and divine synchronicities on Bianca's website, *www.CrazyLoveStories.com* You can read the full story, "There is a story and it has to do with destiny" at: *http://CrazyLoveStories.com/there-is-a-story-and-it-has-to-do-with-destiny/*

There is a story and it has to do with destiny

Yves:
I was having a challenging time in 2010. I had a breakdown and left behind absolutely everything that had defined me and my life up

until that point and headed into a void, letting go of everything. I arrived in Kaua'i, Hawaii at the start of 2011.

The traumatic phase I was in manifested itself physically and I became very ill. At one point, I had a significant experience and felt I had left my body and was floating toward a light. I knew I had to decide to leave this sphere or come back and commit to a new path. I returned committed. My new path was different from the corporate life I used to lead. I started to recommit myself to studying spirituality and living spiritually. In June 2011, I received powerful and profound visions that I had to journey to every island in Hawaii. I knew my purpose was to follow and find as many sacred places as possible and work with all the energies the lands and my higher self had to offer. I just followed my intuition, guided by synchronicity. Doors were opening and gently guiding me along my path (as they do when you are on the correct path!).

I called this my "vision quest." My earlier relationship had ended more than a year before, and I knew intuitively that I would meet my beloved at one point during this journey around the islands. I was ready. I was thinking it would happen at some point during this vision quest. I didn't expect, however, that it would happen even before I left Kaua'i for my big journey.

I was still in Kaua'i, rushing to the airport. I had a brief appointment to meet my friend Tiffany in a café to pay for a reservation I'd made to stay at her place. However, Tiffany was nowhere to be seen. I tried the other café, thinking she might be there instead. I walked in and that's when I first saw Eunjung! She was sitting there, working on her laptop. I had gotten Eunjung's business card at Tiffany's place many weeks before, which had her photo on it. I had been meaning to contact Eunjung for one of the sessions she offered. I'd also happened to notice how pretty she was in the photo on the card, but my intentions were purely professional. Somehow, I'd never managed to book an appointment in the three months since I'd taken her card. And here she was now, in the flesh.

I walked over and introduced myself. She was surprised that I knew her. I explained the story and asked if she could pass the payment to Tiffany for me. I told Eunjung briefly about my vision quest. I had no idea what Eunjung was doing at that point and how similar our paths were.

This is how we met, just like in a movie, for only a few minutes. I dashed off to catch my plane, too hurried to realize the significance of the moment. At the end of my vision quest I returned to Kaua'i, but Eunjung wasn't there anymore. I went back to Switzerland at the end of July, after I had stayed and studied in Kaua'i for six months. I knew in my heart that Switzerland was not the place for me anymore. I had to return to Kaua'i. In the beginning of September, Eunjung reappeared.

Eunjung:
I left Kaua'i that summer and returned to Colorado. I'd been traveling so much that I wished to just stay grounded for a while. It wasn't long before I started getting antsy again and yearning to travel. A friend of mine sent me a message saying she had recently moved into a lovely apartment in London overlooking the Thames and asked me to visit. I loved the idea and accepted her invitation with gratitude. I had long wanted to visit the Rosslyn Chapel in Scotland, a special place, and wanted to be there for the autumn equinox on September 21st. I could combine the journeys.

I sent some invites to people I knew in Europe, perhaps ten people, including Yves. Though we'd had little contact since our brief encounter in Kaua'i at the end of June, Yves confirmed that he would join me in the Rosslyn Chapel on the 21st. I'd arranged to fly into Scotland that day, carry out some ceremonies and meditations in the chapel and fly out that same night.

It was a cold and rainy day. Yves' plane was delayed, and he was slightly late. When he did arrive, he was wearing a black coat. I remember thinking how dashing he looked in that coat. He actually later placed his coat on a bench for me to sit on outside the chapel, as it had been raining and the seats were wet. That was such a tender gesture, it touched my heart.

We went ahead and offered some ceremonies and meditations. It was not a romantic date to begin with; we really focused on what we had come there for. We have beautiful memories of that rainy afternoon in the sacred chapel.

Then we went to have some dinner at an Italian restaurant in Edinburgh. That was when we finally got to know each other on a soul level. Funny, I had sent that invitation to several people and it was interesting that it ended up being only the two of us. Later, Yves admitted it was there that he started to have some romantic feelings about me! I was surprised he'd flown in for just one day.

Yves:
There is a story as to why I flew in that day and it has to do with destiny. See, I knew Eunjung would be in Switzerland, where I was, a week later and I could have easily waited to see her there instead. Here is why I didn't wait: Months before that, I was doing a lot of spiritual work with a healer on Kaua'i. I hadn't even heard of Eunjung at that point. I was spending the afternoon with Howard Wills, a powerful and gifted healer who lives on Kaua'i, and a small group of friends at Howard's place when suddenly he got serious and looked at me.

"Yves," he said, "I have to tell you something. You have to go to the Rosslyn Chapel. There is something that awaits you there. You must go, and you must do it during this year. It is very important for the work you will be doing throughout 2012 and beyond. Please go!"

I hadn't ever heard of the Rosslyn Chapel and asked him where in Hawaii the chapel was located. He told me that the place is in Scotland and had connections with themes in the book *The Da Vinci Code* and the story behind the Holy Grail. At that point, I had no intention of leaving Kaua'i or returning to Europe. So, this information had gone to the back of my mind and I'd completely forgotten what he'd said until I got the invite from Eunjung five months later. It gave me chills! I strongly felt the presence of my healer friend, remembered his words and knew I had to go. It was a prophecy and it had to be fulfilled.

And there we were, having dinner in Edinburgh, just the two of us. I was slowly starting to sense feelings that were awakening in me toward her. Eunjung had to fly back that night and I'd booked a room for myself for the night. I went to see a movie on my own, and I found myself wishing that she'd just been there right next to me so we could share the movie together. I was really looking forward to seeing her a week later in Switzerland.

Eunjung:
I was also looking forward to seeing Yves. The next week, when we met in Switzerland as planned, we were with a few other friends in a beautiful mountain forest. We felt infused with the pristine energies. We offered ceremonies and meditations again. We both felt incredibly connected on an energetic level due to our previous work in the Rosslyn Chapel. We had a great time, but we couldn't spend any of it alone. I was beginning to like him more and more.

Yves:
We arranged to meet in Kaua'i again one month later. Another friend of mine on Kaua'i, who is a spiritual teacher, was setting up a retreat for lightworkers and wanted me to act as her assistant. Not only was this job something that I loved to do, it gave me a great opportunity to go back to Kaua'i.

The retreat itself was wonderful, with a profound experience to be had every day. I was in bliss and it was truly magical. The retreat ended on October 29 and we had a community event to celebrate it that evening. I'd had a vision in 2008 and knew I had to be in Kaua'i at the end of October 2011—and I was. It was at the community event that I saw Eunjung again.

Eunjung:
I had just arrived that day and went to the community event in the evening. Yves and I had been messaging each other before, just to discuss logistics and accommodation. I was walking and we came across each other and hugged. He told me it was nice to see me again

and that he'd watched some of the videos on my website and found them helpful. Then, out of the blue, he gave me a small kiss on the lips.

Yves:
I was on a short break, but I just had to give her a little kiss. It was completely unplanned. That was it for the day. I was off work for the next few days. There is a beautiful cave in Kaua'i called the Blue Room. It's considered sacred for many reasons. A mutual friend of ours was going to conduct a crystal bowl meditation there and I knew I had to go.

The energy in the cave the next day was perfect and I felt peaceful. I had my eyes closed and was happy. When the meditation ended, people started to sing. I still had my eyes closed in blissful silence, enjoying the chanting. Just then I heard the most powerful voice join in, a familiar voice. It was Eunjung.

Eunjung:
I heard about the sound gathering in the Blue Room cave and felt I needed to be there. When I arrived a bit late, I was pleasantly surprised to see Yves again, sitting in meditation. That day was amazing and I felt a lot of energy coming, moving me to sing.

I channeled "Rainbow Goddess Shantara" for the first time. It was absolutely amazing, powerful. When it was over, people slowly started to leave. I just stood there and saw Yves coming over. He gave me a warm, long hug. That's when we had our first real kiss, in that magical cave. We have been together since!

We got married two years later in South Korea. We also had a spiritual ceremony on Kaua'i the following month. I can't believe it's already been a year!

We've been working and traveling together ever since. We've already been to so many countries, spreading love and healing. I must admit it's been challenging at times with all these energies we are working with. But we have so many blissful moments that we feel like we are constantly floating from one honeymoon to the next!

Questions and Answers About Relationships

Question: What advice do you have for anyone who's looking for love?

Eunjung:

Be completely in love with yourself first and follow whatever your passion is. When you follow what lies in your heart, you'll meet the person who shares your passion.

Yves:

I agree. You have to love yourself unconditionally, really love and accept who you are. Also, you have to have a vision. Eunjung and I do counseling and energy work for couples' therapy, and I ask the people we work with four questions: "What do you want to bring to the relationship? What do you want your partner to bring? What do you want to create together? What do you want to experience with your partner in your world?" As I noted earlier, when you have clarity on these questions, you'll attract the right type of partner. Remember, always ask what you want to give before you ask what you want to receive!

Eunjung:

Writing it down is also important. I had a ceremony in Kaua'i to invoke my love and my partner a few months before I met Yves. I wrote down what I wanted to experience in love, and all the qualities I wished to have in my partner. I was with my girlfriends and we had the ceremony on a beach in the south of Kaua'i on a beautiful day. We were surrounded by all the colors of Mother Nature and I released my written prayer into the ocean.

I immediately spotted a heart-shaped purple stone and a smaller, heart-shaped pink stone on it in the waters where we sat. I recognized this as a sign that my wishes would be granted and knew that I would soon be united with my love. I felt a surge of strong energy. And here we are now, loving one another and also helping and healing other couples on their own journey as part of our work. It really is wonderful.

Question: What advice do you have for couples going through a hard time?

Eunjung:
Always remember the essence of each other—why you fell in love in the first place. Challenges always arise and they always pass. Always focus on the essence, the core of the other person and yourself. We are all growing ourselves, and helping each other to grow. Don't lose yourself in another person. Allow the energies to harmoniously dance together, without trying to change the other person.

Yves:
Don't be afraid to go to a place of solitude. Take time out to contemplate. Don't use all your free time to go socializing or meet other people. Instead, take time to go to a place of stillness and silence. See what emerges.

Question: Please tell me how you would end this sentence: "One thing that I have learned about love is...."

Yves:
It was always there around me, even in the moments I forgot it the most. Love is always around...love just is.

Eunjung:
Love is present in every moment. Be persistent in remembering that. Don't let the other person forget it either.

Kalihiwai Beach, Kaua'i

Magical Experiences in South Korea

We all have certain places, regions or countries where we feel particularly inspired, because they open our hearts and bring us closer to our purpose.

I'm repeatedly overwhelmed and touched by the hospitality and friendliness I'm welcomed with in South Korea. With every return, I feel embraced by the soul-full spirit and kindness of the South Korean culture, people and land. I also resonate with the South Korean flag. It has a remarkable deeper meaning we can embrace, especially in steering toward a purposeful life.

The flag of South Korea, also known as the "*Taegukgi*," has three parts: a white rectangular background, a red and blue "*Taeguk*" in the center that symbolizes balance, and four black trigrams—selected from the original eight—on each corner of the flag. When we find our life's purpose and share our gifts and talents with the world, we are in balance.

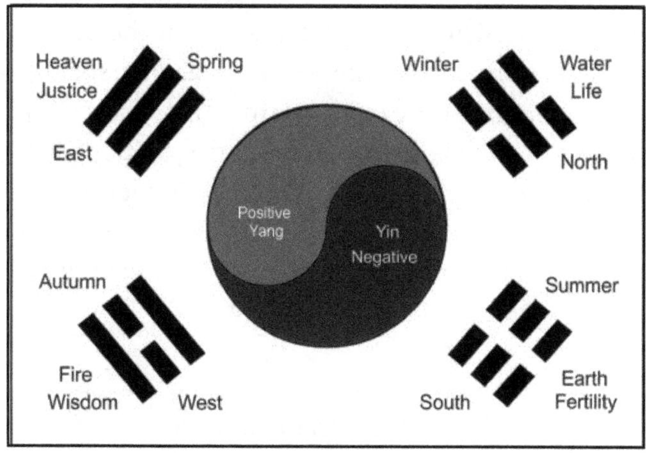

The white background = The nation
The circle = The people
The four trigrams = The government

South Korean Flag

The flag's background is white, which is a traditional Korean color. In fact, Koreans were originally called "white-clad people." The color white represents purity, innocence, peace and wholeness, among other virtues. It also carries the meaning of a completely new beginning. We human beings too start our journey with a clean slate, with a white background upon which we can paint our unique visions and dreams.

The circle in the middle of the flag is derived from the philosophy of yin yang and represents the balance of the universe. The blue section represents the negative cosmic forces, and the red section represents the opposing, positive cosmic forces. When we tune into this natural flow of the universe, we can reach the optimum empowered state of balance and harmony—graciously giving and receiving while living our purpose.

The trigrams together represent the principles of movement and harmony. Each trigram represents one of the celestial bodies (heaven, sun, moon, earth); one of the seasons (spring, autumn, winter, summer); one of the cardinal directions (east, south, north, west); and one of the elements (heaven, fire, water, earth); as well as one of the archetypal family members (father, daughter, son, mother). When we are connected with nature and its elements, we are in alignment with the cosmic forces weaving through all aspects of our lives.

When we connect with nature,
we align with the cosmic forces weaving through our lives.

When Cats Become Tigers

During our first visit to South Korea in August 2012, Eunjung and I wanted to hike in nature. While we were having breakfast in a café, we learned there was a sacred mountain nearby, right in the middle of Seoul. I saw a magazine on an adjacent table and felt I had to open it. The first word I saw was "shaman."

The magazine article said that "Mount Inwang" is a sacred place, which has been used for many ceremonies by local shamans throughout Korea's long and rich history. This piqued our curiosity, as we love to visit spiritual places. We decided to pay a visit to this sacred place that afternoon.

Seoul is a huge metropolitan city with a population of 10.3 million. It is built around many wonderful mountains as well as the impressive Han river. This makes it easy to gain access to one of these peaks via subway or bus. After about forty minutes on a subway, we were at the base of Mount Inwang. We first hiked to "Seonbawi Rock." This geological landmark got its name because early residents thought the two huge rocks resembled a Buddhist monk standing in his robe and called them "Seonbawi," which means "rocks associated with seon" (Buddhist meditation).

There were several trails but rather than consulting a map, we followed our intuition. We were guided to a little cave with a sign in Korean reading "Grandmother Dragon's Spring," so-named because this place was traditionally believed to be the home of a grandmother dragon. The cave is filled with spring water and we drank from it and felt energized. In Korea, dragons are believed to be auspicious, mystical beings who bring good luck and power.

On the way up, we passed three shamans chanting and making offerings, and we felt privileged to be able to see their sacred ceremony. Not many people think of South Korea as a country with shamans. I've learned, however, that shamanism was one of the first spiritual practices in South Korea and is still practiced today.

After about an hour of hiking we finally made it to the top of the mountain, where we enjoyed a beautiful, wide-open vista over Seoul and the surrounding forests and mountains. When I see the world from above, whatever concerns I have shrink. I'm reminded of how vast the world really is, and what a small space I occupy.

On our way back, we passed the place where we'd seen the three shamans earlier. They were gone, but we were welcomed by two cats. Cats are experts in sensing energies and, I believe, at traveling through different dimensions. When Eunjung and I see cats in a sacred site such as a temple in our travels, we know they are there as guardians. We decided to offer a ceremony and meditation of our own at the same place, with the altar on a rock against a huge boulder formation.

During our meditation, we encountered many animal spirits, including two magical and powerful tigers. We felt that the two cats who'd greeted us had shape-shifted in our meditation into these majestic tigers. By showing up as tigers, these two small cats were teaching us that we too have a tiger within—our greater self, who can show up when needed to help us accomplish our mission of fulfilling our higher life's purpose.

Seonbawi Rock, South Korea

Listening to the Sound of Silence

In the autumn of 2013, Eunjung and I returned to South Korea, and travelled to a magnificent Buddhist temple complex, Tongdosa (meaning "salvation of the world through mastery of truth"), located in the region of Yangsan City. The previous year, we'd stayed at this temple overnight through the temple-stay program and participated in a six-hour meditation led by one of the head monks. We'd had profound experiences at Tongdosa and were eager to return.

Tongdosa, the largest temple in South Korea, is steeped in the sacred. There are thirty-five buildings and pagodas and fourteen smaller temples in its vicinity, yet you won't find any Buddhist statues in its beautiful grounds. This is because the authentic "*Śarīra*" (pearls or bead-shaped crystalline objects) of Shakayumuni Buddha are preserved here. Śarīra are purportedly found among the cremated ashes of Buddhist spiritual masters.

When the Buddha passed away, there were thousands of Śarīra and these most precious Buddhist treasures can be found in the pagodas of many temples around the globe. Tongdosa is the "Buddha Jewel Temple" because it enshrines the Buddha's relics in the "Geumgang Gyedan" (Diamond Altar), a platform for sacred ceremonies.

To reach the Diamond Altar, you must first enter three separate gates of spiritual significance. The first is called "One-Pillar Gate" because, when viewed from the side, the gate appears to be supported by a single pillar. This symbolizes the support of the world and the one true path of enlightenment. This is the boundary between the spiritual realm and the secular world.

The second gate is "Guardians of the Four Directions" (four Heavenly Kings), each of whom watches over one cardinal direction. They are the protectors of the world and fighters of evil, each able to command a legion of supernatural forces to protect the dharma (Buddhist teachings).

The third gate of the temple is known as the "Gate of Non-Duality." The world beyond this gate is one of non-duality, where there is no distinction between the Buddha and human beings, being and non-being, good and evil, fullness and emptiness.

After Eunjung and I walked through these three gates, we finally came to a place called "Daeungjeon" (the Main Dharma Hall) and behind this building we reached the most sacred place of all, the "Geumgang Gyedan" (Diamond Altar) where the Buddha's Śarīra are preserved. We first asked the spiritual world for permission to enter this sacred site, and our request was instantly answered by monks who started to recite mantras inside the Dharma Hall right at that moment.

We were gifted with a precious opportunity to sit and meditate next to this altar for almost an hour. The previous time we'd visited, it was crowded and it was not possible to sit down to meditate. The faraway refrain of mantras recited by the chanting monks, and the occasional magical sound of birds in the background brought us even more deeply to a space of stillness and surrender.

Tongdosa Temple, South Korea

In our meditation, feeling the Oneness that unites everyone and everything, we asked, "What wisdom can we receive and share with others right now?" The answers that came ignited our hearts and souls: "The power of imagination makes us infinite" and "Be present while you listen to the sounds of silence."

I hope you also can take time to go within and receive your own pearls of wisdom while listening to the sound of silence, the whispers of your soul. I believe this will help you imagine the life you're truly meant to live and inspire you to reach your highest potential.

Heart-shaped Island in Thailand

People who are in search of meaning and purpose in their lives sometimes look for guidance from spiritual organizations or teachers.

I've worked with a few spiritual teachers in the past, and have followed the teachings of some spiritual groups. They've all played important and unique roles in deepening my understanding of who I was, who I can become and how I can best serve in this world.

Along my journey, I've also learned that teachers are only human—even those who can impart the most brilliant and profound lessons. They aren't immune to human shadows such as over-identification with ego and the misuse of power, money, control and fame. Knowing this has helped me avoid falling into a similar trap, and has sharpened my sense of discernment.

By erring—and thereby showing me contrast—some of these teachers and organizations have given me even more clarity in terms of the kind of teacher and mentor I want to become. I have the greatest respect for teachers and mentors who 'walk their talk' in class, onstage and behind the scenes. They are my greatest role models.

In this section, I share the story of how a sick dog helped me see through the façade of a yoga school in Thailand and how our friendship deepened one of my greatest passions, which is animal healing.

I decided to start the new year of 2014 mindfully, away from the internet as much as possible and taking good care of my body, mind and soul. So, Eunjung and I headed to Koh Phangan, Thailand for a month of rejuvenation. My intentions were to focus on yoga, meditation and healthy living and to help others, should I encounter anyone in need.

Based on my experience in Koh Phangan, where I had spent time at a yoga school during the summer of 2013, I felt the campus and community would provide me with the perfect circumstances to help me stay focused on my practice. In the end, I completed a 150-hour yoga program. Along with fostering personal growth and health, I aimed to learn new tools and techniques to incorporate into the workshops and individual sessions Eunjung and I provide. The intensive Level 1 course I took at the yoga school was great. It was the most comprehensive, informative yoga instruction I'd ever encountered in terms of learning many new techniques and gaining insight into how to improve the wellbeing of myself and others.

Every morning and afternoon we had a two-hour practice, followed by an evening lecture lasting from one and a half to two hours. During the practice classes, teachers would explain in detail where to focus during and after each asana (yoga posture), how asanas influence the *chakras* (energy centers), and how we can heal ailments by incorporating certain poses.

I enjoyed most of the music meditations that were part of the course, and had profound experiences during and after the final relaxation pose, called *Shavasana*. I also felt that the practice enhanced my healing gift by augmenting my ability to focus and direct energy.

Most of the teachers I had during the program were supportive and dedicated. When I asked them questions about my yoga practice, however, they couldn't answer if it wasn't in their script. Their answer was usually, "I first need to ask Swami," referring to the spiritual leader and founder of the school. What's more, the wording that was used during classes to instruct students on poses was almost identical, regardless of who was teaching the class.

Eunjung and I later found out there was a huge disconnect between what certain key people in the community taught and what they put into action outside class. We witnessed a certain degree of inauthenticity at the yoga school, which I feel compelled to share. It was a resident dog on the campus that helped us see through the facade to find deeper truths around the organization.

I met this special dog on my first day of the program, while I was having lunch at the campus restaurant. He looked sick and vulnerable. I saw a big tick above his right eye and a huge lump in his throat, but I didn't yet realize how bad his physical condition really was. He approached me as if he were needing some healing and affection. Since connecting with and healing animals are among my biggest passions, I find that animals are naturally drawn to me, especially when they're sick. Thanks to our heart-connection with the dog, our Thailand yoga trip ended up being one of the most profound, heart-opening journeys we've ever experienced.

From the first day I met the dog, I spent a lot of time with him after every yoga class, playing with him and doing energy work on him because I felt a deep bond and strong heart-connection. After about a week of doing healing work on him, focusing on the big lump in his throat, it shrank considerably.

Unfortunately, he was developing many other small lumps all over his body. Some red lumps he developed under both his eyelids were especially problematic. As the days passed they got so bad he often had bloody eyes and was literally crying tears of blood. Seeing him in that condition just broke my heart. He would sit down and let me clean his eyes with tissues.

After the dog's condition worsened, we found an animal care organization called Phangan Animal Care (PAC) about fifteen minutes from the yoga campus and went there to ask for help. PAC is run by a small group of wonderful and goodhearted volunteers from all over the world. When we explained the dog's situation, some of the people at PAC knew about him and told us the dog had been fighting cancer for a while. These amazing volunteers gave us some medicine to administer to him twice a day to reduce inflammation and pain.

From that day on our mission was to help the dog feel loved, and to help him live with less pain and discomfort. We'd go to a local convenience store called 7-Eleven and get a sausage, which we'd use to hide the medicine we gave him twice a day. It became our daily ritual. Sometimes we wondered what the employees of 7-Eleven thought of us, because we always came around the same time of the day just to buy one piece of sausage.

One evening, when Eunjung and I asked him for a name, surprisingly, the dog communicated to us mentally that he'd like to be called "Dolphin." He carried a lot of dolphin energy, and was playful and pure despite his terrible health condition. Dolphin taught me how he liked to be cared for and touched, and he responded particularly well to spinal massage. Sometimes when I was working on Dolphin on campus, other students would come over and express concern for the dog. I'd tell them the story of Dolphin, and show them how they could also do spinal massages for him.

The friendship between Dolphin and I grew and deepened every day but, sadly, his overall condition was deteriorating. Some days, he looked so terrible around his eyes that some of the students and staff on campus seemed afraid and shied away from him. Of course, we also met several kind-hearted people who were caring enough to sit with Dolphin and send him loving energies. Dolphin opened many people's hearts, awakening their compassion, as well as connecting people through a thread of tenderness. On campus Dolphin had a lively animal friend, a female dog who wanted to be called Muffin.

Muffin never treated Dolphin as a sick dog. Instead, she played wildly with him. Dolphin seemed to forget his pain when they played together, if only temporarily. One evening, as Eunjung and I sat with these two dogs while giving medicine to Dolphin, Muffin showed us in a vision that she was an angel dog with wings! She was helping and protecting other dogs in pain. I was so grateful to witness this genuine love between these dog friends.

After I found out Dolphin had cancer, I spent at least two hours every day taking care of him—administering medication, walking around with him, massaging him and sometimes just holding him in my arms. One day, though, I looked at Dolphin's eyes and realized that our best efforts of giving him love and healing work wouldn't save him. It completely broke my heart.

Still, we wanted to see if a surgery removing the tumors from his eyes could help him. After discussing the matter with PAC, we took the day off on the first day of our fourth week in the yoga program. We traveled by boat to a larger animal clinic in Koh Samui, a larger neighboring island, accompanied by Dolphin and a PAC volunteer who brought another dog that needed urgent care.

Our trip started at 6:00 a.m. with a gorgeous, luminous sunrise on the boat, which reminded us that light is always there to guide us in all stages of life. It was quite a journey to get to the clinic with two ill dogs. We finally arrived at our destination in the late morning.

After examining Dolphin, the doctor at the animal clinic said he'd never seen a dog with so many tumors. A blood test revealed that Dolphin had the most aggressive form of cancer, which had originated in his testicles and spread everywhere quickly. In addition, his kidneys were failing and he was suffering from blood parasites and tick fever.

The doctor said there wasn't much that could be done for him, medically speaking, and told us that Dolphin didn't have many days left. With this sad news, we returned with some more medication and eye cream, to lessen his discomfort.

After returning from the clinic, Eunjung and I continued to care for Dolphin with love and energy medicine. Dolphin seemed to know that his days were numbered, but he was always so happy to see us and smiled at us. I can still picture him, following us around when we went to the restroom across the campus and waiting in front of the yoga hall until we finished our practice.

Dolphin connected us with many other animal-loving students on campus, who also noticed his worsening condition. We'd gather around Dolphin, share snacks with him and do energy work for him. Some students suggested we collect funds to pay for Dolphin's medication and to support Phangan Animal Care's work by placing a donation box either at the registration desk or at the campus restaurant.

When I asked a woman at the registration desk if we could place a donation box there, her response was not at all what I would have expected from a person associated with a yoga school that teaches spiritual evolution, balance and harmony. Even though I told her that I was asking this on behalf of a group of students, she gave me a quick, condescending glance as if I were wasting her time and sarcastically remarked, "No, that's none of our business."

During our classes, we spent many hours doing *asanas* (yoga postures) and awareness exercises focusing on the heart chakra to develop and expand our capacity for compassion and universal love. There were also lectures on topics like the virtues of cultivating a pure heart, karma yoga (doing good work) and vegetarianism. In one of those lectures, I heard that "ignorance creates suffering." And yet, right outside of the yoga hall where I'd heard this quote, a dog was suffering.

I believe we need to extend whatever we practice on the yoga mat to our daily lives. So, the staff member's response was shocking and disconcerting to me. I wasn't just a random person who stopped by the school. Eunjung and I were both students, who had paid fees to the school to be part of the program and community for an entire month. I had simply voiced something many of the students were concerned about.

Knowing I couldn't place a donation box at the registration desk, I asked the manager of the campus restaurant—which was booming, thanks to so many yoga students—about putting the donation box there. He also took good care of the dog, but I learned from him that it wouldn't be possible either because the owner, who also ran a detox center on the island, didn't like to have the dog there.

Only two days later, in the evening after one of the yoga lectures, I had a brief encounter with the restaurant owner, while I was giving Dolphin a massage. This man (who is originally from Greece) looked down on me and the dog and I perceived anger in his eyes, which made me uncomfortable. Later, I read in his online biography that a healing massage from a Buddhist monk on the island had accelerated his spiritual transformation. If I'd received such a miraculous healing on this island, I'd be honored to repay the blessings I'd received by helping resident animals and locals.

I considered Dolphin, not the people who had important titles or proclaimed their spiritual mastery, to be the true teacher on campus. It took a humble, loving dog to impart and model unconditional love and compassion.

After my unpleasant experience with the receptionist, I now wanted to meet with Swami, the spiritual leader of the yoga school, to learn his views on the situation. To my disappointment, however, it wasn't possible to get a private meeting with him due to his busy schedule. I would have loved to share with Swami that what matters most to me is how we can use our spiritual growth to be in service for others and the planet. Spirituality serves different purposes, and each of us has our unique path.

My experiences involving Dolphin gave me the biggest growth opportunities while I was studying at the yoga school. I learned more about myself—about my own discernment and authenticity, about conducting a spiritually-based business, about spiritual teachers and gurus—and about how I relate to challenging situations or people.

I learned that when we sense things are wrong or out of balance, it's important to stand our ground, tell our truth, and not give up on something that has deeper spiritual truth and meaning for us. It's not about convincing others to honor our truth and inner authority. The fact that we don't need to have an agreement with others to live a self-empowered life is a liberating realization.

Don't give up on something that has deeper spiritual truth and meaning for you.

With Dolphin, I was gifted with an opportunity to see and perceive things with greater clarity and detachment. He also taught me that integrity, "walking the talk," is of paramount importance to me. He showed me I can trust my intuition about when and where integrity has been compromised. I know that I have spiritual gifts of healing and intuition that can serve me and others, and I choose to use and share these gifts with authenticity, love and compassion.

A wise person once said, *"The greatness of a nation can be judged by the way its animals are treated."* It's important to highlight that the people I had these unpleasant experiences with were not local Thai people; they were Europeans living and working in Koh Phangan. They seemed to forget they were borrowing land from the Thai people, and that Dolphin had lived on the land longer than they had. The veterinarian at the clinic in Koh Samui estimated Dolphin's age at around twelve, so he'd almost certainly lived on the island before the yoga school opened its campus there.

Thailand being a Buddhist country, Thai people treat animals with kindness. They see animals as having perhaps less intellectual ability than humans, but as being no less capable of feeling happiness or of suffering. Animals possess Buddha nature and therefore also possess the potential for enlightenment.

Moreover, according to the Buddhist belief in reincarnation, sentient beings currently living in the animal realm have been our brothers, sisters, fathers, mothers, children and friends in past lives. Therefore, one can't make a hard distinction between moral rules applicable to animals and those applicable to humans. Ultimately, humans and animals are part of a single family—we're all interconnected.

After our return from the clinic in Koh Samui, Eunjung and I started to spend even more time with Dolphin each evening. Our connection became deeper and more profound. I often held Dolphin in my arms, close to my heart, to comfort him. He could then completely relax and communicate more about his life with us.

We learned that Dolphin had decided to be on this campus for a reason. He had a purpose. He was a guardian and helped people on the campus transform some lower vibrations, while helping them see beyond the veils of illusion and find truth within. Dolphin also showed me images from earlier in his life when he was completely healthy and happy, even scenes when he was still a puppy and playing with his brother and sisters.

One late evening when Eunjung and I were sitting with Dolphin, we saw a beautiful, luminous firefly dancing in front of us, creating an amazing, dancing trail of light. It was so beautiful and touching. Later, we looked up the spiritual meaning of fireflies and learned that they are magical symbols of inspiration and encouragement. They are the promise of accomplishment through hope and effort.

Fireflies remind us that we've laid the appropriate groundwork, and from it will spring great reward. For those to whom the firefly appears, it's time to trust in your own rhythms, both physical and spiritual. Your hopes will begin to manifest, and your ability to inspire others will grow.

Dolphin transitioned to dog heaven on February 3, 2014. In his last days, some of the areas on his body where he had many small lumps started to grow together as big tumors. His lungs and belly began to cave in, making it increasingly difficult for him to breathe. By the end, he was tired most of the time and didn't have much energy left to play with his angel friend, Muffin.

When we went to the campus on the last day, Dolphin wasn't in his usual resting places—on the grounds of the restaurant or in front of the main yoga hall. Instead, we found him sleeping under a bench in the middle of the garden, away from everyone. When the time for transition comes close, many animals like to find a place of solitude and calmness to prepare for their journey home.

Dolphin went on to his next journey, into the light, in my arms. I was holding him just the way he had liked to be held all the evenings before. When Dolphin transitioned, time stood still and everything became calm and peaceful. Eunjung saw that many angels were sending a beautiful column of rainbow light to bring Dolphin home.

Even after over four years, Dolphin always stays in our hearts. We'll never forget the journey we took together in early 2014. Eunjung and I are so grateful for all the teachings and insights he gifted us with. Despite his physical suffering, Dolphin was a loving, joyful and courageous dog until the end. He was truly another amazing teacher on my journey.

Four years ago, we shared the story of Dolphin on our Facebook pages. Through the power of social media, many people were touched by this courageous dog and sent him prayers and healing energy. They reported that they felt a strong heart-connection with Dolphin, who even appeared in their dreams!

If you look at Koh Phangan on a map, it's shaped like a heart. There are many places on the island where we felt powerful heart energy. My experience with Dolphin led me to the most profound heart energy of all. When I was travelling from Colorado to Thailand, I saw a BBC documentary called *The Secret Life of Dogs*. I highly recommend watching it on YouTube. This short feature will help you understand dogs and the way they perceive life and relate to us on a deeper level.

Finally, I'd like to acknowledge and give thanks to the countless people who work and volunteer at animal care centers around the world. They dedicate their time and energy to helping animals in need, usually without any public recognition. If you'd like to donate to the cause of helping animals, Phangan Animal Care (*www.pacsthailand.org*) is one of these amazing places that need and would so appreciate your help. For me, these volunteers are true examples and teachers who walk their talk of love, unity and compassion for all beings.

Koh Phangan, Thailand

Detours on Bali

The journey is the reward, and sometimes we need detours to find our destination.

Such detours may originally appear difficult and strenuous. However, isn't it true that when we look back, the detours we take can be valuable and gift us with new insights and realizations? We can also find new answers to our questions, and even define new goals and receive new visions by taking a longer journey.

Five years ago, in the first half of 2013, I lived in Bali for two and a half months. In August 2010, the film *Eat Pray Love,* starring Julia Roberts and based on Elizabeth Gilbert's best-selling memoir, was released in theaters. Many who saw the movie, including me, were fascinated by the lush scenery of the rice fields and calm beaches and by the spiritual traditions practiced on this exotic island.

My time in Bali was marked by many contradictory experiences. Before Eunjung and I decided to go there, we'd met many people who told us how much they loved Bali—especially Ubud. Ubud is a hill town and a cultural and tourist center, and it was becoming a thriving hub for spiritual seekers as well as teachers and students of yoga. You can also get wonderful massages and eat a variety of healthy, fresh meals at restaurants while paying much less than you would in western countries.

At first glance, there are so many beautiful sights to see in Bali. The island has incredible architecture and the temples you can find around almost every corner are impressive, like works of art. Many of the locals we met were welcoming, friendly and helpful. Most of all, I remember their beautiful smiles, and I found their hospitality genuine and authentic. As with anywhere you visit, however, there are positives and negatives. As you stay longer in one place, you begin to see beyond the surface and start observing hidden, less glamorous aspects.

Beyond the picturesque rice fields, we started to notice trash and pollution. The sight of people burning trash was common. This practice worsened the air quality, which was already bad because of all the traffic and the heavy clouds of incense being burned in religious ceremonies. Ubud isn't close to the ocean, so there wasn't too much wind to clear the stagnant air.

Bali, located approximately ninety miles (144 kilometers) from west to east and fifty miles (eighty kilometers) from north to south, is home to about four million people, plus an abundance of tourists visiting the island. During the time we were there it was overpopulated, with lots of traffic in most of the places we visited except for some areas in the north.

But it's not just citizens and tourists that inhabit this beautiful island—there's a high population of spiritual beings too! In Bali, there is a keen awareness that there are good spirits and bad spirits. Balinese people spend their lives and their energy trying to appease both types of spirits—they make offerings to the gods so that the gods will be happy, and they make offerings to the demonic spirits so that the demonic spirits will leave them alone. One of many rituals is the *Bhuta Yadnya,* which is intended to neutralize the evil power of the *Bhutakala* (evil spirits).

Unlike any other island in largely-Muslim Indonesia, Bali is dominated by Hindu religion and culture. Every aspect of Balinese life is affected by religion, and the most visible signs are the tiny offerings (*Canang Sari*, or *Sesajen*) found almost everywhere.

To hold offerings such as rice and flowers during ceremonies, the Balinese make palm leaf trays daily. The trays can contain an enormous range of offerings. One of the drivers we employed during our stay told us he spends an average of $200 each month for ceremonies and to help support temple priests. That's a lot of money, considering what the average Balinese person makes in a month.

There are an estimated 20,000 temples (*pura*) on the island, each of which holds ceremonies (*odalan*) at least twice yearly! Balinese people are religious, and the Hindu observance of *Nyepi*, which means "keep silent," falls after the first two boisterous and active days of the Balinese New Year celebration. The island goes into hiding to protect itself from evil spirits. No incoming or outgoing flights are allowed, hotels are urged to cover their windows, shops are shuttered and the streets are empty. According to tradition, the spirits are fooled into believing that Bali—enveloped in an atmosphere of complete tranquility and peace—is a deserted island.

Before this trip to Bali, Eunjung and I had been with a group in Cyprus leading a retreat. Our journey to Bali took us over thirty hours; we took some detours and had a long layover in Athens. Our first few days in Bali were incredibly intense, physically, energetically and spiritually. At that time, there was a combination of a full moon, a lunar eclipse and powerful solar flares. Our jet lag added to the intensity of our experiences. Especially during the first days, I felt oddly disconnected on many levels and sometimes experienced overwhelming waves of energy. As I started to connect further with the field of energy in Ubud, I began experiencing intense and unpleasant dreams at night. It wasn't easy to be with these energies. I was, however, grateful that we'd just arrived at an amazing and beautiful sacred island and aware that it was a good place to go through this uncomfortable experience!

We knew that the first few days after arrival in a new country can be challenging physically and spiritually, because in 2012, we'd traveled to sixteen countries and many sacred sites within the space of just a year. But on this trip to Bali we had much more difficulty than usual. In one of the places we stayed, situated near a rice field, we were even woken up repeatedly by some spirit (not a benevolent one) who was hanging around the area.

Looking back five years later on these intense and difficult times, I am thankful for the powerful transformation I allowed myself to go through. I recognize again the hidden blessings in disguise. Every hurdle we faced only strengthened our power of discernment.

When our soul grows to its next level of development, we are forced to step back from our daily activities and start to look inward. Such experiences can be mistaken for depression or even as burnout. Such soul calls happen when we become ready to reach a new level of understanding about ourselves and how we can better serve in the world.

For our first week in Bali, we stayed at an ashram near Ubud, an ideal spot for a spiritual retreat. This place gave us the opportunity to dive deep into the core of our beings, experience a meditative state of mind and access our inner selves. Every morning at 6:00 a.m., we participated in a thirty-minute meditation, followed by a powerful fire puja for energetic purification and one hour of Hatha yoga. There were also noon and 6:00 p.m. meditations dedicated to different sacred purposes. The ashram sometimes hosted gatherings with wonderful local people. We participated in one of these special events. It was such an honor and blessing to be part of such a welcoming community—to feel their hearts and see their beautiful, authentic smiles and the bright lights in their eyes.

Four days after our arrival, Eunjung and I explored the area around Ubud for the first time and visited three beautiful temples and sacred sites: Tirta Empul, Goa Gajah and Gunung Kawi.

Tirta Empul (the most sacred spring in Bali) has a large healing pool, where we prayed, drank from the holy water and purified ourselves by pouring the water over our heads. Goa Gajah (or Elephant Cave) also served as a sanctuary. It's an unforgettable destination. At the cavern's facade, carved right into the rock, is a relief of various menacing creatures. The final highlight was our visit to Gunung Kawi, a magnificent ancient site right next to a river in a lush valley. There are ten large rock-cut *candi* (shrines) carved into the cliff face, and there we experienced a strong initiation through toning. In one particularly powerful spot within the site, we also received various messages through Eunjung's channeling.

As we were settling into the prayerful life in Bali we heard about "Ida," a Balinese high priestess known to give powerful healing blessings. We were intrigued and wanted to visit her. A few days later, our driver came to pick us up at the ashram to take us to "Ida." We were running a bit late, so we asked him to call Ida to say we'd been delayed. The driver assured us that we didn't need to worry, since HE was already waiting at the temple.

When we arrived, we were told Ida would be there soon. We waited for two-and-a-half hours without HER showing up, so we decided to let it go and return another day. We called her to reschedule our appointment and, two days later, our driver took us back to the same temple we'd visited earlier. The wait was much shorter this time, but the high priest who came out definitely didn't look female. We realized immediately that we may have been at the wrong temple.

Also, from the first moment we saw the high priest, we didn't feel in resonance with his energy. Until that moment, we thought that the name of our high priestess was Ida, but we quickly learned that all priests and priestesses in Bali (no matter if they are male or female) are called "Ida" followed by another name. So, the driver had taken us to an "Ida" he knew instead of the "Ida" we wanted to see!

Once again, we called the high priestess Ida we wanted to meet and explained the situation. Luckily, we were told we still could drive to her temple to see her that morning for a purification ceremony and water blessing. The driver still had to drive around town before we found the right 'Ida temple,' because there were simply too many Ida's in this area. After some detours, on our third attempt we finally arrived, in the right moment, at the right place and with the right person! We've had similar experiences during our travels around the world, where we made it to the right place or person on the third try. We instantly felt that the meeting with the Balinese high priestess would be special.

While we waited for Ida briefly, the energy at her temple felt different compared with the place we'd spent so much time in earlier. It felt more feminine, loving and pure, whereas our earlier encounter and the energy of the former temple were harsh and unbalanced and felt like controlling masculine energy.

It seems to me that through our contrasting experiences, we could appreciate and validate the final experience even more. The meeting with the high priestess herself was another highlight of our sacred journey. From the first moment, we felt comfortable in Ida's presence and at her temple. I was surprised at how youthful she looked.

She first guided us into a separate temple area and asked us to meditate and use a special breathing technique to empty our minds. Meanwhile, she prayed over the water to be used for the upcoming ceremony with mesmerizing, powerful mantras and she invoked guiding spirits for about an hour.

We were then finally ready to receive a Balinese purification and water ceremony. After our one-hour meditation and right before Ida started the ceremony, we felt powerful ancestral energies coming in as well as energies from many of the other sacred sites we'd journeyed to so far.

Eunjung and I stood in front of Ida as she poured the sacred water over us from above while reciting sacred healing mantras. Sometimes it was really tough to find space to breathe because the way she poured the water was so powerful. Nevertheless, it was an intense and beautiful healing experience, mostly on an emotional level.

Both Eunjung and I broke into tears, crying hard toward the end of the water blessings. Through crying we could release so much.

After the ceremony, Ida told us she's the youngest female high priestess in Bali. Throughout Balinese history, high priests (or *Pedanda*) have traditionally been male. She told us that she began to have out-of-body experiences during meditation and had received several of what she referred to as "transmissions." Ida was then officially recognized and ordained as a high priestess one year later at the age of twenty-one, defying tradition.

We realized with humility and deep gratitude that the ceremony was also dedicated to everyone who had come before us, and to the energies of all the lands we had previously visited.

Later we learned that, according to Robert Coon, author of the book *Earth Chakras*, Bali is a global purification site, connected with other power sites through sacred water energies.

The amount of water in the human body ranges from fifty percent (for an elderly person) to seventy-five percent (for a newborn). As we cleanse and purify, we're penetrated by light. When we cleanse this water-being that we are, the light penetrates us. After all, if our water is filled with dirt, there will be less penetration of our water—the light will be unable to shine through. This is why it is so important to purify ourselves: when the body is without its source, we are unplugged from the divine. I learned from my friend Howard Wills that when we cleanse and purify ourselves, we're making way for the light to be received within us again. It's an opportunity for us to reunify with the light or source of everything and to heal ourselves, body and soul.

Part of my life's purpose is serving as a healing facilitator, and I like to emphasize that healing is not given from one human being to another. Healing happens when people cleanse themselves of the burdens that they and their ancestors carry. In essence, my role as a healing facilitator is to help people cleanse and purify their stuck energies, unhelpful emotions and thought patterns as well as any negativity they may carry from others and their environment.

I am grateful that experiencing the entire spectrum of the light and the dark while in Bali gifted me with an all-important insight: When we want to heal, when we want to overcome obstacles that hold us back from fulfilling our life's purpose, all we need to do is free ourselves from negativity regularly—physically, mentally, emotionally and spiritually. As Howard Wills says, "Once we purify ourselves the light penetrates, and in light there is perfection. Then our bodies can reunite with divine energy, which is perfection itself."

When we want to heal,
we need to free ourselves from negativity regularly.

There's a quote about obstacles that has stayed with me since the first time I saw the movie *Discover the Gift*. Director Demian Lichtenstein says, "When you start off on your path, one of the very first things you notice is that the biggest obstacle you have is you." How right he is. It would benefit all of us to reflect on the role we may have played in creating any challenges we're facing—to examine the deeper reasons behind the appearance of such obstacles.

If you're committed to finding your purpose and improving your life, you need not only cleanse negative energy regularly, but also make a conscious choice to change the habits and patterns that may be hindering your growth. Otherwise, the momentum behind these tendencies will likely bind you to the same life you've have been leading.

Near Ubud, Bali

Egyptian Mysteries

I feel blessed to have travelled extensively in recent years. Eunjung and I have visited sacred sites around the world. Throughout our journeys, we've had out-of-this-world, magical and profound experiences. We've witnessed amazing transformations in our workshops and bonded deeply with people from other countries—many of whom we initially thought were so different from us.

Many people dream of visiting exotic places of natural beauty and cultural and historic significance such as Egypt, Peru, Greece and Hawaii. Many have told us they're inspired by our globetrotting partnership. They've said they wish they could travel the world too, particularly with their soulmates. However, traveling for an extended period while doing energetically intense work can present unexpected challenges. My second journey to Egypt in early 2016 was so grueling, for example, that it nearly grounded me entirely. Afterwards, I longed for a place to stay put for a while. I needed to heal from my illness and integrate the myriad experiences of the past three years of intense travelling.

You'll recall that after my initial awakening experience with Paul in 2008 (described in the introduction of this book), all I envisioned and wished for was to move to Hawaii permanently and settle down. Everything changed, however, when I met Eunjung on Kaua'i in 2011. I've always enjoyed the occasional trip, but I'd never planned to travel so extensively.

So how did I become someone who would travel to countless foreign destinations, including going to Egypt twice within a few years? I have Eunjung to thank for this inspiration! Eunjung had a deep calling to travel to other countries to connect and share with local consciousness groups and communities. She was committed to offering prayers and ceremonies at sacred power points around the world, helping uplift the frequencies of the planet. I was ready to expand my heart-vision and contribute to the transformation of the world in my own way, so I eagerly agreed to become the co-navigator of our global spiritual adventures. So, off we went, on a five-year whirlwind adventure!

One of the most remarkable places we visited was Egypt. It has a captivating history, magnificent antiquities and warm-hearted people. I hadn't read much about ancient Egypt, its temples and all of the *neteru* (gods and goddesses) before my first trip. When I visit a new place, I prefer to dive into experiences first-hand—going in cold, so to speak. Afterwards, I pore through books, websites and literature, finding out the significance of my adventures and connecting the dots between my personal experiences and the accounts shared by others.

One of the joys of traveling to a foreign country is that you learn about its culture in action, not just by reading books or attending a lecture. The Egyptian culture is strongly influenced by mythology. Egyptian mythology is a collection of stories that describe the actions of the Egyptian gods, they translate the essence and behavior of deities into terms that human beings can understand. Each adaption of a myth represents a different symbolic perspective, which greatly influenced the Egyptians' understanding of the gods and the world.

There are twenty-two main gods, called *neteru*, in the Egyptian pantheon. They all express one aspect of divinity and the entirety of who we are, collectively. Each of these *neteru* or archetypes exist within each one of us and can have both light and dark aspects. Interestingly, the number of *neteru* total twenty-two (eleven feminine and eleven masculine), the number of chromosome pairs within our DNA. (There are twenty-three of these pairs in total, however, the twenty-third pair differs between males and females.)

The Egyptian gods and goddesses are celebrated in myths. The Osiris myth is the most well-known and influential story in ancient Egyptian mythology. Briefly, it's about the murder of Osiris, a primeval king of Egypt, and how the murderous event unfolded. In summary, here is how the story goes:

> *Osiris' murderer, his brother Set, takes the throne after succeeding with his dark plan to kill his brother. Meanwhile Osiris' wife, the Goddess Isis, restores her husband's body by finding and putting together the fourteen pieces thrown along the Nile River. This allows Isis to conceive Horus with*

Osiris. At first a vulnerable child protected by Isis, Horus later becomes Set's rival for the throne. Their conflict ends with Horus' triumph, which restores order to Egypt and completes the process of Osiris' resurrection.

The Osiris myth is about the conflict between balance and imbalance, the interplay between the light and the dark and, most significantly, about death and the afterlife. This story teaches us to take responsibility—choosing how to respond when we face challenges. It encourages us to tap into our higher guidance, remembering our magical, creative powers so we can co-create with spirit.

The ancient Egyptians understood that we have both physical bodies and various subtle bodies invisible to the physical senses. They referred to the physical body as *khat*. They were trained to work with its etheric counterpart (known as the *ka*), which includes an extensive network of energy meridians as well as mental, emotional and etheric imprints. The *ka* nourishes the *khat* while extending beyond it. Beyond this is the *akh*, a luminous body of light that can also be referred to as the astral body. With training, the *akh* could function independently of the physical body, traveling through time and space. The soul was known as the *ba*, and there was a body of light directly associated with the soul known as the *sahu*. Initiates who learned to work with the *sahu* could receive the light of the soul directly into their physical bodies. As you can imagine, with my interest in spiritual advancement, energy medicine and wellbeing coaching, I became fascinated with this ancient Egyptian belief system!

As I mentioned earlier, I fell in love with Egypt on my first visit—a journey organized by Greg Roach and Halle Eavelyn from Spirit Quest Tours—after having truly amazing experiences both with them personally and with our travel group.

I believe that a journey starts the moment you're inspired or guided to make that journey. The universe arranges people and situations to make sure the stage is set for the great adventure that awaits you. One remarkable thing happened even before we left for Egypt. While travelling in California a few weeks before the trip, Eunjung and I stayed the night at a hotel near the Los Angeles airport. As we checked out at the reception desk, I felt guided to pick a card from a big jar filled with hundreds of business cards. The name on the card I chose was John D. Riley, a quantum physicist and zero-point researcher. Since Ueli, a close friend of mine from Switzerland, was also interested in zero-point, I kept John's card.

Once we arrived in Egypt and started our journey with a group of about fifteen people, it turned out that John D. Riley, the man whose business card I had picked, was on the same journey! This was no coincidence; there are so many hotels near the Los Angeles airport, and there were hundreds of cards in that jar. John had traveled through Egypt several times, and he was knowledgeable and witty. I really enjoyed his company throughout our Egyptian journey.

I'd had a similar 'precursor experience' when I embarked on my spiritual vision quest over all of the Hawaiian Islands in 2011. I'd expected my quest to start once I'd arrived on the Big Island of Hawaii. Surprisingly, as I shared earlier, I had a life-changing encounter before I even arrived at the airport on Kaua'i—I met Eunjung, opening the energies for my vision quest. And now I'd chosen John's card shortly before we left for Egypt. The universe definitely has a way of preparing you!

My first journey to Egypt took place from December 9 to December 23, 2012. You may remember that there were many predictions and prophecies regarding December 21, 2012, which was said to fall at the end of the Mayan calendar. In 2009, German film director Roland Emmerich even directed an epic disaster film, called *2012*, dealing with one of the more dramatic interpretations of the Mayan calendar's conclusion, the catastrophic end of the world. I had been reading a lot about the 2012 phenomenon, so it was meaningful that Eunjung and I were in Egypt during this potent, energetically super-charged time on the planet.

New Thought thinkers and philosophers presented various ideas about astronomical alignments and posited a variety of numerological interpretations regarding this auspicious date. Scenarios ranged from the dreaded end of the world by cataclysmic events—including Earth's collision with a mythical planet called Nibiru—to a more optimistic New Age interpretation that the date marked the start of a new era when humanity would undergo an unstoppable, positive spiritual transformation ushering us fully into the long-awaited Aquarian Age.

It was very special to visit Egypt with its majestic ancient sites and temples during this cosmically potent time. During our trip, we were guided by Egyptologist Doaa Badawi, who was friendly, gracious and knowledgeable. We learned that most of the Egyptian temples we visited were built along the Nile and that the location of each temple reflects the stellar, solar and lunar influences that were so important to the ancient Egyptians.

I found it fascinating that the construction of the temples was often influenced by the cycles of the sun, moon and stars. Many temples are specially designed to allow sunlight, moonlight or starlight to illuminate statues of Egyptian gods or goddesses during specific times on the calendar, such as at equinoxes and solstices. Every Egyptian temple is dedicated to a different neter and is a symbol or embodiment of the divine. Each of these sacred sites carries a different vibration.

During our remarkable journey, special arrangements were made for us to enjoy private visits to some of the most spectacular temples in Egypt. We saw the Isis temple on the island of Philae (located downstream from the Aswan Dam and Lake Nasser) in the morning, the Luxor temple in the evening, and the mysterious Sphinx and the Karnak temple at sunrise. The most anticipated private visit was to the chambers of the Great Pyramid of Giza on December 19, 2012. That visit fell just two days before one of the most talked-about dates in recent history, one greeted with either great hope or gripping fear.

When you are awarded private time in the temples without other tourist groups around, these ancient masterpieces come alive. It truly felt as if I were walking into a holy temple in another dimension, traveling through time and space. If you can quiet your mind and open your heart, these temple sites will help you find the answers you are seeking.

We were the second to last private group before the Egyptian government closed off the Great Pyramid to the public for three days before reopening it on December 23. I'll never forget the marvelous moment when I entered the King's Chamber, and what it was like to chant while lying in the granite sarcophagus. So much has been written about the true purpose of that legendary sarcophagus. According to various sources with spiritual perspectives, this simple-looking stone coffer was used as an initiation chamber for pharaohs. Some say it also functions as an ascension chamber, assisting those who seek spiritual evolution. My own powerful encounter with it seems to support that view. It felt as if I were falling into a great abyss and, at the same time, rising into the vast universe, hearing my voice echoing a thousand times throughout the stars. Through these multi-dimensional vibrations, I could feel myself viscerally as a universal being unbound by space and time. That moment alone was worth the trip to Egypt!

Before we went into the Great Pyramid I had no idea what to expect, and no clue what was waiting for us. People who visit these energetically potent sites have vastly diverse, unique experiences.

Spending time in the pyramids and temples made ancient Egyptian mythology vivid and palpable to me, physically, emotionally and spiritually. It provided me with profound insights. The Egyptians saw time in the present as a series of recurring patterns inspired by the cycles of nature. Recurring themes include the conflict between the keepers of balance and the forces of disorder, the importance of the pharaoh in maintaining societal harmony, and the continual death and regeneration of the gods.

I'm inspired to conclude the highlights of my first time in Egypt with two unforgettable experiences....

On December 12, 2012, a day we were told held powerful cosmic energies linked to December 21, 2012, we got up very early in the morning to watch the sunrise at the Karnak Luxor temple from the Holy of Holies, the ancient temple's innermost and most sacred chamber. Our group gathered in respectful silence. It was an emotional moment when the sun rose above the horizon. Its bright, golden rays illuminated the stone wall of the chamber. We were standing in a path of light leading to the dawn of a new era. I was grateful that I was greeting this new beginning with my beloved Eunjung and this special group. We could feel that from the Holy of Holies, the Gods and Goddesses of Egypt were preparing us for entering the new age.

Nine days later, December 21, 2012—the day I'd done so much reading and research about—finally arrived. By that time, we had flown back from Luxor to Cairo to prepare for this special day. In the late morning of this historic day, we went to the Step Pyramid at Saqqara—which is known to be a portal to the stars—and had a powerful ceremony to honor the anticipated and celebrated solstice. In the four years since my initial awakening with the Hawaiian mystery healer, Paul, I'd been driven to prepare myself and others for this monumental day, and I was grateful the world did not end! We played our crystal bowl and chanted and prayed together for peace in the new world.

When we returned to our hotel room, the crystal bowl we'd used inside the Step Pyramid unexpectedly dropped out of my hands and fell to the floor. It was the only spot in the entire room where there was no carpet! We watched in utter disbelief as—as if in slow-motion—the bowl crashed onto the hard floor and broke into many pieces. We'd worked with this beautiful-sounding crystal bowl countless times since the first ceremony Eunjung and I conducted together in Switzerland at the end of September 2011.

At first, we were saddened and couldn't understand why this had happened on such a special day. After we regained our composure, though, Eunjung tuned in and received a message that this crystal bowl had fulfilled its purpose of singing to activate many sacred sites we had travelled to until December 21, 2012. Its mission was complete, and it wanted to be free. We kept one small piece of this wise, beautiful crystal bowl. The crystal spirit said that it was now up to us to carry its vibrational songs within ourselves.

As we prepared to leave Egypt, I felt that my first Egyptian journey had gifted me with new hope, courage and inspiration to continue walking on this path of light. I was ready to reveal more of who I truly am and lead my life with purpose and higher visions.

After my amazing first journey to Egypt, I was eagerly looking forward to returning to the land of sacred temples. So, three years later, after spending Christmas 2015 with my family in Switzerland, Eunjung and I flew back to Cairo. Little did I know I was about to get a serious wake-up call about the role my emotions play in my life.

My second journey to Egypt helped me to start taking self-responsibility, reflecting on how I've been a willing accomplice in a variety of life circumstances. My second time there made me aware of the stubborn patterns and deep-rooted conditioning that had influenced me, particularly in the emotional realm, for far too long. I learned what the consequences could be if I didn't identify them and release them. I also started to recognize and embrace the hidden power and gifts in what I had always perceived as my weaknesses, obstacles and shadows. I once believed my struggles were caused by others, or by external events that had nothing to do with me. That view only perpetuated my difficulties.

As I mentioned in the introduction of this book, the precepts of Yoga say that suffering arises for four reasons. One of these is our desire to repeat a pleasurable experience, and the suffering that ensues when that expectation isn't fulfilled. I experienced this on my second journey to Egypt. Because our first trip had been magnificent in countless ways, I expected similarly wonderful experiences when we decided to go back. The universe, however, had a different plan. The return trip turned out to be difficult, pushing me to my limit physically, spiritually and emotionally.

Our emotions are powerful. They are what make us human, and they greatly influence the way we lead our lives. Depending on how we relate to them, our emotions have the power to either destroy or heal our lives. Ideally, we can use them to guide us to a place of peace and evolve us into a better version of ourselves. When we sense resistance or blocks, it's important to feel our emotions completely and not to push them away. I've always tended to have difficulties relating to my stronger emotions, often feeling like they control me and my life. So, on our second trip to Egypt, I learned a great lesson about not over-identifying with my feelings or losing myself in them—and how to surrender when the obstacles life places before us are too burdensome to overcome.

Once we returned to Egypt for our second journey, we stayed at the Mena House, one of the most unique, stunningly beautiful hotels in Cairo. This palatial hotel, which boasts a rich and colorful history, is located in the shadows of the Great Pyramids of Giza and is surrounded by forty acres of verdant green gardens. We were welcomed with a long hug from our friend Mohamed Nazmy, the president of Quest Travel, who had arranged our trip. His company is among the top ten travel companies in Egypt and specializes in organizing customized spiritual journeys. We had met Mohamed during our first trip in 2012, and we were happy to see each other again. Mohamed emits warmth, love and kindness, and he truly cares about everyone he interacts with.

Although he hails from a very different culture, Mohamed feels like a family member to me. He inspires me hugely because he is truly living his life's purpose. I learned his story through the book *Nazmy—Love is my Religion*, a biography of Mohamed written by Sharlyn Hidalgo. In the early '80s, Mohamed heard a voice while he was visiting the King's Chamber in the Great Pyramid. It said, "You are to be of service." Mohamed says that spending time in Egypt can open your heart, helping you to remember who you are and what's truly important to you. I agree.

Mohamed owns a gorgeous, well-built luxury sailing boat called the "Afandina." The Afandina, which has ten cabins and room for twenty people, offers the unforgettable experience of sailing on the Nile privately. I felt blessed to have navigated the Nile on such a stately boat during both of my journeys to Egypt—it was an unforgettable experience and I absolutely loved it. On the Afandina, the delicious Egyptian-style meals are prepared by an excellent chef. What I was most impressed with and touched by was that the entire staff was so dedicated and passionate about providing excellent service and hospitality. Their commitment is a testament to Mohamed's heart-based leadership. I learned a lot by observing how the staff on the Afandina were interacting with each other, with Mohamed and with us guests. They were kind, friendly and eager to serve, one of the most valuable qualities any human being can possess when it comes to creating a peaceful, respectful and happy world.

When you travel on the Afandina, over time you start to develop friendships with the crew. During my second voyage on the Afandina, our group was honored to be joined by Mohamed and his friends Tarek Lofty, marketing director for the Mena House, and Mohamed Hegazi, a former ambassador of Egypt, who was accompanied by his lovely wife. Their company added lively conversations and depth to our journey. It taught me to appreciate the deep connection I was starting to make with these wonderful Egyptian friends.

There is a backstory about how Mohamed Nazmy and his friends came to join the Nile cruise on the Afandina with us. Mohamed usually does not travel with his Quest Travel clients;

he has his tour guides accompany them. However, at that time, he decided to join us with his friends, making the high operating cost of the beautiful luxury boat Afandina worthwhile. Around the time Eunjung and I were planning our second trip to Egypt in 2015, there was a flurry of concerned remarks and comments coming our way regarding the safety of traveling to Egypt. The media seemed to be focused on a few, isolated negative incidents that had occurred in Egypt, a perspective that deterred many tourists from visiting the country.

As this included people who may have been interested in joining our journey, we didn't have enough participants to form a group to make this private trip possible. Undeterred, our kind and generous friend Mohamed Nazmy said, "No matter what, this trip will happen!" And it did. Eunjung and I never felt unsafe during either trip to Egypt, nor did anyone in our group.

While travelling the Nile on the Afandina, I facilitated two energy healing sessions for Mohamed Nazmy. I'd never had someone come to healing sessions so prepared. For both sessions, he'd showered beforehand and was elegantly dressed. It was an honor for me to facilitate these sessions in his room while floating on the Nile on this gorgeous yacht. If you'd like to learn more about Mohamed, his company and his purpose, I highly recommend reading the wonderful book about him.

There was a funny episode on the Afandina involving me and Tarek Lofty, the marketing director of the Mena House and a close friend of Mohamed Nazmy. One morning, while Eunjung went on an excursion with our group to a temple site, I decided to stay on the Afandina to rest because I didn't feel well. I left our room and walked up to the lounge and dining room on the upper deck. I was listening to healing music on headphones, wearing a pullover with a hood similar to the one Tarek was wearing. Later I learned that Mohamed (the former ambassador) and his wife thought that I was Tarek, who was still sleeping in his room at the time. Since that day, whenever Tarek and I write to each other, we start with, "Hi, me." I am always touched by the depth of the relationships one can build with others from such different cultures when one travels with an open heart, an open mind and an adventurous spirit!

When we embarked on our second journey to Egypt on December 27, 2015 all seemed fine and it looked like another great adventure was awaiting us. However, on December 29, during a short flight from Cairo to Luxor, I started to feel out of balance. We entered the new year of 2016 while floating under the stars on the Nile. It should have been a transcendent moment. Instead, the feeling of imbalance and weakness increased, affecting my mood and sense of wellbeing.

I first wondered if these disorienting feelings were because of jet lag, or if I had caught some kind of cold or flu while traveling. I got some good rest on the boat on January 3 and rejoined our program the following day. After eating breakfast—always served al fresco on the upper deck of the Afandina—we headed for the Karnak temple, where a private visit at the statue of Sekhmet had been arranged.

I'd had a powerful healing experience with Sekhmet's statue three years prior, so I expected to receive further healing on this visit. Once we arrived at the entrance of the Karnak temple and were about to walk into the large temple complex, though, I suddenly felt an invisible energetic wall in front of me. I couldn't walk through the wall, no matter how hard I tried. It felt like I was not allowed to visit the temple and Sekhmet that day.

The energies at the Egyptian temples can be extremely powerful, especially combined with what you bring to the table—your intentions, your attitude and your prayers. I wondered if my physical and emotional states needed to improve before I could enter this mighty temple complex.

The energies at the Egyptian temples can be extremely powerful, especially combined with your intentions, your attitude and your prayers.

I told Eunjung and Amro Munir, our friendly and witty tour guide, about the energetic wall I'd encountered and said I'd like to go back to the Afandina to get more rest. The driver who had brought us to Karnak had already left, so I had to wait in the cold, air-conditioned welcome center for more than two hours until the group returned. After an hour-long stop at a famous jewelry store in Luxor, I was finally able to return to the boat.

Meanwhile, my symptoms had gradually worsened. Earlier, I'd felt something was off in my body. By the time we were back on the Afandina, I saw the world around me in wavy motion. Although the boat was stationary, I assumed I was having intense symptoms of sea-sickness.

The next morning our group left early without me for a day-long excursion. The trip included many hours of driving to Dendara, the temple of Hathor. I hoped my condition would improve after a day of rest. Instead, upon waking I still felt weak and the sensations of the world moving around me were even more severe.

I talked to Mohamed Nazmy, who immediately arranged for me to stay at a hotel for three days before all of us flew back to Cairo. We realized that staying on the Afandina would not help me recover, especially with my intensifying dizziness and sea-sickness. From my hotel room, however, I could hear the loud noise from the streets, even with the doors closed. After a restless night during which my symptoms worsened, I needed to move to a calmer hotel nearby. The Hotel Pavilion Winter Luxor seemed like the perfect place to recover, because there was a wonderful garden on the property with many trees and birds.

Although I could now hear the beautiful sound of singing birds instead of traffic, my condition was still deteriorating. Now, everything I saw was lopsided—the whole world around me appeared slanted to the left, with on-and-off wavy feelings. I had never had this problem before, so I was completely perplexed and a bit scared.

I saw a friendly and humorous hotel doctor a few times. His diagnosis was that I had severe vertigo, possibly originating from an ear infection. He gave me a lot of medication to reduce my symptoms. I hoped the symptoms would improve during the three days before our flight, but they didn't. Now my world was slanted, wavy and spinning, and my doctor advised against taking any flights. I couldn't imagine being on an airplane in this condition anyway, so I stayed behind in Luxor at the hotel while the rest of the group left for Cairo. This included Eunjung, as she was the group leader. I was saddened to be alone in this condition and had to muster my courage.

I had never experienced anything like this in my life. Every day, the weird symptoms of vertigo intensified. No matter if I was lying down, sitting or standing, everything was spinning at an accelerating speed, both within and around me. It felt as if I were on a cruise ship in a colossal storm, being tossed in the waves, with no land in sight.

I endured the most severe spinning on the day I reconnected energetically and remotely with our group for a final ceremony inside the Great Pyramid. I felt immense, profound energies during their ceremony inside the King's Chamber. That night, the relentless spinning got so intense that no matter what I tried—including holding tightly to the bedpost in my hotel room—I felt outrageously dizzy. I feared I wouldn't survive the night. I ended up losing consciousness and woke up the next morning, alive but with no idea what to do anymore. I had no choice but to surrender completely to what was happening.

Over time I became extremely nauseous too, probably from the combination of vertigo and the strong medicine. I was devastated that I'd failed to find relief from these crazy symptoms, even after taking medicine and finding refuge in a nice, calm hotel. As I tried to recover, my emotional state went through a huge, inner storm. Alone in this hotel, with Eunjung and the group still traveling, I was buffeted by varying degrees of sadness, hopelessness, anger, confusion and depression.

I started to wonder if there was a bigger picture as to why my imbalanced state hadn't improved. After a few nights at the hotel, I had a prophetic dream. I was travelling through space and looking down at the Luxor temple from a bird's-eye-view. The dream reminded me that the hotel I was staying at was located just about 150 meters southwest of the Luxor temple.

After I woke up from the dream, I went online and found out that R.A. Schwaller de Lubicz, an Alsatian mathematician, philosopher and Egyptologist, had worked on a fifteen-year onsite study of the great temple complex of Luxor. In the temple of Luxor, he found a record of the Egyptians' understanding of the cosmic laws of creation and the way spirit becomes manifest as matter. Together with his wife and daughter, he measured and mapped the temple at Luxor. They looked at everything that might provide information about Sacred Geometry and proportion. According to R.A. Schwaller de Lubicz, the Luxor temple describes the structure of the human body, including its chakras (energy centers). Built as a representation of the perfect man, it expresses the process of creation and growth of the human form.

I found out that the top of the Luxor temple, this symbolic representation of the human body, was directly facing the location of the hotel where I was staying. This meant I had been sleeping above the crown chakra of the Luxor temple for many days. I wondered if this experience was perhaps a powerful initiation orchestrated by the Egyptian gods, conspiring to release me from emotions, habits and patterns that no longer served me—by tossing me into an energetic washing machine.

After the formal journey ended and our group left Cairo, Eunjung flew back to Luxor to be with me as I still could not travel. Even after the revelation of the Luxor temple's structure resembling a human body and my proximity to its crown chakra, I still experienced the strong waves of energy and the lopsided view of the world around me. But I was at least united with my love, Eunjung. With her holding my hands, walking became easier. We felt that visiting the statue of Sekhmet might help with my condition, so we went back to the Karnak temple. This time the energetic wall that had stopped me from entering the temple complex was no longer there, signaling it was okay for me to proceed.

In Egyptian mythology, Sekhmet is a warrior goddess as well as a goddess of healing. Sekhmet's name comes from the ancient Egyptian word *sekhem*, meaning "power" or "might." She is portrayed as a lioness, the fiercest hunter known to the Egyptians. She was seen as the protector of the pharaohs. She led them in warfare and it was said that her fiery breath formed the desert. Sekhmet is also a solar deity, sometimes called the daughter of the sun god, Ra, and often associated with the goddesses Hathor and Bastet.

While in the presence of the Sekhmet statue, located at the back of the Karnak temple complex, I felt a tremendous healing power rising from her. I cried and prayed from the bottom of my heart for healing and that the symptoms of vertigo would finally disappear. I knew my prayers would be answered. A few days later I could finally fly again. We decided to go stay at an Ayurvedic healing center in the south of Sri Lanka where I could receive more holistic treatments and care to deepen my healing process.

When I completely recovered from the vertigo four weeks later, I felt a huge sense of relief and gratitude that I'd found balance again. As I reflect on this second time in Egypt, I realize that—though it was one of the most difficult experiences I've ever faced—it forced me to release the emotional states and thought patterns that had until then had a powerful grip on my life. I came to understand that emotions are like waves of energy that pass through us but do not define us, which helped me surrender to the now-moment and divine grace.

When I'd been by myself in Luxor without Eunjung, I had to totally feel my emotions around the vertigo and the resulting existential crisis. There were moments I feared that I wouldn't survive and would never see Eunjung again. I noticed that when I became overwhelmed by emotions of despair and hopelessness, the vertigo got stronger. When I was able to calm down rather than over-identifying with my emotions, the vertigo symptoms lessened slightly.

Life's lessons come in many forms and, through this ordeal, I learned a priceless life lesson. We need to embrace both the light and dark, the archetypal qualities represented by the *neteru*, in order to have true balance in life.

My yoga teacher Rod Stryker shares that to be teachable, we need to be as open to learning from failure as from success. Nature seems to know that hardships will eventually break down your resistance and loosen your attachments, allowing you to finally embrace the lessons that life has long been trying to teach you.

Surrendering completely in Egypt to something that spun me so completely out of balance was a starting point. It taught me to embrace myself fully, light and dark, without getting too attached to either of the two aspects.

I'd like to conclude this chapter with another favorite quote from the movie *Discover the Gift*. At the end, Demian says, "And after this long journey of my own, if there is any wisdom I can offer, it is simply this: Follow your heart, discover your gift and get ready for the greatest adventure of your life."

When I saw the movie for the first time in October 2010, I embraced Demian's words. I started to follow my heart and discover the gifts I brought into this world. Looking back, since that moment of decision, I've truly been having the greatest adventure of my life, including these mysterious experiences in Egypt.

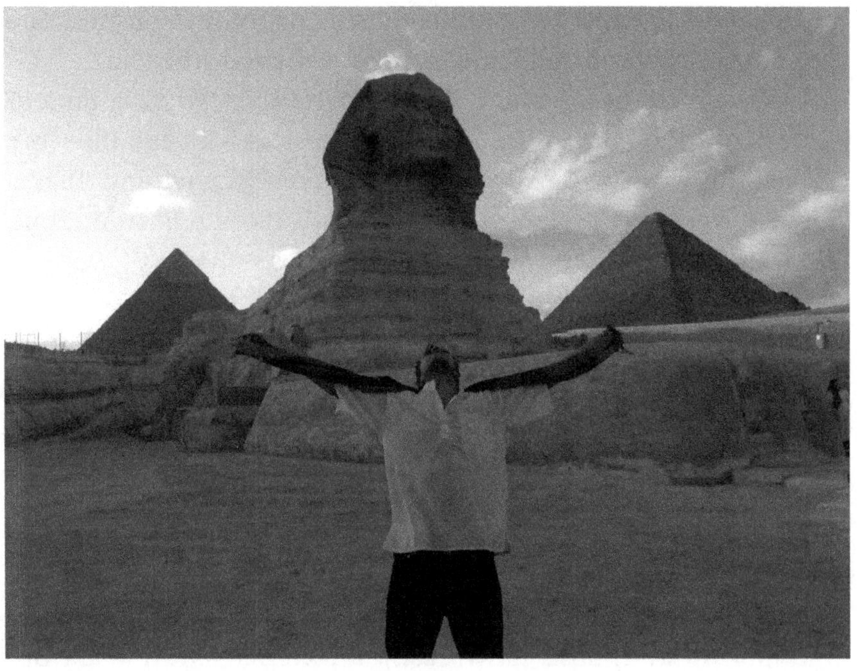

Giza Plateau, Egypt

Exploring the World with Ilahinoor

How do you explain something so profound that it can't be described with our limited human language? That is perhaps the greatest challenge when it comes to imparting the concept of Ilahinoor.

Whenever people ask me what Ilahinoor is, I start with the etymology of the word. I explain that Ilahinoor means "divine light" in Turkish and Arabic, and that it is deeply rooted in spiritual and shamanic traditions and initiatory rites, including those of the ancient Egyptians and the mystical Islamic tradition of Sufism. I also tell them that Ilahinoor is much more than just another form of energy healing. Through profound personal experience, I've learned that it allows us to tap into the ancient morphogenetic field, balancing the soul imprint that serves as the pattern for our existence. This can provide deep personal healing and allow us to experience multi-dimensional consciousness and a profound sense of wellbeing, contentment and freedom.

The nineteenth century Persian poet Rumi wrote a famous verse about the human experience of oneness with the universe. "Something opens our wings," he wrote. "Something makes boredom and hurt disappear. Someone fills the cup in front of us: We taste only sacredness." Rumi's mysterious choice of words—*something, someone*—underscores the ineffable quality of Ilahinoor.

When I explain to others what Ilahinoor is, I share that it is a divine light that has the potential to activate and awaken us, and the earth itself, to our infinite potential. Many questions still arise, however. What is this divine light? What is this morphogenetic field? What is multi-dimensional consciousness, and how can we improve our own lives and the lives of others by accessing it? What does it truly mean to awaken to our infinite potential and to find our life's purpose? And how do we choose, individually and collectively, to make our unique contribution in co-creating peace, bridging heaven and earth in a world seemingly spinning out of control?

I've found that I can be most effective in teaching others how to heal and awaken when I share transformative events and epiphanies that I've learned personally and authentically. I've heard from others about the miracles they've experienced too, and I hope that this will inspire you to find your own answers to such questions and share your insights with others. And I hope that learning more about Ilahinoor will bring miracles into your life. It certainly did for me.

Reconnecting with Hawaii

I first met Kiara Windrider, an author, researcher and spiritual teacher and the mentor who taught me about Ilahinoor, in Switzerland in

2009. He had tapped into the cosmic energy of Ilahinoor a few years earlier, and was traveling around the world to spread the message of its healing and awakening potential.

I had a strong, immediate sense that my meeting with this remarkable man and my firsthand experience of the Ilahinoor field would change my life drastically, forever. I could not have imagined, however, how profoundly my life's journey would shift. I could not have anticipated that I'd start to travel around the world and finally make Kaua'i my home.

It was also beyond my wildest imagination that I'd begin teaching Ilahinoor, together with my beloved Eunjung, to hundreds of people and that I'd practice Ilahinoor at sacred sites around the world. I also had no inkling that we would continue to meet Kiara at some of these spiritual places throughout our travels, as we most recently did again in Assisi, Italy during the summer solstice 2018.

In 2008, a year before my initial encounter with Kiara, I traveled for the first time to Hawaii where, you will recall from the story I shared with you earlier, I experienced a profound healing miracle with a Hawaiian healer named Paul. Once Paul had finished working on me, I was blissful. I had tasted heaven on earth in an altered state of consciousness. It was like dreaming while awake! It was a momentous occasion. Recall I told you the amazing story of how Paul and I were standing in a clearing in a tropical forest on a cloudy day, and how the whole space was full of the melodic chatter of birds. Paul raised his right hand and snapped his fingers. Suddenly the clearing was filled with a huge, bright column of light. Paul snapped his fingers again and we stood in absolute silence—the birdsong stopped.

I was fully present in that moment. I savored the power of the silence. A few moments later, Paul snapped his fingers again. Instantly, the birds started to sing, the opening in the sky closed and the clouds returned.

This fateful meeting with Paul changed the course of my life, starting me on a mystical journey of healing. It gifted me with a rebirth after a time of crisis and desperation, which reached a climax when a series of deaths occurred in my family in 2005. I shared my initial rebirth experience in the introduction of this book, and in a book I contributed to, titled *Inspired by the Passion Test.*

The time with Paul was a starting point for a quest that led me around the world, seeking answers to the questions of why humanity is suffering, and how I can contribute personally to the release of suffering and teach others to do the same. After my healing miracle, my deepest heart's desire was to help others heal as Paul had done for me. I studied healing and energy work, both by taking courses and reading books, which was an invaluable starting point for my quest. First, I became a Reiki master, and then continued to study many other forms of healing and energy work. As eager, excited and grateful as I was to learn more about healing and how to facilitate it, however, I was unable to reconnect with the power of the initial healing miracle I'd experienced in that tropical forest above Honolulu in Hawaii.

Led by synchronicity

Luckily, I only had to wait eleven months until I met Kiara in Zurich. He was teaching a one-day workshop at a large, four-day conscious life exposition called "Lebenskraft," which in English means "life force."

I had participated in many spiritual seminars since my return from Hawaii, seeking answers to the burning questions in my heart. I decided to get a four-day pass, so I could attend as many workshops as possible and talk to some of the more than 150 exhibitors who were part of this event.

Kiara's workshop was scheduled for the third day of the expo. By this time, I had begun following intuitive guidance when it came to deciding which events to participate in. Instead of trying to decide which workshop to attend logically, based on the workshop descriptions and presenters' biographies in the official program, I chose to follow my gut feelings and look for synchronicities in deciding what session to join.

I clearly remember March 7, 2009 when I experienced Ilahinoor for the first time. I hadn't been able to sleep much the night before. When I woke up, I remembered some vivid dreams about my experience with Paul and, surprisingly, about ancient Egypt, a country that I had not yet traveled to and had no calling to visit at that time.

I woke up early and arrived at the location much sooner than I had on the first two days. It was a cold, sunny day, and the air was crisp and clear as I walked from the train station to the venue near Lake Zurich. Because I'd arrived early, it was much less crowded than it had been during my participation over the previous two days. There were quite a few workshops from which to choose, they all started at 10:00 a.m. I decided to follow my intuition and, drawn to the workshop area, I went inside the different seminar venues to find out how the rooms *felt* when I sat down in silence.

After checking out three rooms I stepped into a fourth, which had a slightly different vibration. It felt immediately comfortable and peaceful. I decided to stay there, no matter who the presenter or the topic was, knowing I could leave and join another workshop if I didn't resonate with the presentation, presenter or the group energy there.

I chose a seat in the middle of the room and meditated for a while, and suddenly my vivid dreams of Hawaii and Egypt came flooding back. With my eyes still closed, I sensed more and more people coming in, and then the workshop began. When I opened my eyes, I looked directly at a radiant and beautiful Indian-looking man with shining eyes—Kiara.

What Kiara talked about was intriguing and fascinating and it resonated profoundly within me, although I could not yet fully understand all the concepts and theories. The presentation was based on his research for his newest book, which had just been published. I was fascinated by some of the personal experiences he shared. He and his partner, Grace, had just arrived from Egypt and he talked about visiting ancient temples there, as well as about swimming with dolphins and whales in Hawaii. As Kiara spoke, I felt immense gratitude that I'd happened upon his workshop. My dreams from the night before served as confirmation that I'd been guided to the right place and the right person.

After lunch, Kiara and Grace started to introduce us to Ilahinoor. Some of us in the group were initially doubtful that we could learn how to practice a modality within half a day. Many of us had taken other healing courses, and they had generally required several days of learning and integration before we felt confident enough to practice them ourselves. This doubt disappeared completely once the energy filled the room.

I mentioned earlier the column of light that had filled the space in Hawaii, as well as the profound silence that occurred once the birds stopped singing. Here, that experience came back. I had finally found what I had been seeking so desperately. For the first time since my initial experience with Paul, I found not only an expanded and peaceful state of consciousness, but I was learning a technique that even included an element called the "column of light!" Ilahinoor brought immense peace, calm and stillness to my mind and opened my heart wide. The other participants I worked with that afternoon said the same thing about tapping into Ilahinoor energy.

When I left later that evening, my heart was wide open and felt expansive. I also noticed something unusual. I felt physically very tall. Whenever I walked through a door, I ducked because I thought I might hit the doorframe. Later, as I sat waiting for the train back home at the busiest station in Switzerland, the overwhelming feeling of peace and calm remained despite the hectic noise and many people that surrounded me.

When I got home, I fell into a deep and restful sleep.

When I awoke the next morning, my body felt incredibly light. Once I got up, I felt like I was walking on clouds...while at the same time feeling clear, grounded and present in my physical body. It was another miracle for me. How could I feel so anchored in my physical body and yet have such a strong feeling of expanded consciousness?

There was one more day left at the expo. All day long I met many people, and was excited to share with them about my transformational experience. I had hoped to see Kiara and Grace one more time, but I learned their visit to Switzerland was brief and that they'd already moved on to another country.

When I found out that Kiara would return to Switzerland in just four weeks for a four-day seminar, I signed up without hesitating. I had powerful experiences during this second course with Kiara and a group of about thirty people who gathered from April 3 to April 6, 2009. It was wonderful to learn and practice the different Ilahinoor steps for an expanded period of time.

I still remember how beautiful it was when I watched the sunset outside after the seminar was over. I felt as though I was merging with all nature around me, and it was just as wonderful, blissful and magical as watching the sunset after my miraculous experience with Paul in Hawaii.

The name of Kiara's workshop and seminar was "Energie des Erwachens," meaning "Energy of Awakening" in English, and Ilahinoor indeed became a strong and yet gentle awakening energy during this transitional time of my life. You can check out Kiara's Ilahinoor work on his website at *www.kiarawindrider.net/ilahinoor.*

I kept rereading Kiara's books, and repeatedly watching the few videos I'd found of him online. I also began sharing Ilahinoor with friends and family members, something I'd been hesitant about doing with other healing techniques. Though some people I worked with using Ilahinoor had never received any energy work, they reported positive and pleasantly surprising results.

Expanding our Horizons with Ilahinoor

One year later, in 2010, I went through a severe burnout experience. While I kept experiencing an exquisite state of oneness and unity while in nature, it became increasingly difficult to keep up with my job as a business consultant in addition to spending thirty percent of my time in rigorous life coaching education. At the time, I was studying four modalities: integral life coaching, business coaching, mental coaching and emotional coaching. It was a challenging time, and as I was immersed in soul work, I had no choice but to look at many hidden aspects of my own personality. As taxing as this self-scrutiny was—confronting parts of me I was not fully aware of and had not yet faced—this experience gifted me with immense personal growth. Ultimately, as I noted earlier, the personal work I did at that time guided me back to Kaua'i, where I studied presence-centered awareness therapy, bodywork and other healing and counseling techniques for the first half of 2011.

Once I completed my studies at the end of June 2011, I embarked alone on a vision quest. I began by travelling across the Hawaiian Islands for three weeks. As I shared earlier, my intention during this journey was to travel to as many sacred sites (called *Heiau* in Hawaiian), as I could. I had starting feeling drawn to these sites after my miraculous experience with Paul in 2008, but did not yet really understand why. My journey culminated on Kaua'i where I hiked eleven miles to the remote Kalalau Valley, located at the gorgeous Na Pali Coast, and stayed there for two nights.

I ended up visiting more than fifty Heiau. During this vision quest, I started to gain a deeper understanding of my attraction to these sites. In particular, I found doing the holographic *Merkaba* activation—an important element of Ilahinoor—to be especially beneficial when I was in Heiau with the natural elements around me.

Earlier I shared with you that Eunjung and I met for the first time when I was on my way to the airport on Kaua'i, right before leaving for my vision quest. After we came together later the same year, we became committed to and passionate about performing ceremonies and activations around the world together—by ourselves, with friends or in groups. Both of us work with energy and are sensitive and highly intuitive. When visiting these places, we feel and see much more than what can be perceived through just the physical senses.

Since learning about Ilahinoor in early 2009, I'd shared it with many people and at various sacred sites. I never had thought about teaching Ilahinoor with a group, however. This suddenly changed when I found myself back in Cyprus in October 2012.

Cyprus is a beautiful island in the Mediterranean Sea, west of Lebanon and Syria, northwest of Israel and south of Turkey. It's a wonderful, relaxing place, full of history. Cyprus is well known for its archaeological sites, its ancient temples (connected to the Goddess Aphrodite) as well as its beautiful coastlines. Eunjung and I had had a wonderful experience in July 2012 with our friend Mikaela, the founder of Serenity House in Nicosia. As Eunjung had to return to the U.S. for work, I travelled back to Cyprus by myself in October for a week-long vacation.

Mikaela was not on the island during this time, however, she had introduced me to Guytane, the founder of Gaia Wellness Center in Larnaca. After I gave an Ilahinoor session to Guytane, we decided to offer a three-hour introduction to Ilahinoor at her wellness center. It was a last-minute decision without much time to prepare, so I was nervous at first. I was uncertain if my introduction to Ilahinoor would have the same profound effects on people as it had had on me when I first encountered this life-changing energy and vibration.

The gathering started at 7:00 p.m. and turned out wonderfully. Once the first three hours were over, no one in our small group of five felt ready to leave. We kept practicing for three more hours and finally went home after 1:30 a.m.

A remarkable side-note to this story is that the ground on which the Gaia Wellness Center stands used to be an Egyptian shrine! Guytane told me that this part of the island of Cyprus had belonged to Egypt long ago. She said that upon receiving Ilahinoor during our pre-workshop meeting, she felt 100 percent certain that this building had been the site of Ilahinoor initiations in the past.

I recall that over a number of years—and especially at the end of 2012—many people, including Kiara Windrider and others in the energy healing arts and spiritual movement, were discussing a fascinating and intriguing topic. What would happen to the planet and humanity at the end of 2012, which marked the end of the Mayan calendar? There were many kinds of predictions including some beliefs that we could expect total destruction of the planet—or, on a more positive note—that all of humanity would fully awaken by then.

I mentioned earlier that I was amazed Eunjung and I had ended up with a group in Egypt for a two-week stay. Recall that our visit had included the special day of December 21 and that we were the second to last group to enter the King's chamber of the Great Pyramid on December 19 before the Egyptian authorities closed the site for a few days. It was an amazing journey and I've always wondered if the special, multi-dimensional consciousness of Ilahinoor had orchestrated our whole Egyptian adventure!

As Eunjung and I cruised along the Nile, we started our days early in the morning. We went to the upper deck with our group and shared Ilahinoor together at sunrise. We had wanted to practice Ilahinoor at the temples we visited, but were unable to do so because there were only a few visitors and many guards, who do not allow personal activities on the site, unless a private visit for the group has been arranged in advance.

I still hold the memory of my first journey to Egypt as incredibly magical, adventurous and enchanting. In one of the temples, we even found a hieroglyph where we could clearly see two gods engaging in a form of energy transmission that resembled the "pinky activation" that is part of Ilahinoor. The pinky refers to the little finger, which is connected to the small intestine and heart organs, as well as to emotions such as nervousness, anxiety and lack of self-confidence. The pinky activation was one of the Ilahinoor elements that Kiara had shared enthusiastically with us while he visited Zurich in 2009 after his own trip to Egypt.

One participant in our Egyptian journey was Diego, who is from Ecuador. Diego became our dear friend. He loved experiencing Ilahinoor on the Nile with us, and invited us to visit him in Ecuador. So, as you know, the world did not end on December 21, 2012, and it was only two months later that Eunjung and I found ourselves on another magical tour that brought us to Costa Rica, Mexico and Ecuador. While we were in Ecuador, we had an opportunity to share a one-day Ilahinoor workshop with a group of twenty people in Quito. Diego and another person translated the workshop from English into Spanish. This time, I had more preparation time than I'd had back in Cyprus. I added background information to my introductory presentation and did my best to summarize some of the concepts Kiara shares in his books, drawing from his experiences along his journey and the incredible research he has conducted over many years.

The focus and intention of our workshop was to give everyone enough time to experience Ilahinoor firsthand and to help them gain enough clarity and confidence to share it with others.

After my great initial teaching experience in Cyprus, and with Eunjung and Diego co-facilitating and translating the Ecuador workshop, I felt more relaxed and confident about teaching the Ilahinoor steps to such a large group. We had a wonderful time creating a feeling of peace and unity for the day we were together. However, the biggest miracle of the workshop occurred without us being aware of it.

A few days later, we received feedback from Margarita, the owner of the yoga studio in Quito where we'd held the Ilahinoor workshop:

> *"I am the owner of a small yoga studio in Quito. I've been renting this beautiful space for my studio for two years. The owners of the building are a seventy-year-old lady and an eighty-five-year-old man. The man had cancer and diabetes and, two months ago, had an accident and broke his leg and hip. His wife broke her arm the same day in*

a different accident. She used to take care of him and the injury was hard on her, physically and emotionally.

After the surgery on his leg, the old man's condition worsened until he could no longer walk, go to the bathroom on his own or even talk. He and his family were suffering a lot. Meanwhile, we'd been preparing a meditation to be held in the yoga studio with Eunjung and Yves for Saturday, March 2, 2013. About twenty people met at the studio that afternoon, where we practiced meditation and the Ilahinoor healing technique until 9:30 p.m. that night. Two days later, on Monday, the boyfriend of the old man's daughter called me and told me the old man had died.

"I'm so saddened about your loss," I told him. "At least we were able to practice a meditation on Saturday night to fill the house with light." He surprised me by saying, "Yes, we could feel it. It was so strong!" I was a bit apprehensive about whether his response was positive or negative, because the family doesn't practice yoga or anything similar. When I asked him what they experienced, he replied, "We felt a lot of peace, a lot of love. It was beautiful and powerful."

After that night, the old man passed away. Since this event, the family has had peace again. It was a beautiful and peaceful transition. This truly is an amazing life experience for me."

Boundaries between past, present and future dissolve once we reach the expanded shamanic state of consciousness.

After our journeys to Hawaii and Egypt, Eunjung and I found ourselves in Central America, where shamanism—one of the ancient traditions Kiara talks about in his books—is practiced. Our experiences with Ilahinoor proved that boundaries between past, present and future dissolve once we reach this kind of expanded and shamanic state of consciousness.

When this bridging occurs between the upper world (representing the higher levels of the mind), the middle world (representing the rational human mind) and the lower world (representing our subconscious instincts and deep patterns of conditioning), we can experience multi-dimensional consciousness, transcending all limitations of time and space.

It is remarkable that the Hawaiian priests known as Kahunas, although located many thousands of miles away from South and Central America, similarly assert that the middle self cannot directly communicate with the higher self without connecting with the lower self. According to the Kahunas, for true healing to occur, the inner child, an aspect of the lower self that holds the subconscious memories, needs to be included.

Science confirms that our personality is mostly established at a young age. Many studies show that our preference for sensing or intuiting, which is very important when we want to heal and transform our lives, greatly develops by around the age of seven. How we think and feel is mostly developed during adolescence, and how we perceive and judge is developed by our early twenties. At the age of seven, we can already exhibit signs of traumas that will remain with us throughout our lives, unless we take active responsibility to heal and transform what is stored in our subconscious.

Ilahinoor is an excellent energy work technique that provides links between the higher, middle and lower selves. I include Ilahinoor as part of my healing sessions with individuals, and I keep noticing that it is by reconnecting with their inner child and their original state of innocence and childlike wonder that people experience the release of suffering and begin to heal. This reunion of the selves, in turn, improves their relationships with family and friends.

The field of Ilahinoor doesn't only bring healing and transformation on a personal level. It also brings peace and unity on a planetary level. Eunjung and I practice this energy work on power points, or vortices on the planet as part of our rituals and ceremonies, wherever we travel. Once, just a day after we met with Kiara, we were in Stonehenge, England and did the Ilahinoor work for the land there. The entire area of Stonehenge seemed to open to us and was filled with frequencies of peace and harmony.

Another unforgettable Ilahinoor activation experience unfolded when we went to Punalu'u Beach, also known as Black Sand Beach, on the Big Island of Hawaii.

As we were on the way to the airport, leaving from Kaua'i, our friend Howard Wills prophesied that we would meet three Honus (sea turtles) at this place. Once we arrived at this beautiful beach, there were indeed three Honus waiting for us on the sand in a triangle position! When we arrived, there were still other people there, but as soon we sat down to meditate and practice the holographic Merkaba activation, everyone left, leaving us alone with the Honus.

We merged with a unified field and received messages about multi-dimensional consciousness and realities. We believe the Ilahinoor energy is one powerful way to merge with Gaia and the cosmos, and to bring and anchor peace on the planet.

A Pilgrimage to India

We'd spent five years traveling, giving workshops and facilitating prayers and ceremonies in sacred sites in more than thirty countries. As I noted earlier, we'd seen hieroglyphs in Egypt that showed the "pinky activation," and we'd practiced it while cruising on the Nile. We'd had firsthand experience with sea turtles in Hawaii and with dolphins and whales—representatives of the powerful cetacean consciousness. Cetacean consciousness refers to the cognitive capabilities or intelligence of the Cetacea order of mammals (such as whales and dolphins). These experiences in Hawaii further activated our Holographic Merkaba. (Activating the *Holographic Merkaba* allows us to connect with our multi-dimensional selves and higher realms. The "Holographic Merkaba" is a vehicle of light in the shape of a Star Tetrahedron (two interlocking three-dimensional pyramids, one pointing up and the other pointing down). The Merkaba represents the energetic body of a human being. "Mer" means Light, "Ka" means Spirit, and "Ba" means Body.) And we'd been transformed by profound shamanic experiences during our visits to Costa Rica, Ecuador and Mexico.

Eight years after my initial experience with Ilahinoor, however, I realized that one important destination was missing in terms of what had influenced the creation of the Ilahinoor technique. We'd never traveled to Kiara's home country, India.

In February 2017, we finally got a powerful call to travel to India for four weeks. It turned out that Kiara and Grace were in India at the same time, and we decided to meet them in Auroville. Eunjung and I had crossed Kiara's path three times before—at the sacred British site of Glastonbury and in Denver and San Diego in the United States. Our 2013 meeting in Glastonbury had been special; I hadn't seen Kiara since his four-day course in Switzerland in 2009. I feel so grateful to him for introducing me to Ilahinoor and for the many healing miracles I'd witnessed while sharing and practicing Ilahinoor with others.

Eunjung and I started our first visit to India in Auroville, and concluded our journey with Kiara and Grace in Pondicherry at the ashram of the amazing sages, Sri Aurobindo and The Mother. Mirra Alfassa, known to her followers as "The Mother," was a spiritual guru, partner and collaborator of Sri Aurobindo. Sri Aurobindo considered her to be of equal yogic stature to him and called her by the name "The Mother." She was born in France and moved to Pondicherry permanently in 1920 after meeting

Sri Aurobindo during her first trip to India in 1914. The Mother founded the Sri Aurobindo Ashram and established Auroville, an experimental township with no national barriers and a universal town, which influenced and inspired many writers and teachers on the subject of Integral Yoga.

It was more than sixty years ago, on February 29, 1956, when The Mother proclaimed that *the supra-mental field*, a consciousness higher than the human rational mind, was finally able to penetrate into this realm of density. Through the practice of Ilahinoor we can connect with this supra-mental field and bring it into cellular consciousness.

Since Eunjung and I learn most powerfully through direct personal experiences, our meditations in Auroville and at the Sri Aurobindo Ashram fundamentally deepened our understanding of the concept of the descent of supra-mental consciousness, which Sri Aurobindo and The Mother talked about in depth. Both Eunjung and I had a profound and mystical experience of how the field feels on a cellular level when we meditated in the grand hall of Matrimandir (Temple of The Mother) in Auroville and visited the Samadhi of Sri Aurobindo and The Mother at the ashram in Pondicherry. Through these experiences Eunjung and I realized that the supra-mental field is not something we can grasp with our logical minds or express truthfully with words but something that has to be felt in our beings.

Of all the content from Kiara's work, the concept of the supra-mental field had always been the most difficult and it has been challenging for me to explain it—and for others to grasp it intellectually. After all, as I said at the beginning of this section, how can one explain something so profound that it can't really be described in human language?

I would like to express my deep gratitude to the Ilahinoor field and to Kiara for his teaching. I'm grateful too for all the wonderful experiences Eunjung and I have shared with others, while experiencing the Ilahinoor field at sacred sites around the world.

Looking back on the incredible journey I've undertaken since my first experience with Paul in Hawaii, I realize I've been pushed many times far beyond my perceived limits. Just like the column of light that pierced through the clouded sky on that amazing afternoon with Paul in Hawaii, Ilahinoor offers a powerful channel through which we can heal, transform our suffering and ultimately awaken to our infinite potential. Kiara's book, *Ilahinoor: Awakening the Divine Human*, has rewarded me immensely, as have the teachings from Sri Auribindo and The Mother.

Ilahinoor not only assists us individually to heal and transcend our personal limitations, it also has incredible potential for planetary healing and peacemaking. Once Ilahinoor's healing energies clean our energy fields, clouds of our perception part and we see clearly again. Then, we can experience oneness and unity with everything and everyone around us. We are free to make our unique contribution toward creating heaven on earth!

Abydos Temple, Egypt

Mapping Your Inner Landscape

When you start doing your inner work and have more clarity about the map of your life, the next question is discovering how you can fine-tune your life map and share your gifts and talents with others. This section is about how you can map your inner landscape and start living your purpose, and how you can serve others.

As I noted earlier, one of things I'm passionate about is a sport called *orienteering*. My intention in writing this section isn't to give you a full introduction to this amazing pursuit, but I believe a short explanation could be beneficial. Here's a summary of orienteering I found on the website for the Colorado-based Rocky Mountain Orienteering Club (RMOC: *www.rmoc.org*).

> *You use a map and compass to locate a series of checkpoints shown on a specialized topographic map. You choose the route, either on- or off-trail, that will help you find all the checkpoints and get to the finish line in the shortest amount of time. Each checkpoint (or 'control') is a distinct, mapped feature such as a trail junction, a boulder, a hilltop, etc. The controls are marked with orange-and-white flags. Orienteering is often called 'the thinking sport' because it requires map reading, problem solving and quick decision-making skills in addition to athletic ability and general physical fitness.*

After moving from Switzerland to the United States, I had made Denver my home base between 2014 and 2016. The main reason was that Eunjung had moved there from California in 2000. I find some similarities between Switzerland and Colorado, especially when I spend time outside in nature.

There are high mountains in Colorado—fifty-eight with an elevation of at least 14,000 feet (there are just twenty-four in Switzerland above 13,000 feet) and many lakes. Colorado is home to more than 2,000 natural lakes, reservoirs and enough rivers to keep any water-lover happy. Switzerland too boasts several thousand lakes.

After my move to Denver, Eunjung and I went for many hikes and excursions in the beautiful Rocky Mountains. From the beginning, I thought some of the areas I'd seen would provide excellent terrain and landscapes for orienteering, and I imagined how wonderful it would be to create some maps here. I asked Urs, a friend from Switzerland with whom I'd collaborated on several map projects, if he knew how I could find an orienteering club here and I also did some online research. That's how I found RMOC.

After my initial meeting with Doug, the president of the club, RMOC decided to go ahead and have me start creating some maps for them. I first mapped a 1,360-acre (5.5 km^2) area called "White Ranch," an open-space park with thousands of rocks, boulders and small cliffs near Golden, Colorado. In autumn 2016 I finished another, even larger, map project entailing 2,340 acres (9.5 km^2) and covering the area of Tahosa and Beaver Reservoir near Nederland, near Colorado's Rocky Mountain National Park.

Orienteering maps are among the most detailed topographic maps available. Although they are somewhat similar to standard topographic or hiking trail maps, they are bigger (at a finer scale, usually 1:10,000 or 1:15,000), have more mapped features and are much more accurate and up-to-date. These maps take a substantial amount of time, sophisticated skills and extensive experience to make. They incorporate a standard symbology designed to be useful to anyone, regardless of their language.

In addition to indicating the topography of the terrain with contour lines, orienteering maps show an array of significant features: forest density, water features, clearings, trails, roads, earthen banks, rock walls, ditches, wells, pits, fences, power lines, buildings and boulders. For a map to be reliable, accuracy is essential. It needs to be relevant to a competitor by showing the lay of the land with neither too much nor too little detail.

For as long as I can remember, I've been fascinated by maps. From a very early age, when I looked at a world map, I imagined how exciting it would be to travel to other countries and explore other parts of the world. So far, as noted, I've been to thirty-five countries, and I don't think there has been a single country I haven't looked at from the perspective of a mapper. When I later began studying geography at school, I spent many hours poring over an atlas and, most of all, I kept looking at all those beautiful maps from all over the world.

My parents chose to live in a place close to nature with a nearby forest, so that my (two years younger) brother Alain and I could play outside in nature instead of watching too much TV or playing computer games. From a young age, I was an excellent runner, especially in longer distances, and was known as the youngest organizer of a running competition called "Studweidlauf" in Switzerland. What started with nineteen runners in the first race in 1985 grew into a large event, with about 300 kids running in 1994.

While I always found freedom when I went for a run, I felt a little bored just running on streets or on hiking trails. At age twelve, I discovered orienteering. I did my first orienteering competition together with Alain, without having had any proper training in how to read such a map. Before we started I was convinced it would be no problem at all, because we were both fast runners and had already spent many years playing in forests.

The first experience was devastating: it took us more than an hour and a half to complete a short 3K course. We got lost many times—even though the course was in a forest with many trails and was designed for beginners—and we both fell into a swamp hole. When we finally reached the finish line, we were covered from head to toe with mud and the organizers were already dismantling the event facility.

It was late fall, so it got dark early. We were the last to arrive and, with our mother waiting for us at the finish with increasing concern, the organizers were just about to start searching for us. My ambition was triggered, though, and the following spring I decided to take a weeklong orienteering course to learn everything needed in order to have a better experience while out in the forest.

Shortly afterwards, I took my first steps in mapping. Again, at first I had no proper training and no introduction. I was working without a base map; I just used a blank piece of paper, a pencil and my compass. I first started to map our neighborhood and areas near my school, plus some tiny sections of forests near Spiez, my hometown in Switzerland.

My enthusiasm for mapping was noticed in the orienteering club I belonged to. In the summer of 1991, at fifteen, I joined a more experienced friend in drafting the first "official" map of the forest I'd always played in and explored with my brother.

At first, it took me more than sixty hours to map an area of about 123 acres (0.5 km^2) whereas now, twenty-seven years later, depending on the level of detail and the complexity of the landscape, it takes me about thirty to forty hours to accomplish fieldwork for 250 acres (1 km^2).

Since then, I've mapped about twenty different terrains, culminating in my project at Tahosa, Colorado, which I finished in October 2016. This undertaking was extraordinary for many reasons. First, Tahosa lies at a high altitude. The area I mapped is located between 8,600 and 9,700 feet (between 2,600 and 2,950 meters), and is the most spectacular setting for mapping or orienteering I have undertaken. There is a lot of variety: mainly gorgeous and open mountain forest, some dense vegetation, some swampy areas and only a few hiking trails. The glaciated terrain is pristine and features magical areas with little mountain lakes.

One of the main reasons RMOC decided to go ahead with this map project is that it's located at the Tahosa High Adventure Alpine Base of the Scouts of America. The facilities at Tahosa range from rustic campsites to buildings from the 1800's that have been renovated with modern conveniences.

The remote location provides a wilderness setting ideal for hiking, canoeing, mountain biking, fishing, stargazing and many other activities. For other mapping projects, I always had to drive to the terrain I was mapping and then drive home. This time, however, I could stay in one of the small cabins and just get out of the cabin each day and start mapping.

To accomplish this project (as noted, a 2,340-acre (9.5 km^2) field survey), I was out in the wilderness for a total of 290 hours, divided by forty days and eleven stays. I had profound experiences while sharing the land with the regional wildlife, or more appropriately, while the wildlife shared their home with me.

Because the area is so remote and high up in the mountains, wildlife included animals like moose, elk, bears and mountain lions. Of course, I'd experienced many previous encounters with animals while mapping for other projects, but this was a more intense, higher-level situation. I'm grateful all went well for the duration of my fieldwork, although twice I had an encounter with a male elk ready to charge at me—terrifying in the middle of mating season, which starts at the end of September.

I had another hair-raising encounter with a moose in one of the denser swampy areas. The day before my last day of fieldwork, I heard a loud sound—almost like a dinosaur roaring in one of the *Jurassic Park* movies! I had goosebumps all over my body. It was clear that this moose didn't like having me in its territory. I did what I've been told to do in such situations: run away as fast as you can and look for a big tree or rock where you can hide. You don't do this in all animal encounters in wilderness, of course. For example, if you see a bear or mountain lion, you need to stand your ground and make yourself bigger. But in the case of moose, there's no chance you'll win by doing that. Happily, I lived to tell the tale!

On a lighter note, I also saw many smaller, cuter animals like birds, rabbits and squirrels. They were curious about what I was doing, and we became friends over time.

Having these intimate interactions with wildlife and being surrounded by pristine, untouched wilderness and stunning landscapes are just a few of the many benefits of orienteering. I recommend it to anyone who has an outward-bound spirit!

The title of this section is "Mapping Your Inner Landscape." I think everyone who's spent an extended period of time alone in a remote wilderness setting would agree that you become raw and, one might say, naked. It's harder to have this type of experience when you're in a city, because there's so much distraction and so many others sharing the space.

While working on this Tahosa mapping project, I mapped what I thought would be useful to people who will try to find their way through the mountainous terrain in the future. As the mapping project progressed I became more and more aware of my thoughts, emotions and physical sensations. With no one else around, I grew more conscious of both my outer and inner environment. As I mapped the outer landscape, it became obvious that I was simultaneously creating a map of my own inner landscape.

I mentioned earlier that orienteering maps show many details. In the same way, when we spend time in nature, we become increasingly aware of our surroundings and we can find, symbolically, similar aspects in what I like to call our "inner landscape." The experience of mapping is similar to a walking meditation. For example, say you are trying to accomplish a goal. Sometimes you must climb over (or find a way around) huge obstacles. Or, you may come to a crossroads on your path where you must decide where to go next. Or, you may meet others who have put fences around what they think is their territory. In navigating unfamiliar terrain to reach your goal, you may discover new ditches, wells and other resources within yourself. When breaking a new trail on your life's journey, you can experience immense joy and gratitude as you find your way to clearings that open you up to a new awareness of who you are and where you are positioned in your life and in the world.

I recently came upon a quote by Rod Stryker, with whom I have had the good fortune to study yoga. In his book, *The Four Desires: Creating a Life of Purpose, Happiness, Prosperity, and Freedom*, Rod says:

> *Our world is getting more and more complicated. And as it gets more complicated, we have fewer answers for the difficulties that we are going through. That's a beautiful thing because it's forcing us to look more deeply at what is truth and what is real. We are being forced to go deeper, and to ask the right questions…about who we are, about what our nature with the world is, and how we can unveil this mystery of what it means to have a life, and to be a full person.*

Before you read on, I invite you to reflect for a moment on the following three questions inspired by the Rod Stryker quote above and my recent mapping project in the Rocky Mountains:

- How often (a day, a week, a year) do I stop my activities and become aware of what my inner landscape looks, sounds and feels like?
- How often do I stop to recognize both the immense beauty and the denser and swampier aspects of my inner landscape?
- How often do I truly recognize the inner landscape of someone I share a moment with, or walk with for a stretch of my life's journey?

After you find some answers to these questions (and, ideally, write your answers in your journal) take time to reflect on these questions:

- What is true and real for me in my life?
- Where do I come from?
- Where do I choose to go?

- What paths are available to guide me to my goal?
- What kind of checkpoints (or controls) are on the path I choose?
- What kind of checkpoints do I want to leave for others?
- Where (and who) am I in this moment?

While I worked on the Tahosa mapping project, I got lost once, ending up in an entirely different section of forest than the area I had demarked on my base map. It took me quite a while to find my way out. After I tried unsuccessfully to find my way back to one of the small mountain lakes I had mapped just the day before, all I could do was take my compass and head north. I hit the next hiking trail about forty minutes later.

When I look at my inner landscape, I realize I've also gotten lost on my life's journey a few times, and it has taken me way longer than forty minutes to find my way back! This is one of the reasons I feel so passionate about creating orienteering maps to help others find their way through unknown terrain, and, through my work as a life coach, creating maps to help others navigate their inner landscapes. Are you ready to map yours?

So far, I've written about the first of the two main requirements to accomplish a map project. The first is fieldwork or land survey, the second is actual map design. When it comes to creating the design of an orienteering map, I have an established process.

I start by scanning the extensive handwritten notes I've made in the forest. I then incorporate them into the design of an actual map, which I create with the help of a special program called OCAD. The company that creates the OCAD program was founded and is based in my homeland, Switzerland. Since I first worked with a much earlier version of the program in 1993, there have been many updates to the software.

Whenever people ask me what fascinates me about creating these kind of maps, I always respond that creating a map is just like "putting nature into art." I spend more time on a nice design and layout than many other mappers, because I appreciate orienteering using a map with good readability. It also helps me trust the mapmaker more.

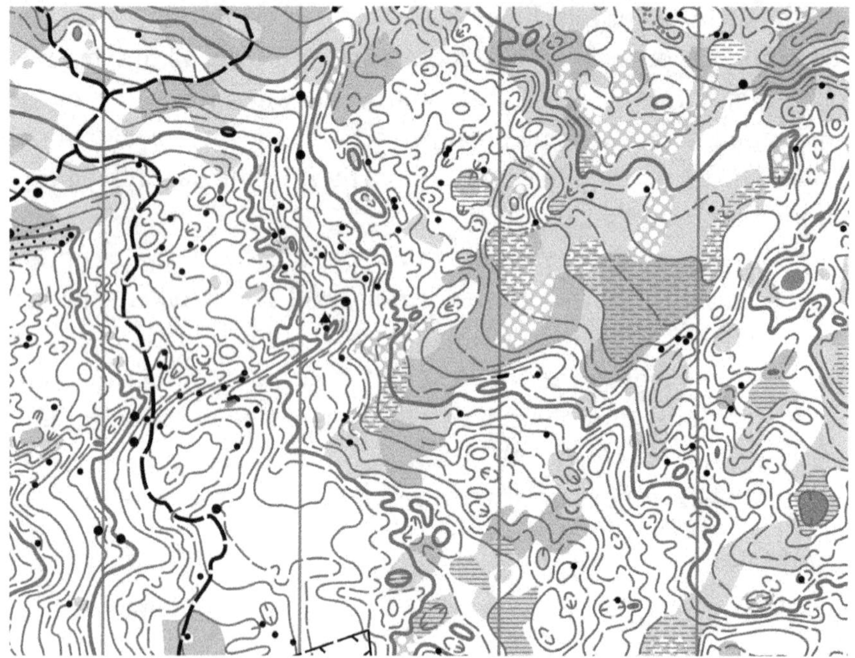

Orienteering Map, Tahosa, Colorado

At this point, you may be wondering, "How does mapwork relate to my current life situation?" "How does orienteering map design relate to mapping my inner landscape?" Well, we're all born with certain gifts and talents to share with the world, and they're related to our life's purpose. Once you start doing the inner work and get more clarity on your life map—which can be seen as a guide to your life's purpose—the next question becomes, "How can I further refine and express my unique gifts and talents?"

Once you've mapped your inner landscape, it becomes an art to discover how best to communicate and express your gifts. As you put more time, energy and other resources into sharing them with the world, more opportunities calling for your unique contribution arise. Whatever your passions are, you can share them with the world through creative and artistic expression.

Sometimes I marvel at how, during the Tahosa project, I managed to map for eight to nine hours a day, up to six days in a row. All the while, I was working at an extremely high altitude. I knew it was important to keep myself fit and that began with staying hydrated. I drank up to six liters of water a day. Meanwhile, I was being nourished by the energy I received from the unspoiled setting—it was teeming with plants and animals. It was as if I was being bathed by the pure, nurturing energy of the forest.

This idea of communing with nature is called "eco-therapy" or "forest bathing." Forest bathing—which is basically just being in the presence of trees—became part of a national public health program in Japan thirty-seven years ago, and is scientifically proven to improve health. Compelling evidence shows that it lowers heart rate and blood pressure, reduces stress hormone production, boosts the immune system and improves overall feelings of wellbeing. If you're interested, you can read the entire article about it at *http://qz.com/804022/health-benefits-japanese-forest-bathing/*. At the end of the article, there's a description of a great practice I've tried a couple times and have taught some of my clients to do. I'd like to take this opportunity to share it with you. Here's how it works: *At the beginning of your next nature walk, simply pick up a rock, put a problem in the rock and drop it.* If you believe that you can't drop your problem so easily, you can always pick up your troubles again on your way back. However, after spending some time in nature, people rarely do.

To start mapping your own inner landscape and unveil the mystery of what it means to be alive, take time to connect with nature. Ask yourself the questions noted above, write your answers down and share your experiences and insights with others.

Tumblesom Lake, Colorado

Connecting with Nature

We're all energetically connected with one another, since we're all part of the natural "World Wide Web." Spending time in nature will help you discharge from technology-driven connections and restore your natural connection with the energy of wellbeing so richly found in forests, ocean, rivers and mountains. As you get closer to living your life's purpose, you'll notice even more acutely how interconnected everything and everyone is. How? Synchronicities will occur frequently.

In his brilliant book, *Gaia Luminous: Emergence of the New Earth*, my friend Kiara Windrider writes:

> *Our bodies are electromagnetic entities aligned with the magnetic fields of the Earth. Our memories too are based on magnetic fields held within our auras synchronized with the memory fields of the Earth. This includes our personal memories, our collective memories, and also the morphogenetic field of our human species. Most of our conscious memories are held within the linear mind, composed of all the imprints and sensory input we have received from birth onwards, aggregated into a personality. Our identity is held within the electromagnetic fields of the lower physical, etheric, emotional, and mental bodies. This is who we think we are.*

In recent years, there's been a lot of discussion about the "Schumann resonance." This refers to the base frequency of the earth, measured in cycles per second, which had been stabilized at around 7.83 Hz for a long time. Many scientists from around the world now assess that this frequency is rising, quickly and exponentially. According to some reports, it has spiked up to 36 Hz as of early 2017, meaning that the heartbeat of Mother Earth has increased.

By reading Kiara's book *Gaia Luminous: Emergence of the New Earth*, I was able to see a bigger picture. A scientist friend of Kiara's, Dr. Paul LaViolette—a researcher and author of four books—coined the term *Galactic Superwave* to refer to cosmic ray bombardment. Dr. LaViolette was the first to assert that high-intensity volleys of cosmic ray particles travel directly to our planet from distant sources in our galaxy, a phenomenon now confirmed by scientific data. He suggests that cosmic ray particles and the consequent cosmic dust emanate from the super-dense center of the Milky Way galaxy. The resulting effects on our sun and the earth's climate, he says, are primarily due to the cosmic dust. When cosmic dust and debris bombard the sun's surface, the magnitude of solar flares increases exponentially. This, in turn, causes the sun to engage in continual flaring activity and to spew out massive coronal ejections.

A geomagnetic storm is a temporary disturbance of the earth's magnetosphere caused by a solar wind shock wave and/or a magnetic field cloud that interacts with the earth's magnetic field. The solar wind also carries with it the sun's magnetic field. This wind has energetic bursts, contracting and expanding the magnetosphere, thereby increasing the base frequency of earth, the Schumann resonance.

Kiara ponders whether this shift in Earth's Schumann resonance might be enhanced by the bombardment of high-frequency cosmic rays that move through our bodies. If, like me, you're intrigued by this topic, I highly encourage you to read *Gaia Luminous: Emergence of the New Earth*.

In Fall 2014, Eunjung and I went for a walk in a pristine mountain forest in Leysin, located in the western part of the Swiss Alps, with our friend Beth. While we walked in the blooming, magical mountain forest, we breathed the crystal-clear air into our lungs. We received wonderful energies from the nature around us and the sun above, and we integrated the gifts this beautiful area offers. At the end of the mountain trail we came upon an opening in the forest, which offered a stunning panoramic view of the mountains on the other side of the valley. We sat down and offered a ceremony to the land and picked up a message to calm our minds, become fully present and to listen and receive with our hearts. We went into a deep meditation and became aware that we were in the presence of a powerful portal.

A little spider joined us in our meditation. She confirmed that the portal supports the weaving of a new dimension. Her presence reminded us that whenever two or more gather in prayer, in meditation or in a ceremony in nature, it helps increase and weave higher vibrations of peace and harmony within ourselves and on the planet.

Just a few days later, solar flares hit the earth's magnetic field and sparked two days of geomagnetic storms. In the meantime, Eunjung and I were back in the area where I grew up. We went for another walk in a fairytale-like park near Lake Thun.

During this walk, the whole energetic field felt unstable. We also heard about some strong earthquakes in other parts of the world. We walked with my mother's dog, Joy, and she seemed to feel the instability too. Although she usually likes to play and run around, Joy stayed close and walked between the two of us. Probably animals perceive this kind of powerful energetic shift even stronger than we human beings do.

I mentioned earlier that the solar wind contracts and expands the magnetosphere. It's widely acknowledged that everything is energetically connected. Could it be that incoming cosmic energies influence the process of global transformation as we ourselves contract and expand—both individually and collectively? Although older, lower-oscillating magnetic vibrations haven't completely dissipated, we still witness new, high-vibrating frequencies entering our world these days.

As a result—those people who are more sensitive to the earth's vibrations are becoming increasingly aware that there is a separation occurring within the collective consciousness. All around the world, there is an ever-expanding gap between those who are awake, who follow their hearts and get clearer about their purpose and those who continue to allow the fear in their hearts to control their lives. Just as the earth's base frequency has risen—and Mother Earth's heartbeat has quickened—many of us, especially those of us who are not in touch with our true selves, are literally stretched beyond our comfort zone.

We have a choice to make, both individually and as a collective, about whether we want to be part of a culture which no longer represents our values, or if we want to follow our hearts and connect with nature and the invisible forces that can guide us to something much greater than our individual ideas of who we are. If we choose the latter, I believe we can live a life that is true and meaningful.

It's your choice if you want to be part of a culture which no longer represents your values, or if you want to follow your heart and connect with nature.

I believe that the change in the earth's magnetic vibrations is one of the reasons that many people are going through such challenging times. During this transitional phase of our planet, we're called to let go of everything that doesn't serve our purpose, and to become clearer on what we really intend to create and experience in our lives. As you become clearer and start noticing the increasing gap in the collective consciousness, you can choose to inspire and encourage others to step out of their fear and into freedom. And, one of the ways to remember what freedom feels like is to get back to nature and to reconnect with your spirituality.

I believe that when we connect with nature, or visit sacred sites and powerful portals, we receive a lot of energetic and spiritual support for our process of rebirth. This is why, I believe, so many people visit sacred sites such as Stonehenge in England, the pyramids in Egypt and Machu Picchu in Peru. Even those who are not spiritually inclined have an awareness that there is something "special" in these places.

The many uplifting spiritual experiences Eunjung and I have had while we've spent time in nature and at sacred sites prove to us that we human beings are multi-dimensional, moving between many layers of energy and through many dimensions. Wherever we connect with nature we feel the amazing force of the elementals, the true guardians of nature who honor and love their home.

Over the past five years, in our trips to many countries around the globe, Eunjung and I have sensed that there's a configuration, realignment and connection happening through nature's many portals. These portals and openings are expanding powerfully. Connecting with nature can help us to realign ourselves to the higher realms.

You may be thinking, "How does this relate to us as human beings collectively?" "How does it relate to me, reading a book about finding my life's purpose?" Well, many people say that the increase of the Schumann resonance is scientific proof that higher frequencies are arriving on earth and that there's a real shift in consciousness taking place. This shift impacts our individual biorhythms and health, our emotional and mental states, our sleep and dreams at night and our overall wellbeing. Why? Because as the earth raises her vibration, we also raise our vibration. It doesn't matter if someone is aware of the connection or not. The earth, which is influenced and supported by increasing solar flares, is raising her vibration. It's up to us to decide: do we follow this path—increase our vibration and live our truest purpose—or hold onto our patterns, habits and old versions of reality?

As we participate in our evolutionary journey with planet Earth, raising our vibration means releasing old patterns and stuck energies. In the process, you may feel depressed, alone, confused—you may even get sick. Sometimes you may think there's no way out—that you'll never be able to change your current life situation and that you can't make a positive contribution to the world.

But remember, when we increase our vibration, whatever is not yet in resonance with these higher frequencies comes to the surface to be cleared. Shadow aspects of ourselves—things we didn't want to see or haven't been aware of—come to our attention to be recognized, transformed and healed. So much is being revealed during these times in which we live, individually and on a global scale. We must face our problems in order to clear them in a conscious and centered way.

It doesn't matter if you're just embarking on the path toward finding your life's purpose or if you're someone who's already done a lot of personal work. If you find yourself going through a phase of intense clearing, please remember you're not alone. There's nothing wrong with you, and it's important to take time for yourself and rest before continuing your work and focusing on what you desire. Connecting with nature is an ideal way to de-charge from symptoms of negative energy.

Here are five simple, basic de-charging techniques that may be helpful:

- Holding a rose, a black stone, a crystal or any other power object, with the intention of de-charging.
- Taking a bath or shower with the intention of de-charging stress and emotional and mental burdens.
- Walking or standing barefoot on the earth to ground your energy.
- Visiting sacred sites or power spots, holding the intention to clear negative energy.
- Creating a bubble of light around you, using sounds, sacred geometry or any energy modality that resonates with you.

It's wonderful and beneficial to spend time in nature and connect with animals, nature spirits and elementals. As I mentioned, I grew up in the Swiss countryside and as a child and young adult, I spent a lot of time in nature. It helped me become who I am. I invite you to do this as well!

We truly are connected with each other and to the entire universe. We are part of the natural "World Wide Web"—and we are weaving it individually and as a collective. It's our birthright to have this deep connection with the earth and the elements and to receive healing and transformational support from nature's energy field.

When people feel disconnected from nature, they may experience confusion, disillusionment or disempowerment. Simply by reconnecting with nature, no matter how long they've been disconnected, they can remember who they truly are. We all need to get out of the cities, connect again with nature and integrate the dimensional and energetic shifts that are taking place on our planet. When we go out into nature, it is always a powerful and profound experience—and it gets more and more potent with each passing day!

White Ranch Park, Colorado

Making Peace with My Father

This section is dedicated to my dear father, who had a passion and a gift for jazz music and a love of being in nature hiking in the mountains—and who passed away in 2005 at the age of 58. I'm thankful for the life we shared together and the gifts and purpose he pursued and shared in his unique way with me and with the world.

The time around the passing of my father and grandparents was the most difficult phase of my life. It became the starting point of a lengthy and arduous journey of finding myself, my gifts and my purpose. It was a long, curvy and bumpy journey before I felt the powerful call of my destiny and answered the question, "What am I here for?"

Do you remember the song "The Living Years" from a group called Mike + The Mechanics? I heard it for the first time when I was thirteen, on a compilation of rock music ballads released just before Christmas 1989. I listened to it with my brother, Alain, who was eleven at the time. There were thirty-six great songs on the compilation, and this was our favorite. Having grown up in Switzerland speaking Swiss German (and I'd just started studying English), we didn't understand the lyrics. Still, the melody of "The Living Years" inspired us so powerfully that we felt compelled to listen to it over and over again.

Over the years, I forgot about this influential song. I heard it again nearly two decades later, in May 2008, when I participated in a four-day personal transformation training seminar in Honolulu. In the meantime, my English had improved a lot. This song was played as a part of the program to help us look deeper into the relationships with our family members and how they've influenced our lives.

As soon as it started to play—even before the lyrics started—the song hit me like a flash from heaven and I burst into tears. I'll never forget this profound moment because I realized how accurately "The Living Years" described my relationship with my dad, who'd passed away three years earlier.

Through online research, I learned that the "The Living Years" was written to tell a story about the disagreements between a band member, Mike Rutherford, and his father who had recently died. In an interview, Rutherford said, "The lyrics were written by BA Robertson and the song is about something he went through [too]. He lost his dad and it's about the lack of communication between him and his father before he died." Rutherford reports that both he and Robertson had similar experiences with their fathers so the lyrics really resonated with both artists—as they do with many people.

I learned during my research that Paul Carrack, who had performed the original lead vocal, has made several solo interpretations of "The Living Years." Carrack's father died when he was eleven, bringing authenticity to his delivery. You can find this song on YouTube if you want to listen to it.

After the death of a family member, dear friend or pet, some people experience a spiritual awakening. Similarly, after facing an accident, illness, breakup, near-death experience or a large-scale event such as a natural disaster or a tragedy like 9/11, profound shifts can occur in people's personalities, conscious awareness or life path. Others might awaken to a new reality through a magical event or even simply through noticing the majesty of nature—seeing a gorgeous rainbow, sunrise or sunset can be a remarkably life-changing event.

So, there are different reasons that people choose to begin following a more conscious or spiritual path than they have done previously. I believe strongly that whether or not we consciously follow a spiritual path, we are all spiritual beings who are always connected to "Source." Whatever you like to call this invisible, all-permeating field of light and love—God, the Infinite Light, the Universe—it's always aware and present, around and within us. Sometimes, though, you can get lost on your path. You may think you're all alone until you find yourself and realize your connection with source, as I did in my journey.

Some people find they can improve their lives in many ways when they become more conscious of their spiritual nature. It's a chance to let go of the unhealthy habits, belief systems, ideas and concepts that have been part of them for a long time.

Some people find more peace and calm through meditation or other practices. Others go through different phases of awakening while recovering from burnout, grief, sadness or depression.

Do you remember when you had your initial awakening? I invite you to close your eyes, take a couple of deep breaths and connect with your heart space. Take a moment and become aware of that moment. Really engage with your heart space and see *how* it led you to where you are right now, reading this book, contemplating your future and learning how to find your life's purpose and manifest your dreams.

My awakening and the consequent decision to follow a more conscious spiritual path occurred at different stages in my life, beginning when I was young. When I look back today, however, I can pinpoint the year 2005 as having an especially strong impact, not only on my own journey but on the lives of my close family members, including my mother and brother. I vividly remember the moment I received a phone call in the early morning of February 12, 2005. I learned my father, who had suffered from cancer for many years, had passed away the previous night.

When my dad received the diagnosis in autumn 1998, just a few months after he had returned from Hawaii, the doctor told him he had, at most, one to two years left, even with chemotherapy. My dad received holistic therapies in addition to conventional medical treatments, and most of the time his mental capacity remained strong. This added four more years to the time he was able to spend with us.

Throughout my life, despite our challenges and differences, my dad was always a great mentor for me. When I was a teenager, he introduced me to the work of author Dr. Joseph Murphy. Dr. Murphy emphasized the connection between our thoughts and our realities, saying, "Change your thoughts, and you change your destiny."

Like many other young adults, as a teenager I suffered from a lack of self-worth, disempowerment, depression and an inability to clearly express what I was going through. Through reading Dr. Murphy's book, I gleaned the importance of positive thinking and belief in oneself. At that age, however, it was hard for me to truly understand the concept and how to best apply it in my life.

I shared the background of the song "The Living Years" above. The song is about someone losing his father, and it's also about the lack of communication between the writer of the song and his father before he died. My father and I did the best we could, but our relationship was not always easy. He had had a difficult relationship with his own father, and there were many other unhealed relationships on my father's side coming through our whole lineage. Even when we knew he would make his transition soon, my father and I were still unable to clearly communicate how much we loved each other. We remained unable to forgive ourselves and each other, right up to the day he passed away.

I still remember the afternoon I saw my dad alive for the last time. It was four days before he died and right before I left my parents' house in Spiez. I lived almost two hours away from them. There was a silent moment that occurred when we were saying goodbye; we looked at each other and somehow, we both "knew" we wouldn't have another opportunity to share our thoughts and feelings.

For many years, I suffered from regret that I couldn't tell my father in his "living years" how much I loved, honored and appreciated him—exactly the way he was, for everything he'd shared with me and for the huge impact he'd made on my life and the lives of others. The death of my father was just the first in a series of three deaths of close relatives that affected me greatly. My father made his transition in February, my maternal grandmother died the following

July and my maternal grandfather died that same year, in October. Our relatives and friends gathered three times within eight months, not to celebrate a wedding or the birth of a new child, but to say goodbye to people who were dear to our hearts.

After that, my life was never the same. No matter what goals and visions I tried to achieve in my career, finances and personal relationships, I felt I was failing at everything. I maintained a façade of strength in the following years, but deep within I felt myself getting weaker, helpless and depressed. It got to the point where I wanted to put an end to the pain by leaving this world.

On Christmas Eve of 2007, almost three years after my season of loss, I walked alone through the streets of my town. Through the windows of their homes, I saw families celebrating their reunion, while children opened their presents with shining eyes. I started to cry. Suddenly, I found myself in front of a church I'd never noticed before. My inner voice told me to go inside the church and pray. The church was empty. I lit a candle. For the first time in many years I prayed for help, desperately and deeply, from my heart. Only three months later I was on a flight to Honolulu, where a whole new world and a completely new path would open right in front of me.

One of the many reasons I was guided to Oahu in 2008 was that my parents had lived in Hawaii for a month in the spring of 1998. They were unaware that only a few months later they would face the grim diagnosis that my father had a rare and incurable form of cancer. It was their last happy and light-hearted holiday together. My brother had visited Oahu in 1997 and everyone in my family encouraged me to go to Hawaii, telling me I would love it.

However, I lived a different life then and the timing was not yet right. So many things have changed since then and I am grateful for every experience, whether positive or negative, that led me to the life-changing decision to go to Hawaii. Looking back, I can see it wasn't coincidence that led me to my Hawaiian rebirth but instead, it was divine guidance. There, I finally learned how to forgive myself and my father for not speaking our truths to each other.

I feel inspired to share two effective tools that can help you with forgiveness and peacemaking. I wrote earlier about the ancient and transformative prayer, Ho'oponopono. My friend Howard Wills shares this on his website: *www.HowardWills.com*

> *The native priests of Hawaii, called Kahunas, say that thoughts are physical, alive and have substance, even though they are invisible. Thoughts are powerful and thoughts influence feelings. If we have negative, harmful, hurtful or hateful thoughts, we are creating the same types of negative feelings. So, simply, the remedy is to think positive blessing, non-judgmental thoughts—simple, happy, positive thoughts. When we allow our thoughts to be simple and positive, we free ourselves of the weight, burden and unhappiness created by negative judgmental thoughts. When we practice the art of forgiveness, and positive, happy, non-judgmental thinking, we start feeling good, happy and free. When we start feeling good, happy, and free, complete wellbeing in all areas of our lives will follow.*

In Hawaii, I learned for the first time how to forgive others and myself, and how to break free of the suffering I'd been holding onto for so long. This process helped me to finally find peace with my dad and within myself.

In 2013, more than eight years after my dad's passing, I was still focusing on healing the relationship between myself and my father. I noticed the clients who came to me for healing or life coaching sessions were dealing with similar life themes and challenges, so I was able to provide insight and solutions from my personal experience—and also to learn from my clients. Despite their diverse cultural backgrounds, many of my clients had unresolved issues with family members. They were having a tough time with suppressed anger and sadness, either because they couldn't forgive or couldn't ask for forgiveness from their loved ones. They reminded me of the great pain and regret that lay heavily on my heart after my father's death, before I was finally able to let go using the forgiveness practice of Ho'oponopono and Howard's prayers.

Many books have been written about the practice of Ho'oponopono, and in recent years, people around the world have begun to practice it as a meaningful and effective ritual for improving their lives. Here are the four simple statements of Ho'oponopono again: *"I am sorry. Please forgive me. Thank you. I love you."*

There is another cleansing prayer that is an invaluable tool for forgiveness and generational peace-making. It's part of a transformational, concise prayer program Howard Wills shares on his website. You can download the entire prayer free of charge.

Eunjung and I use this prayer every day. Howard recommends saying it five times in the morning and five times or more in the evening. You can say "God," "infinite light," "divine light" or whatever term is appropriate for you when referring to source:

> *"God, For Me, My Family, Our Entire Lineage, and all of Humanity*
>
> *Throughout All Time, Past, Present And Future*
>
> *Please Help Us All Forgive Each Other*
>
> *Forgive Ourselves, Forgive All People*
>
> *And All People Forgive Us*
>
> *Completely And Totally, Now And Forever*
>
> *Please God, Thank You God, Amen*
>
> *Thank You, God, Amen."*

On February 12, 2015, I walked into a store in Breckenridge, Colorado to rent some ski equipment. The song "The Living Years" started to play on the radio. The flash from heaven hit me again, just as it had seven years earlier when I'd heard the song in Honolulu. It was extra-special because February 12 was the ten-year anniversary of my father's passing. It was like my dad was sending me a sign from the heavens, acknowledging the peace we now have with each other.

I can't believe it's been thirteen years since my father passed. I marvel at the way my life has changed. I realize how I have grown and how I have become the man I am today. My memories of my father are deep and profound. I remember the impact he had on me and so many others by sharing his gifts and passions in his unique way. I feel honoured to dedicate this story to him.

Taken from Kepuhi Beach, Moloka'i

Loving Memories

In Spring 2015, I received a message that a friend and inspirational teacher from Kaua'i, Lee Joseph, had taken his last breath after a difficult battle with cancer.

Lee was someone who was living his purpose fully, and he inspired me and countless others to live our purpose too. This story is dedicated to Lee and my classmates.

Studying with Lee for six months in 2011 was a huge catalyst for me in transforming my life. Lee quickly became a father figure to me. So, the news that he'd been diagnosed with an advanced form of cancer came as a shock. I couldn't believe it. Five months later, when I heard the devastating news that Lee had passed, it felt like I was dreaming. The surreal, sad news reached me as Eunjung and I were driving to Estes Park, Colorado to spend two days in Rocky Mountain National Park. The immense impact of his passing hit home during our long hike the next day. It was painful to realize that he was no longer here. I spent a long time thinking about how we had met and all the ways I treasured the compassionate and authentic community he—and all of his students—had created together.

After I'd returned to Kaua'i in 2011, I started to study with Lee, taking a six-month long Presence Centered Awareness course at PCAB (the Pacific Center for Awareness and Bodywork). My time there brought me revelations about my life and my purpose. I felt liberated. I sensed on many levels that I was at the right place at the right time. "Right here, right now," as Lee would say. As I mentioned earlier, I'd had a disheartening and contradictory experience in Switzerland in 2010 that led to a burnout. I realized the immense value of Lee's PCAB course.

My program with Lee in 2011 allowed me to reflect on that burnout experience in 2010 in Switzerland and heal the enduring feelings of isolation and loneliness I had carried with me. I realized that what

I had lacked most during that trying phase of my life was a sense of presence and mindfulness. I had spent half a year in Switzerland seeing many doctors and therapists. The practitioners weren't at all present with me during my sessions with them. It was unbelievable to me how many highly-educated professionals just wanted to pass time, not caring about what I had to say or what I was going through. During my meetings with several people managing my case, our discussions were always about the past or the future, never about the present moment—what was happening *right now.*

As it turned out, I had to coordinate the communication between the practitioners in charge of my case. Instead of getting help from them, I had to act as if I were my own case manager. Each time I met with a therapist or doctor, I had to tell them what the others had said previously, which in turn significantly shortened our actual session time. They each treated me as a piece of a problem, instead of as a whole person needing healing, understanding and compassion. The blessing in disguise was that because I did not get the help I needed from the medical system in Switzerland, I started proactively taking care of myself by learning self-healing techniques.

During this challenging time, I was told that I had "unrealistic" visions and ideas, and that it would help everyone involved if I were to face "reality." To me, however, what they referred to as "reality" was a dysfunctional system, because it didn't provide any holistic solutions. Jiddu Krishnamurti, a well-known Indian philosopher, speaker and writer, said it eloquently: *"It is no measure of health to be well-adjusted to a profoundly sick society."*

So, to have the opportunity to study with Lee and to be part of a community of thirty wonderful classmates seemed to me to be divine intervention. It was confirmation that it is possible to share, teach and learn in a simple, yet profound, heart-based way. By studying at Lee's school, I learned firsthand that the core of all stress and disease symptoms are emotions and memories stored in our subconscious minds, and that they manifest physically as disease. I learned how

I could heal and transform myself on ever-deeper levels. During the six-months of training, I gained knowledge and learned new techniques and tools to help me better serve my clients. I was also able to effectively combine and integrate everything I'd studied previously for my sessions, based on a holistic approach.

Since 2011, Presence Centered Awareness (PCA) therapy has provided the foundation not only for my services but for how I conduct my life. PCA helps people live consciously, with more awareness. PCA integrates teachings and practices from many interdisciplinary programs and traditions in the fields of meditation, consciousness and psychology. These include practical applications of meditative awareness from *Vipassana* and *Advaita* and psychological approaches including Hakomi Therapy, psychosynthesis and Gestalt therapy, along with various communication models.

PCA therapy teaches an experiential blend of deepening awareness, presence-full touch and heart-full communication in a relaxed, here-and-now environment. It safely and effectively supports healing old wounds, fosters forgiveness and acceptance and releases unhealthy patterns and habits. This, in turn, allows us to explore higher levels of wellness and creativity.

I remember Lee in countless ways. Two years after our training, at the end of October 2013, Lee and his wife Carole participated in the sacred union ceremony Eunjung and I held at a beautiful beach on the North Shore of Kaua'i. Since they were both important and influential figures for me, it was special that they joined us for this unforgettable afternoon. It deepened the connection I felt with this unique couple.

Lee shared his passions for the immediate experience of presence and love, and for helping others to live happier lives by experiencing their own truth. Some of the things I cherish most about Lee, however, are his endearing personal attributes: his warm, loving and compassionate voice, his blue eyes and the blue shirts he liked to wear most of time.

How I loved Lee's guided meditations and practices! I still have fond memories of the days when we'd escape to a secluded beach nearby instead of having classes at school. The effect of Lee's teachings and meditations was even deeper while we were sitting in the shade of trees, next to a beautiful reef in the turquoise ocean of Kaua'i. I'll forever treasure these special memories, deep in my heart.

Another precious moment was our final graduation day and how I felt when we hugged each other before Lee presented me with the certificate of completion. I had tears in my eyes and such mixed emotions—gratefulness for the wonderful time I'd had and sadness that it was over.

Lee had had profound experiences and insights while traveling in India, and he shared these passionately during his classes. I explained earlier that Presence Centered Awareness therapy includes practical applications from *Vipassana* and *Advaita*. When I look back on my invaluable and transformative time studying with Lee and my thirty wonderful classmates in a tropical setting, it becomes clear that the reason I was able to learn so well was because we were practicing PCA firsthand, instead of just reading theories out of books.

Much later, during my yoga teacher training, I learned that *Advaita*—one of the classic Indian paths to spiritual realization—is based on certain features of Hinduism. The term *Advaita* refers to the idea that the soul or true self is the same as the highest metaphysical reality. *Advaita* posits that there are four states of consciousness:

- The first state is the waking state, in which we are aware of our daily world.
- The second state is the dreaming mind.
- The third state is the state of deep sleep.
- The fourth state is *Turiya*.

Some describe *Turiya* as pure consciousness—the background that underlies and transcends the three common states of waking, dreaming and deep sleep. In *Turiya* the true nature of reality is directly perceived. It's a state of deep meditation.

Vipassana, on the other hand, is part of Buddhism. In the Buddhist tradition, Vipassana means insight into the true nature of reality, which consists of impermanence, suffering and the realization of non-self. *Vipassana* is cultivated by contemplation and introspection, with the focus placed primarily on the awareness and observation of bodily sensations.

In *Vipassana* meditation, you practice a combination of mindful breathing and contemplation of impermanence in order to gain insight into the true nature of reality. When you observe your breath, you become aware of the perpetual changes involved in breathing, and the arising and slipping away of mindfulness. Through the observation of your bodily sensations, you can also gain insight into impermanence.

So how did this experience change my life, and how can it contribute to your own life's journey? The *Vipassana* meditations Lee led so masterfully each morning at the beginning of our classes laid the foundation for everything that was to unfold later in my life. In 2010, I had been under a lot of stress, and it was challenging to maintain mental and emotional balance due to the many obstacles on my path. After I started to unwind, studying and practicing in the nurturing environment of PCAB, many unhealed mental and emotional issues from the time of my burnout in Switzerland came to the surface. Through bodywork practices, I realized that these issues were still energetically stored in my physical body. Studying at Lee's school offered me a breakthrough for true healing and transformation to occur. It freed me from the traumas of the past.

Through a deeper understanding of *Advaita,* I realized how, during my burnout, I had perceived myself as a victim of outer circumstances. I saw how this perspective added more stress to an already stressful situation and further compromised my wellbeing.

I could finally recognize my thought patterns, with the insight that I had a choice to free myself from my own thoughts and stories.

After enduring many years of emotional and mental distress, it was a true miracle for me. I started to feel a deep connection and oneness with myself and others. I could feel and see with clarity, and let go of what no longer served me with ease and grace. Ultimately, I could see the beauty and presence of the divine within and around me again.

I encourage you to take some time to sit quietly for self-reflection and self-study, because it will help you understand yourself more. To live a life on purpose, it's important that you learn how to acknowledge your thoughts and emotions and redirect them toward your dreams. It takes some practice to transform your mental and emotional patterns and replace them with positive patterns, but it's not impossible. And once done, it is so rewarding!

To live a life on purpose, acknowledge your thoughts and emotions and redirect them toward your dreams.

My friend Kiara Windrider, who as I mentioned is rooted in Integral Yoga and the Advaita traditions of India, describes the healing process of self-reflection beautifully in his book, *Gaia Luminous: Emergence of the New Earth*. Kiara says:

> *As we become aware of this truth, and learn to carry this awareness into all the circumstances of our lives, we achieve a freedom from identification with the separate ego and recognize ourselves as one with the infinite source*

of all things. As this recognition grows within our human experience we come into the awareness that nothing happens by chance, and that we are the creators of every aspect of our life. In this knowledge, we set ourselves free.

I was on Lee and Carole's property for the first time on July 28, 2008. A former PCAB student, Indi, whom I had met through my friends Astrid and Blake, had guided me to their place early one morning. On that day, Indi (also known as "The Pirate") who really liked guiding me to amazing places off the beaten path here on Kaua'i, introduced me to this special school. Indi predicted that one day I would return to study at PCAB myself. There are so many people from Kaua'i I'm grateful for. Lee and Carole are two of them.

Larsen's Beach, Kaua'i

I simply cannot express how I truly felt about letting go of Lee, my dear friend and father figure. It was with an immense range of emotions that I said goodbye to Lee. When I look at pictures and videos from my time on Kaua'i in 2011, I feel the energy of this wonderful mentor again and experience all those emotions anew. Since he left us, I've often felt Lee's powerful presence during my meditations and I'm so grateful for those moments of awareness. I'm also eternally grateful that he gifted me with a new perspective and the realization of who I am. Lee taught me to be right here, right now. Instead of saying, "I am sad," "I am happy" or "I am grateful," I've learned to say, "Sadness, happiness and gratitude are present in this moment right now."

Coming Home to Kaua'i

In the beginning of Part III, you read my stories from different Hawaiian Islands. In these stories, I shared some of my transformative experiences and insights from the islands of Hawaii. As you are nearing the end of this book, I would like to guide you to visit the island of Kaua'i, which became my new home in the spring of 2017.

When people hear the word "Hawaii," often they think of Honolulu, Oahu or Maui. But the Hawaiian island chain consists of eight big main islands in the southeastern part of the archipelago. Sometimes they are called the Southeastern or Windward Islands, and they include many offshore islands. In the northwest of Hawaii, there are many uninhabited islands, the so-called Northwestern Hawaiian Islands or Leeward Islands. Except for the Midway Islands, all of these islands belong to the U.S. state of Hawaii.

It is believed that the Hawaiian Islands were uninhabited until the Polynesians first landed about 1,500 to 1,600 years ago, on the Big Island of Hawaii. The name *Hawaii* derives from the word *Havaiki*, the Polynesian name for a homeland. The Polynesians believed they all originally came from Havaiki, and that after they death would return to this homeland.

Kaua'i is the northernmost of the eight main islands of Hawaii. At more than five million years old, it is the oldest island in the archipelago and offers an enormous variety of landscapes on its 552 square miles (1430 km^2). There are about 68,000 inhabitants on Kaua'i. Although hospitality is the largest industry on the island, Kaua'i is less developed compared with Oahu, Maui and the Big Island of Hawaii, with only about ten percent of the island being accessible by car.

On January 20, 1778 two ships of the British navigator Captain James Cook set anchor on Kaua'i. More than 150 years ago, American planters began growing the first commercial sugarcane on the island. Since then, millions of people have visited this magical island paradise, yet the beautiful landscape of Kaua'i still seems to appear in many parts like it has for millions of years.

Mount Wai'ale'ale, at an elevation of 5,148 feet (1,569 meters), was once the volcanic heart of Kaua'i. It's the center of a series of peaks and valleys that fan out around this point, creating some of the most spectacular scenery in the Pacific area. When I first saw this deep core, the heart of Kaua'i, from a helicopter, I was overwhelmed by the utter beauty of this mystical place, its many waterfalls flowing down like the tears of this great-grandmother mountain valley.

There is an ancient legend that the Hawaiian Islands, like other Polynesian Islands, are the tops of the former land of Lemuria or Mu. In 1931, James Churchward, one of the most prominent researchers on Lemuria, wrote in his book *The Lost Continent of Mu* that the Motherland stretched from the Hawaiian Islands to Fiji and from Easter Island to the Marianas.

Some people believe that the Hawaiian Islands represent the seven main chakras of the human energetic body. Sensitive people perceive that Kaua'i, for example, holds subtly—yet powerfully—the unique energies of the third eye chakra and the crown, whereas the Big Island of Hawaii is more grounding and connected to the root chakra. While this association is of course mere conjecture, it does feel as though the veils between this world and the next are thin in some areas of Kaua'i, allowing sensitives to connect and co-create with the divine spirit, and even with other dimensions on Kaua'i.

Because of its beautiful vegetation, Kaua'i is called "The Garden Island." Among its lush vegetation is the heart-shaped taro plant—its foliage flourishes on Kaua'i as well as on other Hawaiian Islands. Polynesian legends describe how the taro plant existed even before the first humans. An ancient chant recounts how Wakea (the god of the sky) had to bury his first son because the child was born as a shapeless mass. The next day, a taro plant grew up from the burial location. Wakea named the plant-child Haloanaka (long, trembling stem). Wakea's second son was a boy whom Wakea named Haloa Naka Lau Kapalili (long stalk, quaking, trembling leaf stem). He was considered to be the first human; the taro plant was honored as the oldest ancestor of all humans.

In ancient times, Kaua'i was regarded as a sacred island that individuals were invited to or called to. Certain places on the island that were used for ceremonies held special energy, since participants were initiated and prepared for specific work on their heart and soul journey.

Hawaiians believe that all things sacred or revered wait for the right time to reveal themselves. Many people feel drawn not only to the sparkling blue-green waters and lush green lands of Kaua'i but also to the sacredness of the island itself, which emanates a sense of purity, freedom and wisdom.

In the beginning of May 2008, on a new moon weekend, I got the inner call and an invitation to visit Kaua'i for the first time. I had been living and studying in Honolulu for about six weeks and I had also started to visit other Hawaiian Islands. I first went for a weekend trip for three days to the Big Island. Two weeks later I was sitting in a plane on my way to Kaua'i.

Only one day before my trip to Kaua'i, I got sick, with strong flu-like symptoms. Despite feeling sick and weak I had a powerful inner call to visit this special island, without knowing whom I was going to meet or what awaited me. As soon as I arrived at the airport in Lihue, everything started to shift around me.

As soon as I set foot on the Garden Island, it felt like I was stepping into another dimension—or even through some sort of a time gate. Everything looked and felt slightly different to me. I realized that somehow things I was thinking or feeling manifested rather quickly in my perception. The longer I stayed, the stronger this wonderful and miraculous sensation felt.

Despite my flu, I felt at home in a place that I had never visited in my life and, from the beginning, I met wonderful and loving people who welcomed me back home. At a new moon gathering on a secluded beach I attended, several people (who didn't know what the others had said to me) told me something to this effect: they'd waited a long time for my return and were happy I'd come back home to Kaua'i.

During my first visit, which lasted only three days, I had many special and wonderful encounters with people I feel grateful to call my friends to this day, and with beings from many different realms. My flu was completely and miraculously gone in only two days. The healing happened not only on a physical level, but it also initiated a profound transformation in my emotional and mental states.

I experienced complete oneness, harmony, balance and love between myself and others, and even with the whole universe and the earth. It felt like an amazing and beautiful dream, which continued for the duration of my first time on Kaua'i. I didn't return to Kaua'i for another ten weeks—I was afraid to lose the best dream I'd had in my whole lifetime.

To me and many others, Kaua'i is a wonderful example of balance and harmony between the seen and the unseen. Kaua'i offers an environment where people can follow their own spiritual paths more authentically and manifest their dreams. On this magical island, I feel the balance of both masculine and feminine energies within me, allowing me to fully connect with my inner child.

I've met many others who have similar profound experiences when they spend time on this beautiful Garden Island. We all are meant to experience such wonderful and magical beauty, oneness and heaven on earth. When you are on Kaua'i, you recognize this not only on the level of the mind but also feel it deeply in your heart.

Shortly before I had to leave for Switzerland again in July 2008, I finally returned to Kaua'i for two weeks and, again, I had more of these amazing, magical and beautiful experiences. It is not possible to share in words how I felt. I experienced more incidences of synchronicity and wonderful encounters. While I explored the island, visiting several sacred sites and powerful energetic vortexes, I also received visions and predictions in my meditations about how my future would unfold—and even about when I would return to the island. I truly experienced a spiritual renewal and received gifts in many different forms.

As it turned out, just as I'd seen in those visions, I came back to Kaua'i three years later, in 2011, after which I lived on the island and studied Presence Centered Awareness therapy with Lee for half a year. As I described earlier, at the end of my journey on Kaua'i, I went on a spiritual vision quest which guided me over all the Hawaiian Islands. Within three weeks, I traveled from Kaua'i to the Big Island, Maui, Moloka'i, Lana'i, Oahu and back to Kaua'i—a whirlwind journey which took me to many heiau and powerful vortices. As I mentioned, heiau are beautiful places of worship, power, history, mystery and magic, and they assist us in connecting with the ancient energies of Hawaii. These places are located at vortices. I repeatedly connected with many of these sacred sites, especially on Kaua'i.

A vortex is a place in nature where the natural energies are exceptionally alive and healthy. In a vortex, the aliveness and health of natural elements are reflected in tremendous natural beauty created by the elements of land, light, air and water. The energy of a vortex acts as an amplifier and opens us up to receptivity. Whatever we bring to such a place (whether on a physical, mental, emotional or spiritual level) is amplified or magnified. I believe that when we gather as a group to meditate, pray or manifest life intentions at such places, it has a significant impact not only in our own lives but also directly on our society and the collective consciousness of all humanity.

Of course, not everyone who lives on or visits Kaua'i has experiences like the ones I had while visiting Kaua'i in 2008 and 2011. However, I believe that Kaua'i is a place that reflects and mirrors our thoughts, emotions and intentions more powerfully than on most other places on earth—especially for those of us who are sensitive and aware enough to perceive it in that way.

It's just like looking into a mirror. Depending on how you feel, you can see both your beauty and inner shining light, or you can suddenly see some shady parts which have been unknown to you before. Maybe this is one of the reasons some people completely fall in love with the island as soon as they arrive and never want to leave, whereas others prefer to leave Kaua'i for other Hawaiian Islands.

In my case, I needed to heal and transform myself when I came to the island (both in 2008 and in 2011) and Kaua'i provided me with the perfect environment for that healing. When we go through a profound transformative phase in our lives, it can be difficult and challenging. However, the incredibly pleasant climate and extraordinary beauty of Kaua'i helps make it easier.

When I came to Kaua'i for the first time, I felt welcomed like a family member returning home. So, I would like to leave you with six practical steps based on the six letters contained in the word "family":

F: ***F**ollow your heart and passions, share them with others, and have **f**un with it.*

A: ***A**ppreciate life. Every day find things you **a**ppreciate about yourself and others and make them into **a**ffirmations.*

M: ***M**editate daily, become aware of the **m**iracles in your daily life and start **m**agnetizing them.*

I: ***I**ntend. Have **i**ncredible **i**ntentions. Keep thinking and speaking about them and write them down.*

L: *Love is the most powerful force in this universe. Love yourself, love others and love **l**ife itself.*

Y: ***Y**es! Say **y**es to life and your passions whenever you are presented with an opportunity, decision or choice.*

I am grateful and happy that, after all these years, I have returned home to Kaua'i with Eunjung. Do you feel the call to join us in Paradise, to awaken your heart and soul vision through the Mana (energy) and Aloha (spirit) of Hawaii on this magical and beautiful island paradise? We are here to guide you, if you choose to visit and experience a powerful transformation in your life. Aloha!

Kalalau Valley, Kaua'i

PART IV
TAKING ACTION

"When you're standing in your purpose, the quality of your dreams and the quality of your life will change. Now, whether you know your purpose or not, it's definitely worth taking the time to drip in, take action, and go deeper into the discovery."

—Marcia Wieder

In the final Part of this book, it is time for you to start taking action. You will receive valuable tips on how to use social media consciously, and how you can start each day conscious and centered. You will also learn more about yourself and others, how to set inspiring and motivating goals, and how to start taking action toward manifesting your vision and dreams.

Using Social Media Consciously

These days, it would be hard for many of us to imagine life without interacting on social media outlets like Facebook, Twitter, Instagram, etc. In essence, the term "social media" can be defined as a host of internet sites that enable people from all over the world to interact with each other. The most popular, of course, is Facebook. Facebook has more active users than WhatsApp, Twitter and Instagram combined. Worldwide, as of the first quarter of 2018, there were more than 2.19 billion active monthly Facebook users, a more than fourteen percent increase over the previous year.

My own first entry into the world of social media was in 2006, when I created a Myspace account for a music project I was involved in for many years. The site was mainly for introducing our music, and there was much less interaction with the people who visited my site than there is now with Facebook.

Two years later, I traveled to Hawaii to study at an international language school in Honolulu and learned about Facebook and Twitter for the first time through my classmates. After hearing what these platforms were about, I joined Facebook and started to use it. At the time, I used Facebook to share beautiful nature pictures and inspiring experiences; both were abundant during my stay in Hawaii.

During the intense burnout I experienced in Switzerland a couple of years later in 2010, Facebook helped me to connect with people all over the world who were having similar experiences—diving deeply within to change the course of their lives by courageously following a path of the heart. It helped me tremendously to know, firstly, that I wasn't the only one going through turmoil, and, secondly, to realize this burnout was another starting point for my awakening.

On the other hand, I started to notice how distracted I tended to get while on Facebook. I was spending too much time on the site, checking feeds and comments and generally getting lost in the flood of communication. I realized I spent only about ten percent of my time on Facebook doing what I wanted, which was sharing inspirational stories or pictures. The rest of the time I was absorbed in what others were posting on Facebook. I was also spending a lot of time reading online newsletters and blogs so I was dedicating a lot of time to the internet.

Years later, however, after taking the 150-hour yoga program in Thailand, I became aware that in order to find our purpose, achieve our goals and complete our projects, *focus* is important. I felt the nudge to take time out of social media and go inward. By March 2014, while Eunjung and I were visiting Sedona—a powerful and well-known energy vortex area in Arizona, U.S.A.—I decided to leave Facebook for an indefinite time.

The break from social media gave me a wonderful opportunity to reflect on how I related to myself and the world around me. It was freeing to stop thinking about what to share and to quit compulsively checking Facebook feeds. I thought deeply about why I was using this vehicle of relating and sharing. After three months of "digital detox," so to speak, I returned to Facebook in June 2014 determined to use it more consciously and with greater awareness.

Not too long ago, our world cherished personal communication and interactions. We used to write letters, call someone and have a conversation on the phone, or walk down to their house to talk to them. Nowadays people are often fixated on their mobile phone or tablet, oblivious to their surroundings. On our travels, Eunjung and I have learned that this is a worldwide phenomenon. In 2015, we saw a remarkable example of a group of people lost in their devices.

We had arrived at a hotel on the Greek island of Rhodes and were astonished and amused by the scene we encountered in the lobby. There were about twenty people there and everyone, whether they were by themselves or with someone, was looking at their phone. No one was talking to anyone else. It was shocking—it reminded me of the lyrics of the song "Connection" by Miten, in which he talks about people being connected on the phone but not really *connecting*.

On that note, I'd like to discuss the pros and cons of social media and suggest that we can use it in a balanced way, with more awareness and mindfulness.

Social networking is a topic that divides opinion. Some people think it's an amazing tool, while others are concerned about the impact it has on people's lives and on society. There's a plethora of information about both the advantages and disadvantages of social media. The advantages include:

- It helps us open up to people, including those who are far away, and makes this world truly one global village.
- It helps people stay in touch as well as create new connections. It makes it much easier to stay connected with family and friends, even those who live on the other side of the planet.
- It's an amazing tool to help you reconnect with people from long ago.
- It can help you find life partners, as it's easier to find and interact with people who have similar interests.
- It can help you network and market yourself, and advertise goods and services.
- It can be a powerful search engine, both for people looking for a new job and for companies seeking new staff.
- It can provide an accessible medium for self-expression and serve as a creative outlet.
- People can easily share their feelings and what's happening in their lives, garnering support and encouragement from their friends.
- It can be harder to feel embarrassment over the internet than in person. Many people—especially those who are

shy—find it easier to interact and vent their feelings on social media sites.

- It can leverage political power for groups that might not otherwise have access.

Every coin has two sides, however, and social media is no exception. Its disadvantages include:

- It can be a waste of time. Some people visit a site to check one thing and end up spending hours staring at the screen. It takes time away from other meaningful activities and can replace real-time interactions. At the workplace, it can mean lost productivity.
- While contact is constant in social media, it's not always meaningful. Pictures and phrases on a wall can take the place of phone calls and face-to-face time with family and friends.
- It magnifies the gap between people who have access to computer technology and those who don't, exacerbating other social inequities.
- It can lead to the spread of rumors, lies and incorrect information. For example, people began to use the term *fake news* to refer to such misinformation.
- It can leave a person feeling exposed and vulnerable and threaten their sense of privacy. It can become a venue for cyber-bullying, a serious problem that can lead to suicides and incidents of self-harm, especially among teenagers and young adults.
- It can force changes in public policy. Employers can now make access to your private social networking history a condition of hiring. Even when it's not an official policy, today's employers often browse the internet to learn

more about a potential employee. Candidates may find themselves passed over because of social media content that employers consider inappropriate or incompatible with the job.

- It presents the risk of getting spammed or having private information taken, resulting in fraud or identity theft. Certain things, such as private pictures and personal information shouldn't be shared on social media sites. If you do share these things, you should limit who can view them.
- People often put their best foot forward on social media, presenting their lives as upbeat, successful and blessed. They're more likely to share their triumphs than their setbacks, and to post photos taken when they're looking their best rather than when they are having a "bad hair day."
- Constantly comparing yourself with others based on likes, status updates and images can lead to a lack of self-esteem and depression.
- Social media can amplify narcissistic traits such as egotism and self-promotion, exploitative tendencies and an obsessive need for social validation. You can find numerous resources, including articles at *www.psychologytoday.com*, that shine light on the psychological issues worsened by social media sites like Facebook.

Social Media can be addictive. According to recent studies, social networking accounts for twenty-eight percent of all time spent online. On average, teens between the ages of fifteen and nineteen spend at least three hours a day using platforms like Facebook, Twitter and Instagram, while users between the ages of twenty and twenty-nine spend about two hours on their social media accounts. Sixty-one percent of Facebook users feel they must check their Facebook feed at least once a day, which is a clear sign of compulsion.

I believe this is affecting the manner of communication used by current and future generations by fostering a culture of anonymity and superficial interaction. Communicating with close friends and family on Facebook is no substitute for real-life social interaction. The more time we spend in the artificial world of social media, the more isolated we become.

We develop social and communication skills through real-time interactions and by feeling the other person's energy field.

We develop social and communication skills through real-time interaction and by feeling the other person's energy field, whether consciously or subconsciously. I believe the best type of human communication occurs face-to-face, where we can see each other's facial expressions and body language and feel one another's energy.

Here are some practical tips on how you can approach using social media with more awareness.

- Take time and think about *why* you're using social media. Write down the reasons and reflect on them. Just considering the purpose of using social media can give you great insights. Weighing the advantages and disadvantages I summarized earlier may also help reduce the time you spend on social media or change how you interact with people on each platform.
- I'd like to challenge you to strike a balance between personal communications and online, social media communications. If you haven't talked to a friend in a long time, give them a call instead of texting or messaging. Better yet, meet with them in person.

- When you get up in the morning, don't automatically reach for your phone to check the latest feeds on Facebook or the messages in your inbox. Instead, start your day with a mindful ritual like meditation, setting an intention for the day or reading an inspirational book.
- Social media, if used appropriately and at appropriate times, can be a great way to learn about the latest information and knowledge in your areas of interest. However, it's essential to develop awareness—to understand how much time you're spending on it and how you feel afterwards.
- I'd like to suggest that you track the time you're on social media for one day, either on your phone or your computer. And after clicking and reading a feed on Facebook, go inward and see how that news or information affects you. Does it make you feel calm and uplifted, or upset and angry?
- If you're using social media for your business, especially Facebook, it's important to have a solid understanding of how the mechanism works. Learn when and how to use it, and which channels to focus on to yield maximum benefits without getting distracted by a sea of unrelated information and news.
- Use privacy settings to control what other people can see and read about you. It would be prudent to protect your private information, such as phone numbers, your birthday and home address. This may seem obvious, but some people don't use enough caution online. A few times, much to my dismay, I've seen people post their passport pictures on their Facebook wall, with all the related information. Such vital information should never be posted publicly on social media.

- It's critical to use discernment when it comes to news from unreliable sources. The internet can be an important tool for sharing alternative information that's been ignored or overlooked by the mainstream media. However, be aware that there's plenty of fake news that "goes viral," collecting tens of thousands of shares or likes. The disinformation is often created by people with the ulterior motive of directing traffic to their suspicious sites, or with hidden political or otherwise self-serving agendas. Manufactured news or news that capitalizes on sensationalism can lower your energy and distract you from what's really important.

In March of 2014, as we sat in meditation on Bell Rock—one of the powerful vortex sites in Sedona, Arizona—Eunjung and I received guidance pertaining to a volatile time that lay ahead for me. This inner voice conveyed to me that during this difficult period—which I'd face before my birthday near the end of April—it would be crucial for me to focus on myself, my resources and my gifts. I'd need to be fully present in order to ride out this challenging time. It was a bit unnerving, but I followed this guidance and unplugged from social media.

Just as the message had indicated, the morning I arrived in Switzerland in early April, I got upsetting news that had to do with my burnout phase in 2010. I had to face a ghost from that time of my life, but found blessings and freedom in completely transforming the last residue—some unhealed parts of myself—from the past. Addressing these unhealed parts of myself prepared me for a clean, new stage of evolution.

During that time, it was vital for me to stay present and to realign my energy toward what I wanted to create. During this digital detox, I started to notice how dependent upon and addicted to using social media I had been at times. I found it difficult to go through this challenging time in Switzerland by myself without connecting with others through Facebook, but ultimately it was rewarding. I realized that there are times when only you—your deeper self, your essence—can guide you. It was a highly valuable experience. I invite you to try it for yourself.

After three months' absence, I returned to social media with higher awareness and more clarity. I promised myself I'd use social media in a way that was aligned with who I was becoming, and balance my time between the real world and the cyber-world by limiting the time I spend on social media and the internet in general. I'm still keeping this promise and, by doing so, I've truly learned to appreciate the deep connection I make with people, animals and nature.

Does the way you use social media bring you closer to or farther away from living your purpose? If the latter, consider shifting your focus and realigning your time and energy. Disconnect from social media and reconnect with your higher self and your inner wisdom.

Blausee, Switzerland

Starting a New Day - Energetic Exercise Series

Introduction

I put together this energetic exercise series to help you start each day fully present to your whole being—body, mind, heart and spirit. This way, you can focus and direct your awareness and energy toward what is at hand in each moment and on what you intend to accomplish and create every day.

You may already have a morning routine that includes energetic movement and that serves you well. You can still try this out and add some variety to your morning practice.

These exercises combine various elements such as body movement, breathwork, Hatha yoga, chakra activation and meditation. They're based on a variety of healing systems and spiritual traditions I've worked with over the years.

Of course, there are many different approaches through which you can come to a similar place of inner peace and balance. I encourage you to explore them, just as I do.

This exercise series is designed to help you go within. Take your time. Let yourself sink into your own experience and create a more loving and energetic space where you can start each new day. If you have limited time, you can pick and practice a few favorite exercises. And, please, be present to your body's condition every day and don't push beyond your limit.

It takes time and persistence to build a healthy new pattern. Practice this routine daily as part of your morning ritual. If possible, do it before you check emails, go online or perform any other activities. If you do energy or healing work, this routine can help you to strengthen your energy field and to become fully present before you work with others.

If you can, keep your eyes closed while you do these exercises. This will help you tune into the resulting energetic sensations that arise. And after each exercise, take a short break for fifteen to twenty seconds and focus on the body part you've just activated.

In each of the following exercises, I describe both the movement and the breathwork involved. I suggest you first create an audio recording of the following instructions, and then play it while you practice. That way you can stay focused on the exercises without having to read the description of each exercise before you perform it.

Before you start, remember to get quiet and allow yourself to merge with a loving and nurturing space within you.

Exercises

**These exercises should be performed at your own discretion. Please be gentle with yourself—don't push beyond your limits. When doing these exercises, if you feel uncomfortable or experience any pain, stop. If you have a medical condition, please consult with your doctor.*

- Standing: Stand with your feet shoulder-width apart, back straight and your knees unlocked. Let your arms hang comfortably at your sides. Ground yourself. Create a connection with the earth through the soles of your feet. Imagine that roots are growing out of your feet, deep down into the center of the earth. Placing your focus on your heart, inhale and exhale deeply through your nose. Feel the energy being drawn upwards from deep in the core of the earth, up through your root chakra, up through your spine, energizing all your chakras. Become increasingly present for about one to two minutes.
- Head rotation: From your standing position, place your hands on your hips. With your shoulders down and while trying not to move the rest of your body, first lower your chin forward toward your upper chest. Then slowly start rolling your head in a circular motion, over your right shoulder, toward the back of your neck, and then to your

left shoulder and to the front with your chin lowered. First move clockwise, then counterclockwise, while inhaling and exhaling through your nose. Repeat seven times in each direction. Rotate your head slowly while breathing into the area of your throat chakra.

- Neck flexion horizontal: Start from a standing position. While doing this step, breathe into your throat area. With your shoulders back and down, rotate your chin slowly to the right as far as you can while inhaling through your nose. Return your chin to the middle while exhaling through your mouth. Then rotate your chin slowly to the left while inhaling through your nose, and return it to the middle while exhaling through your mouth. Repeat seven times each.
- Neck flexion vertical: Gently stretch your neck backwards while inhaling through your nose and then, while exhaling through your mouth, stretch your chin down, toward your upper chest. Repeat seven times. While doing this step, breathe into your chest and heart.
- Shoulder rotation: From a standing position, slowly rotate your shoulders backward ten times, then forward ten times. While doing this step, smile and direct your breath into the area of your spine.
- Alternate shoulder lifting: Smile. From a standing posture, alternate lifting your left and right shoulders as fast as you can without moving your head. While your left shoulder goes up, your right shoulder goes down and vice versa. This movement will activate your spine. Do this for about thirty to forty seconds. Keep smiling and focus on your spine while directing your breath into your spine.
- Arm rotation: From a standing position, rotate your outstretched right arm slowly in a backward circle seven

times and then in a forward circle seven times. Repeat this with your left arm. Then rotate both outstretched arms simultaneously, backward and forward, seven times in each direction. While doing these movements, inhale through your nose and exhale through your mouth, directing your breath into your heart.

- Self-embrace: From a standing position, embrace yourself with your arms by gently placing both palms on the opposite shoulders. Think and feel, "I love and appreciate myself." Inhale and exhale through your nose, focusing on your heart and crown chakras while feeling love and appreciation for yourself. Do this for one to two minutes.
- Upper body stretching: Stand with your feet shoulder-width apart, your back straight and your knees slightly bent. With both arms over your head, stretch your torso backward as far as you can go comfortably, while inhaling through your nose. Then, bend forward while exhaling through your mouth and bringing your arms in front of your body (touch the ground if you can). During this exercise, focus on stretching your spine. Repeat seven times.
- Upper body side stretching: Start from a standing position. While inhaling deeply through your mouth with your focus on your spine, stretch your arms upward. Hold your breath and stretch your sides by leaning to the right and then to the left with your arms overhead. Do this three times. Then, while lowering your arms to your sides, exhale slowly through your mouth. Repeat the whole movement seven times.
- Hip rotation: Stand up straight, with your feet shoulder-width apart and your hands on your hips. Bend your knees slightly and slowly rotate your hips by moving your pelvis in large circles, first to the right ten times and then to the left ten times. Keep your circles parallel to the ground.

Avoid leaning forward and backward when rotating your hips. Try to keep your back straight during this rotational exercise. While you breathe in and out through your nose, consciously focus on your lower three chakras.

- Upper body rolling: Stand straight, with your feet shoulder-width apart and your knees unlocked. Inhale through your mouth and stretch your arms upward with your palms facing the sky. While holding your breath, lean slowly backward as far you can go comfortably, with arms open wide. Stay for about ten seconds in this position and hold your breath. If it's challenging to hold your breath, exhale and inhale through your mouth again. Exhale through your mouth and return to the straight position. During this movement, breathe into your spine.

  From a standing position, take a deep breath in through your nose. While exhaling through your mouth, slowly fold your torso forward over your legs, vertebrae by vertebrae, with your knees slightly bent. Inhale through your mouth and hold this position and your breath for about ten seconds while focusing on your lower three chakras; then exhale through your mouth. If it's challenging to hold your breath, just inhale and exhale through your mouth.

  From this bent position, slowly raise your torso, vertebra by vertebra, while inhaling deeply through your mouth. Once you return to the standing position, exhale through your mouth while focusing on your three lower chakras. Repeat this sequence three times.

- Knee circles: Stand with both feet together. Bend forward and place your palms on your knees. With knees slightly bent, rotate your knees slowly clockwise, then counterclockwise. Do this ten times in each direction. While you inhale and exhale through your nose, focus on your feet and knees.

- Knee flexion: From a standing position, gently fold forward. With your palms pressing on your knees, sit on your heels. Then straighten your knees, with your heels firmly touching the ground. Repeat this movement seven times. Keep inhaling and exhaling through your nose, focusing on your feet and knees.
- Air squat: Stand with your feet hip-width apart, facing forward. With your arms stretched out in front of you at ninety degrees, and while exhaling through your mouth, slowly sit back by bending your hips and knees until your thighs are parallel to the floor. Keep your weight on your heels throughout the movement, and press through them to return to a standing position while inhaling through your mouth. Repeat twenty-one times. You will activate energy in and around your body.
- Hand and foot circles: Start from a standing position. While gazing at a fixed point about eight to ten feet away, make small circles with your right foot and left hand, first clockwise and then counterclockwise. Then make the same movements with your left foot and right hand. Repeat ten times each. While breathing through your nose, focus your attention on your hands, fingers, feet and toes.
- Jumping Jacks: Stand tall with your feet together and your hands at your sides. Quickly raise your arms above your head while jumping out to the sides. Immediately reverse the movement to jump back to the standing position. Repeat this movement thirty to fifty times. Breathe quickly and deeply through your mouth.
- Standing: Return to a standing position, with feet shoulder-width apart and arms comfortably hanging to your sides. With eyes closed, bring your awareness to your crown chakra. Inhale deeply through your nose and

feel the cooling sensation on the tip of your nose. Exhale through your nose and feel the warm sensation on the tip. For about one to two minutes, send gratitude to the energy created through these exercises. Feel the energy within your body, around your body and in the room or space you're in right now.

- Gratitude prayers: Bring both palms of your hands together in prayer position in front of your chest. Give thanks from your heart space for the chance to go through these exercises, for your health and happiness, for life and all creation, and for all the elements of nature (fire, water, earth and air). Give thanks to everyone who has supported you on your path, to your ancestors, to all those who were here before you, and to anyone else you'd like to add. Don't forget to experience gratefulness for yourself. Namaste!

After this exercise series, you can continue with the following meditation, which you can perform either standing or sitting—whichever feels most comfortable. Close your eyes and keep focusing on your breath and the sensations you are feeling within and around your body.

Morning Meditation

- Start your day from a place of centeredness. Start by embracing everything you perceive in this moment with your heart. Perceive the energies of the new day by focusing on merging the energies of your mind, heart and solar plexus. Notice how your mind-chatter stops and your whole being expands.
- Send love and light from this space of centeredness and wholeness wherever you go today. Also, send love and light to all people, animals and plant-spirits you encounter,

communicate with or connect with. Now expand this love to the entire planet Earth and beyond. Embrace yourself and all other beings.

- From this space of centeredness and wholeness, allow creative energies to expand from your heart. Let them enter into all the cells of your body as well as your energetic body (your aura) and then fill up the space around you. Hold positive intentions and expectations for this new day. Trust that your creative gifts and talents will unfold naturally today to help you serve and live on purpose.

- Positively reinforce the notion that you are simultaneously the director, actor and audience of your own life stage. You can create your life in a new way in each moment, no matter how your current circumstances may appear. Remember, you're both the observer and the projector of your realities. Be observant today about what you're projecting outward.

- Now, from your heart space and inner calmness, emanate feelings of deep appreciation and gratitude for yourself and your life. Find at least five things you're grateful for in this moment. This powerful emotional state of appreciation is an expression of your inner life force, which will help you create and experience new miracles every day.

- To close the meditation from the expanded state, take deep breaths in and out a few times. Each breath will help you return to your physical space and your body. Once you feel fully present in your body, slowly open your eyes and start your new day.

Feeling Great Practice

If you don't have time to do the morning meditation, you can do the short practice I share below to help you start your day feeling great.

First, let's get really clear about what we intend to create and experience as we go through our day, and thereby lay a foundation of increased self-awareness for the entire day. As Rod Stryker shares in his book *The Four Desires: Creating a Life of Purpose, Happiness, Prosperity, and Freedom*, "As self-awareness grows, it naturally leads you to new understanding. You see with far greater clarity the deeper meaning and purpose of your life; you understand more about yourself, your needs, and your desires."

In our daily conversations with people, we often hear, "I'm doing *great*," "I'm not that *great*," "Have a *great* day!" and so on. Two years ago, I learned a wonderful new tool that can help us feel great. I really like it, and so has everyone I've shared it with. It's simple, doesn't take a lot of time, and enhances the quality of your day and the way you perceive life. It won't take you longer than five minutes a day. Ask yourself the following five questions every morning:

G: *What am I* ***g****rateful for (five things)?*

R: *What am I* ***r****esolved to focus on today (one thing)?*

E: *What am I* ***e****xcited about today (three things)?*

A: *What do I most* ***a****ppreciate about myself, or what do I* ***a****ffirm today (one to three things)?*

T: ***T****oday I will.... (What concrete steps will I take today to feel great?)*

I hope the exercise series, meditation and practice above will all help you start your day energized and feeling great!

Haleakala National Park, Maui

How Well Do You Know Yourself and Others?

How others perceive us can teach us about who we are, and can help us to develop ourselves. Sometimes, how we perceive ourselves and how others perceive us doesn't match. Our behavior and our body language may communicate something about us that we're completely unaware of.

Main Areas of Perception

These are the four main areas of human perception. In psychology, these are known as the "*Johari window.*" The technique was created by psychologists Joseph Luft and Harrington Ingham in 1955:

1. *Open: Characteristics that both you and your peers perceive.*
2. *Hidden: Characteristics that you self-proclaim but which your peers are unaware of, and which may be inaccurate.*
3. *Blind: Characteristics that you are not aware of, but others perceive about you.*
4. *Unknown: Your behaviors or motives that are not recognized by you or anyone else.*

Actions

Copy the four pages of the following questionnaire nine times. Fill out one of the questionnaires for yourself (self-perception). Give four to people who know you well and ask them to complete the questionnaire and return it to you (so you can understand how others perceive you). Then, fill out the remaining four questionnaires the way you assume the other four people perceive you.

Once you're done, you can exchange the questionnaires with your friends and family and compare the results. You'll probably be surprised by the differences between your assumptions and how others actually perceive you. Any disparities may prompt you to re-examine certain aspects of your personality. The questionnaire covers 100 characteristics. Ask yourself these questions *AFTER* the comparison:

- How do I generally perceive myself?
- How do others generally perceive me?
- How accurate is the way I perceive myself, and the way others generally perceive me?
- For what percentage of characteristics is there a match?

- For what percentage of characteristics is there a bigger difference?
- What is exciting about this result? What makes me happy? What surprises me positively?
- How easy is it for me to accept how others perceive me now? How was it when I was a child?
- How important is it for me to receive feedback from others? What kind of benefits do I receive?
- Which characteristics can I improve, and in which situations?
- Which five characteristics do I most appreciate about myself? (Mark them with a smiley face)
- Which five characteristics do I want to cultivate? (Mark them with an exclamation mark)
- Having reviewed this comparison, what concrete steps can I take now to improve the way I perceive myself and others?
- Which sub-goals will I achieve as I reach for transformation?
- How do I measure whether I've achieved these sub-goals?

Characteristics	-3	-2	-1	1	2	3
	Not present at all <-				+> Strongly present	
Adaptable						
Ambitious						
Appreciative						
Arrogant						
Assertive						
Attentive						
Authentic						
Authoritarian						
Balanced						
Calm						
Caring						
Charismatic						
Communicative						
Compassionate						
Confident						
Conscientious						
Content						
Cooperative						
Courageous						
Creative						
Critical						
Decent						
Detail-oriented						
Determined						
Diplomatic						

Characteristics	-3	-2	-1	1	2	3
	Not present at all <- +> Strongly present					
Direct						
Disciplined						
Dominant						
Dynamic						
Egotistical						
Emotional						
Empathetic						
Energetic						
Enthusiastic						
Ethical						
Flexible						
Focused						
Freedom-loving						
Friendly						
Giving						
Happy						
Helpful						
Hopeful						
Impatient						
Impulsive						
Influential						
Innovative						
Insecure						
Insightful						
Inspired						

Characteristics	-3	-2	-1	1	2	3
	Not present at all <- +> Strongly present					
Intelligent						
Knowledge-seeking						
Likeable						
Loving						
Motivated						
Naïve						
Neutral						
Objective						
Open						
Open to criticism						
Open-minded						
Optimistic						
Organized						
Outgoing						
Passionate						
Patient						
Performance-oriented						
Persistent						
Personable						
Problem-oriented						
Punctual						
Quick-witted						
Rational						
Reliable						
Resilient						

Characteristics	-3	-2	-1	1	2	3
	Not present at all <- +> Strongly present					
Respectful						
Responsible						
Results-oriented						
Self-centered						
Self-confident						
Self-possessed						
Self-reliant						
Sensitive						
Sensual						
Skeptical						
Solution-oriented						
Spirited						
Spiritual						
Spontaneous						
Steady						
Stress-tolerant						
Talkative						
Team-minded						
Thorough						
Tolerant						
Trusting						
Understanding						
Upright						
Versatile						
Warm-hearted						

Ali'i Kula Lavender Farm, Maui

Inspiring and Motivating Goals

Above, I shared how you can start each day feeling more energized and fully present to your own being. I focused on how to use social media consciously, how to gain clarity and how to learn more about the way you perceive yourself and are perceived by others.

These exercises provide a great foundation for improving your life. Without setting goals and taking action toward your vision, however, you may still lack two components that are vital to the pursuit of a purposeful life: focus and direction. If you don't have clarity about what you want, it's hard to move forward.

Get clear about what you intend to create and experience today. If you don't have clarity about what you want, it's hard to move forward.

To accomplish your goals, you need to consider carefully the changes you want to make in your life. Then take steps toward them. Here are five helpful and effective ways of setting your goals:

1. Set goals that inspire and motivate you.
2. Choose SMART goals.
3. Write your goals down and speak them out loud.
4. Take immediate action.
5. Follow through.

Setting and achieving goals provides a point of reference as to whether or not you're moving toward your ideal life. When you start taking action based on goals you've set, you take the commander's seat in your life's journey.

1. Set goals that inspire and motivate you.

It's essential that your goals inspire and motivate you. Along with writing down your goal (the *what*), also write down your motivation (the *why*) and by *when* you'd like to achieve it. Again, when you want to improve your life, your goals must relate to things that have high priority and are meaningful for you.

If you have few aspirations and you're not clear as to why you set a certain goal, there isn't enough value and energy to even start acting on it. If it seems difficult to decide where to begin, I suggest you start setting goals first in the following five areas:

- Family and relationships,
- Health and wellbeing,
- Career,
- Leisure, and
- Personal growth.

2. Choose SMART goals.

You may have already heard of SMART goals. There are many variations on what SMART stands for. Generally speaking, goals should be:

- **S**pecific: If your goals are too general or vague, you're unlikely to reach them efficiently, because they don't provide you with enough direction. Your goals should be clearly defined and as focused as possible. The more clear and specific you get in setting your goals, the better the chances are that you'll achieve them. Think of the benefits, advantages and rewards of achieving your goals when you set them.

- **M**easurable: Quantify (or at least suggest) an indicator that you are making progress. When setting measurable goals, many people fail to take full responsibility in following through with *action*. Are you experiencing blockages? Ask yourself how you'll know with absolute certainty when you've met your aims. Consider also that without making your goals measurable, you'll miss the opportunity to celebrate and reward yourself once you've achieved them.

- **A**ttainable: Become clear as to what you can attain within a certain amount of time. You've probably set lofty goals in the past—with little hope, trust or belief that you can achieve them—and then collected some evidence that it didn't work. Setting goals that are too easy to achieve can be counterproductive. *Balance* is the key word here. Try to set goals that seem realistic and yet a little challenging. Attainable goals stretch your abilities, and yet they remain possible.

- **R**elevant: Your goals should relate to the area of your life you want to improve. When you're in the process of accomplishing your goals, you'll face challenges, obstacles and difficulties. It's a natural part of the journey. At this point, you'll certainly ask yourself if this goal *really* matters to you. If you don't have some real internal motivation to achieve your goal, you're more likely to give up than when your goal is based on your true heart's desire.

- **T**ime-related: Without having a target date or deadline to work toward, you'll most likely either procrastinate or forget about your goal over time. This fifth part of the SMART formula clearly addresses *when* you intend to achieve your goals. It's helpful to break down the necessary steps and assign a deadline to each. Ask yourself: "What can I do in … *months* from now? What can I do in … *weeks* from now? What can I do in … *days* from now? And what can I do *today*?" Then, mark your calendar with the specific days you'll act.

SMART is a well-established tool you can use to set and achieve your goals. Although the SMART acronym is usually used in the business world to ensure that managers and employees share the same understanding of goals, I believe it's equally beneficial for setting goals in any area of your life to help guide you to your life's purpose.

3. Write your goals down and speak them out loud.

If you just think about your goals in your head, or talk to a friend about them every now and then, they often remain in the realm of wishful thinking. In order to give more conscious energy and focused attention to your goals, it's important to write them down while paying close attention to *how* you write.

Instead of "*I hope*" or "*I would like to*" or "*I will*," begin your statement with "*I am ...ing*" to make your intention very clear to your subconscious mind—and to the universe. Frame your goal statements in a positive and inspiring way, and always state them in present-time. Once you write down your goals, speak them out loud on a regular basis.

4. Take immediate action.

After you set your goals and write them down, it's important to start acting *immediately*. We're living in an age of over-stimulation and we are overloaded with information. If you wait too long after setting a goal or intention, if you procrastinate, life happens. Meanwhile, you fail to act and follow through on the aim you set just a few days ago. There's always something you can start doing *today*. You've learned many tools and techniques you can work with. What are you deciding to accomplish *right now*?

5. Follow through.

You've probably experienced this before: you set a New Year's Eve resolution that's probably not serious and to which you lack sufficient commitment. The first two weeks usually go along in a promising way, but by February you're backsliding. Then, by mid-February, you realize that nothing has really changed. By June, you find yourself back where you started and you wonder what went wrong.

It's tempting to procrastinate until the last minute—especially when you set big goals that seem daunting—only to realize that, by now, achieving your goal seems even more challenging. Instead of one step forward, you've taken two steps back.

You're not alone. According to researcher John Norcross and his colleagues, who published their findings in the *Journal of Clinical Psychology*, approximately fifty percent of the population makes resolutions each New Year. Among the top resolutions are to lose weight, exercise more, stop smoking and get out of debt.

Motivation expert Steve Levinson said, "Willpower is both a precious commodity and an unreliable one. You really can't count on it. It often does not come through for you when you need it the most and the best thing to do is to structure circumstances so that you don't need to rely on it."

So, how can you follow through more efficiently? Make a list of friends, family members or colleagues who will hold you accountable to the promises you make to yourself and others and who will encourage and inspire you to follow through on the actions you intend to take. Ideally, find someone who also wants to achieve his or her own goals. Then you can hold each other accountable and celebrate together whenever you achieve a milestone on the path toward your ideal life. Other ways could include creating or joining a meet-up group or working with a life coach like myself.

Let's take some action, right here and now. Please fill out the wheel below, a tool introduced in the beginning of this book, one more time. You'll need two colored pencils for this exercise, one to indicate where you are and another to indicate where you want to be on the Wheel of Life.

By this point in the book, you've worked with all the questions, steps and strategies in Parts I to III. Take some quiet time to think about how doing that work has affected your life. Have there been substantial changes in your life? In what areas?

Now, complete the wheel below. (You may wish to photocopy it first.)

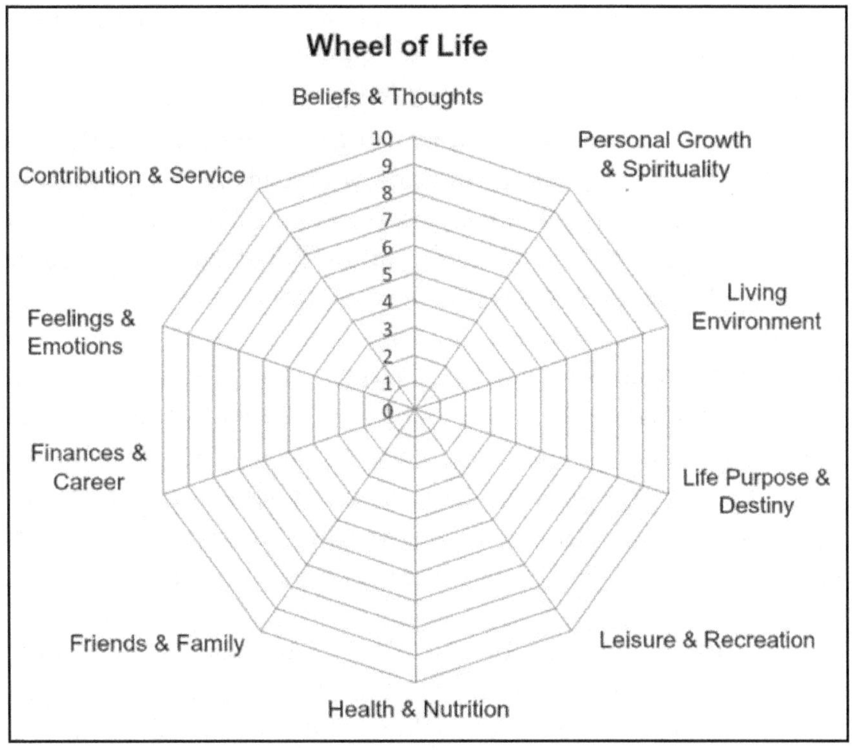

Then, compare your new scores with the results you got when you filled out the Wheel of Life in the beginning of this book. Are they the same, or has there been improvement? Please answer the following questions:

- What contributed to higher scores in certain areas of your life?
- What concrete steps are you committed to taking within the next seven days?
- Where do you intend to be thirty days from now?
- Where would you like to be three months from now?
- How will you reward yourself upon achieving your heart's desires?

For this exercise, I recommend choosing three months into the future as your first milestone (although it is entirely up to you to choose a shorter or longer timeline) by indicating where you want to be in each area. Then, connect the dots using a different colored pencil from the color you used to indicate your current circumstances. When you have clarity about where you want to be in the different areas of your life in your preferred future time frame, it will guide you to a purposeful new direction of your life.

I recommend you work with the wheel of life and the five questions above on an ongoing basis. Fill out a new wheel of life every three months (mark it on your agenda!) and decide what steps you'll take within the next seven days. Get clear about your intention for the next thirty days, and find clarity as to where you want to be when you fill out the wheel of life again after another three months.

To live a life on purpose, it's essential to have balance in all areas of your life. Working with the wheel of life is helpful in getting an overview of how you're currently doing and where you'd like to be a few months from now.

To bridge the gap between your current and future life circumstances, you can set goals in each of these areas. Most importantly, you need to be inspired and committed to following through with what is meaningful for you.

Below you'll find valuable statements you can complete for the ten areas on the wheel of life. These statements are meant to help you dive deeply and reflect on different aspects of your life. They'll give you more clarity in terms of where you are and where you want to be, and they can inspire and motivate you in setting and achieving your goals.

Using your journal or a few empty pages of paper, fill out all the statements (or choose those you resonate with or that are appropriate for your life visions and goals). Some of these statements are inspired by the work of Brendon Burchard, *www.brendon.com* who is one of the most watched, quoted and followed personal development trainers in the world. As I noted earlier, his book, *Life's Golden Ticket: A Story About Second Chances* is among my ten favorite books in the self-help and transformation category.

1) Beliefs and thoughts

   - Some words I'd use to describe my *current* beliefs and thoughts are…
   - The way I think and my current belief system affect my life in this way…
   - Some words I'd use to describe my *ideal self* would be…
   - The *deeper reason* I chose each of those words is…
   - To live these words more fully in my life, I need *to stop* doing these things…
   - To live these words more fully in my life, I need to *start* doing these things….

2) Personal growth and spirituality

   - Some words I'd use to *describe* my personal growth and spirituality are…
   - My personal growth and spirituality *influence* my life in the following way…
   - I would feel happy, content and fulfilled *at the end of my life* if…
   - When I'm gone, I hope I leave these *ideas and values* with those who knew me…

- Before the end of my life, I hope I will have *experienced* these things…
- Before the end of my life, I hope I will have *created or given* these things….

3) Living environment

- Some of the advantages and disadvantages of my *current* living environment include…
- Some words describing the *perfect* environment I can imagine myself living in are…
- Some words describing the ideal environment *for everyone* living on earth are…
- The *deeper reason* I chose each of these words is…
- Some ways I can personally improve the current living environment *for myself* are…
- Some ways I can personally help improve the current living environment *for others* are….

4) Life's purpose and destiny

- The *books or inspirational movies* I'm dedicated to reading / watching in the next six months include…
- Some of the *classes* I'm inspired to take online or in person in the next twelve months include…
- The *mentors* I need to find are people or organizations that have the following knowledge…
- Some of the habits I'd have to *diminish or completely let go* of in order to learn and grow are…
- Some of the habits I'd have to *develop* in order to learn and grow are…

- The *lessons* I've learned in my life that I'm inspired to share with others are....

5) Leisure and recreation

- The way I am *currently* spending my leisure time is...
- What helps me most to *rejuvenate and relax* is...
- If I had more time, the things I'd love to *receive and experience* outside of work are...
- If I had more time, the things I'd love to *create and contribute* outside of work are...
- To improve the quality of my leisure and recreation time, I would have to *stop*...
- To improve the quality of my leisure and recreation time, I would have to *start*....

6) Health and nutrition

- Some words describing my *current* health and nutrition are...
- Some words describing my *ideal* health and nutrition are...
- The *reasons* I'm going to start caring better for my body, mind and soul are...
- If I described my ideal health, this is how I'd *feel* every day...
- To become more fit and healthy, I would have to *stop*...
- To become more fit and healthy, I would have to *start*....

7) Friends and family

- Some words I'd use to describe the *meaning* of having family and friends in my life include...

- Some words I want to describe my *interactions* with my loved ones are…
- I would like the loved ones I interact with to *describe me* using these words…
- The *deeper reason* I chose each of those words is because…
- To live those words more fully in my life, I need to *stop* doing these things…
- To live those words more fully in my life, I need to *start* doing these things….

8) Finances and career

- The things I *already have* an abundance of in my life, and that I'm grateful for include…
- The things I would *buy and invest* in if I had more resources are…
- The best things I can do to *save more money* right now are…
- Other than receiving a salary for my work, these *other benefits* matter to me…
- The things I'd like to learn and master *in the next twelve months* of my life include…
- If I learned just three new skills *in the next two years* that would catapult my career, those skills would be….

9) Feelings and emotions

- Some words I would use to describe my *current* emotional state are…
- Some words I would use to describe my *ideal* emotional state are…

- Some words *my best friends* would use to describe my emotional state are…
- Some words describing *how I relate* to my feelings and emotions are…
- To be (even) more balanced emotionally, I would have to *stop*…
- To be (even) more balanced emotionally, I would have to *start*….

10) Contribution and service

- Some words I'd use to describe what contribution and service *truly mean* to me are…
- The main things I'd love to create and contribute in my life at this point *by myself* are…
- The main things I'd love to create and contribute in my life at this point *together with others* are…
- The most meaningful things I think I could create or contribute *in the next month* are…
- The most meaningful things I think I could create or contribute *in the next twelve months* are…
- The most meaningful things I think I could create or contribute *in the next two years* are….

Once you've completed all of the above statements (or those you most resonate with and find most appropriate for your life visions and goals), apply the six strategies below to help you achieve your aims.

Six Strategies for Achieving Your Goals

1. Write down markers.

In the Passion Test process, there is a powerful tool called *markers.* A marker is evidence that you've accomplished your goal. It's meant to be a signpost, signaling that you've turned your vision into reality. Don't think about *how* your markers will be achieved, just write them out. Everything important to you can be included. Find five markers for each of the ten areas (or the areas you choose to work with) from the wheel of life. Here is an example of mine to help you get started:

Living environment:

- *I keep our place clean and organized daily.*
- *I spend time outside in nature every day when the weather is nice.*
- *I find ways to volunteer and contribute with a focus on nature and animals.*
- *Every day I express my gratitude and appreciation for the paradise I reside in.*
- *I raise awareness on how to protect Kaua'i's beautiful natural environment.*

2. Work with a partner.

Find a calm and peaceful setting where you and your partner will be undisturbed and can be present and focused with each other. This is a beneficial way to deepen any relationship or friendship. Decide who will read first. The first person reads out loud the goal and their markers, while the other person listens attentively and repeats what the first person said. Shift roles after completing one of the areas. Here is an example:

First person: "*I* spend time outside in nature every day when the weather is nice."

Second person: "*You* spend time outside in nature every day when the weather is nice."

If you can't find a partner to work with, you can still do the same exercise by yourself. You may want to make an audio recording so you can listen to it again later. This is one of many powerful and effective approaches to programming your subconscious.

3. Create a ritual.

After Eunjung and I completed writing the statements above on December 31, 2017, we decided to read our sentences aloud to each other. During the following full-moon night on January 1, we went to a quiet place where we could sit near the Pacific Ocean under the stars and the bright, shining moon. We also brought some of our sacred power crystals and objects to place on the sitting area. It was a magical and powerful experience.

On the following new moon on January 16, we were guided to repeat the ritual at the same place after we completed writing markers for each statement. Any full moon or new moon is a great time to create such a ritual, because during these days your intentions, emotions, thoughts and speech are amplified by the powerful waves of lunar energy.

Any full moon or new moon is a great time to create a ritual to amplify your intentions, emotions and thoughts.

---

4. Prepare a sacred space.

In the introductory section, I noted that *Your Hidden Riches* by Janet Bray Attwood, Chris Attwood and Sylva Dvorak is among my ten favorite books in the self-help and transformation category. In this inspiring book, Janet writes, "Rituals are conscious, intentional habits. They help you manage your time, your energy, and your thinking to create balance and rhythm. I believe that creating a sacred space is one of life's most precious attainments."

Put the list with your goals and markers in a place that's special and meaningful for you. Eunjung and I created an altar with our favorite sacred objects, and we put our lists there. Next, mark in your calendar when you'll work with your list again. To get the best results from this exercise, I recommend you reread what you wrote in your list and re-listen to your recording at least once a month, ideally on a full moon or a new moon.

5. Evaluate regularly.

Regularly evaluate where you are in terms of achieving your goals. For each marker you've accomplished, you can give yourself two points. If you're still working on the marker with positive results but haven't fully accomplished what the marker indicates, you get one point. If you haven't taken any action, you get zero points. Once you've fully achieved all five markers for each area of the wheel of life, you will have gained ten points. Of course, this is a simplified approach and if you'd like to, you can fine-tune your scoring.

6. Adjust and rewrite.

Mark your current score in each of the ten areas (or the areas you choose to work with) of the wheel of life. When you evaluate your progress again, ideally one month later, set new goals. Also, adjust or completely rewrite your markers or replace some of your markers with new ones. You'll realize that the more you work with your goals and markers, the more inspired and motivated you'll be. This will significantly increase the chances you'll follow through with your dreams and goals and start living your life on purpose.

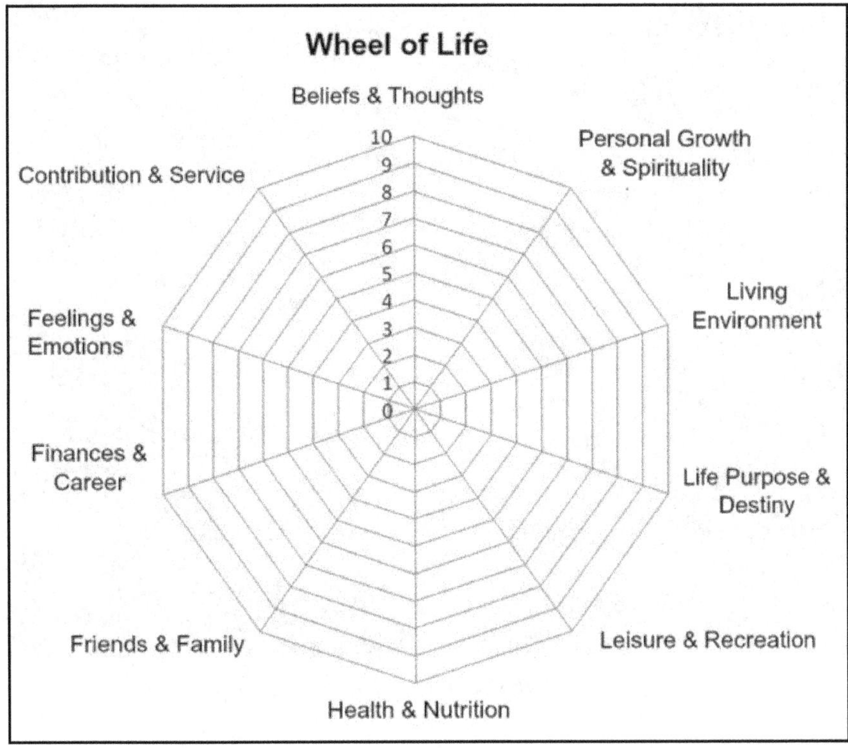

I sincerely believe you can use what I've shared in this section as tools for navigating the grand ocean of your life, charted or uncharted. As you unfold your highest destiny on earth, I hope you'll enjoy, love and appreciate each step of the way.

Lake Geneva, Switzerland

At Any Given Moment, We Have a Choice.

When you connect your deepest purpose with the goals you set, those goals will be achieved. When you understand that there is an accessible pathway to the most magnificent dreams you can dream, you'll get yourself on that path. When you are ready, life is here to fully live.

—Ralph Marston

We've come to the end of this book, and your journey of finding or living your purpose more fully has begun.

When I sat down and tried to find some appropriate words for this closing section, I was flooded with mind-chatter. I felt blocked, unable to write anything. I noticed that I wasn't connected to my heart space, nor was I connected to the present moment. I kept thinking about what I could write, or what I'd written about so far.

I decided to put my laptop away. I closed my eyes. I started listening to what I heard, both near and far. I smelled the fragrance of the air, and felt the gentle touch of the air on my skin. I suddenly became present, aware I was sitting outside on a balcony at our place in Kaua'i.

With my eyes still closed, I saw inner images of the many spiritual adventures I've shared with Eunjung and others for the past five years in thirty-five countries around the world. I also saw beautiful scenes of the magical island of Kaua'i. I realized I'd come full-circle, from my initial awakening in 2008 in Honolulu, Hawaii to finally making this paradise island, Kaua'i, my home. Waves of gratitude filled my whole being. I remembered why I wanted to write this book—to help others to find their home in their heart, by navigating this sacred journey called life while following their true passions and purpose.

Feeling immense gratitude, I opened my eyes. The first thing I noticed were the beautiful leaves of palm trees shining in the sunlight and swaying in the gentle breeze near the ocean. It reminded me of a Hawaiian legend about palm trees I'd read in an article called "Tree of Life" in *Hawaii Kaua'i Dining in Paradise 2016 - 2017*. I'd like to quote it here:

> *Another well-known legend recounts the story of a young Hawaiian boy, the son of Hina and Ku, the goddess of female spirits and the god of male spirits, respectively. After returning to his homeland of Tahiti, Ku is longed for by his son in Hawaii, who solicits the help of his mom. In*

response, Hina chants to their ancestor, the coconut tree, singing "niu-ola-hiki" (oh, life-giving coconut of Tahiti). She continues with "niu-loa-hiki" (oh, far-traveling coconut), when a coconut tree sprouts in front of her. She wakes her son and instructs him to climb the tree and hold on while she continues to chant. The coconut palm tree sways and bends, stretches and grows. It stretches over the ocean until its leaves rest on Tahiti, and son and dad are reunited.

There's so much powerful and inspiring symbolism in this beautiful legend. I was especially moved by how the father and son were reunited by the palm tree. In closing my book, I'd like to give you my own interpretation of this symbolism.

To me, the son represents you. The mother represents your intuition—divine guidance—while the father represents your true home and highest destiny. The coconut tree is your unique gift and purpose.

Even as life places obstacles before you and at times brings a storm, you can remain true to your purpose and grow your talents with flexibility and openness. Then, you'll reach and be united with your highest destiny.

I'd like to leave you with a helpful exercise. Draw yourself as a tree. A tree is a powerful symbol, and can reflect many facets of the many layers in your life. It's a great tool for self-insight and self-awareness.

This process will help you get in touch with your emotions and, through symbolism, can help you to explore your gifts, talents and strengths as well as the challenges and obstacles in your life. It may also help reduce anxiety, increase self-esteem, address stress symptoms and reveal parts of yourself that you're unaware of. Ultimately, it can help you fine-tune your life's purpose.

Find some paper and drawing materials. Create a peaceful setting, and play gentle, inspiring music. Make sure you won't be disturbed while you work on your drawing. Gift yourself with sufficient time for your drawing. One hour is good.

Take some time to become present and centered. Be aware of where you are on your life journey, and then start drawing a tree to represent it. Your creation can be any kind of tree that wants to represent you.

During the drawing session, think about the following questions:

- What elements of a tree do I know about?
- What season of the year do I want to represent in my drawing?
- Does the tree bear fruit or flowers?
- What do the branches and leaves of this tree look like?
- What does the tree's root system look like?
- How old is the tree? And how long will it be alive?
- Are there any animals, or people, living on or next to it?
- Is it a single tree, or is it part of a forest?
- Where is the tree located? At the border of a forest? Next to a lake or a beach? In a city park?
- What is the tree's contribution to this world?

Once you're done with the drawing, write down any insights you gained from the exercise. You can also show your drawing to a friend or family member you can trust. They may be able to give you additional insights and perspective.

And now, it's time to forge your own path. Where you place your focus is your choice. And the way you move your focus from now on will move your life experience.

It's also your choice as to how you work with the questions, ideas and strategies I've presented in this book. Stay committed to working with them and you'll realize that you and your life's purpose are being reunited, just like father and son in the Hawaiian legend.

We have a choice at any given moment. To quote Janet Bray Attwood and Chris Attwood, the authors of *The Passion Test:* "It's very simple. You either move toward what you're most passionate about, or farther away from your heart's deepest desires." Remember one more time what the master teacher and wisdom keeper, Pilipo, the wisdom keeper from Moloka'i (whom I met during my vision quest in 2011), said: *We can keep accumulating knowledge without acting on it, or let our wisdom flow into creating our ideal life.*

You can keep accumulating knowledge without acting on it, or let your wisdom flow into creating your ideal life.

Pilipo shared with me an ancient Hawaiian healing modality known as "*La'au Lapa'au,*" which he said can be translated as "curing medicine." Pilipo told me that *La'au* is all about how you connect yourself to spirit, and how you connect others with spirit. *Lapa* means the whole plant, and *'au* means to improve vitality and wellness. He highlighted that for *La'au Lapa'au* practitioners to take on such a responsibility, they must be willing to follow a healthy lifestyle and remember that the wisdom is already within for those being called to it. The practitioner must ultimately have a strong, deep-heart calling. Conversely, anyone a practitioner works with also needs to be dedicated to taking a lot of *Kuleana* or self-responsibility.

To me, Paul, the healer from the Big Island—who changed my life forever—had mastered and embodied the principles of *La'au Lapa'au.* This made him uniquely qualified to facilitate this profound process, which became the turning point for my rebirth to an entirely new life.

The essence of the teachings of *La'au Lapa'au* are at the heart of this book. I believe the questions, tools, techniques and steps I've shared are simple and easy to follow and when you use them, you will tap into a renewed vitality, improved wellness and a deep connection to spirit. However, shifting your life to realize more greatness and fulfillment takes commitment. It requires your inspired and focused action, and your patience, perseverance and self-responsibility.

My intention in writing this book has been to provide help and support as you find your life's purpose and ultimately fulfill your destiny. In the end, however, it is only you who can take the self-responsibility to follow through on what you know to be true.

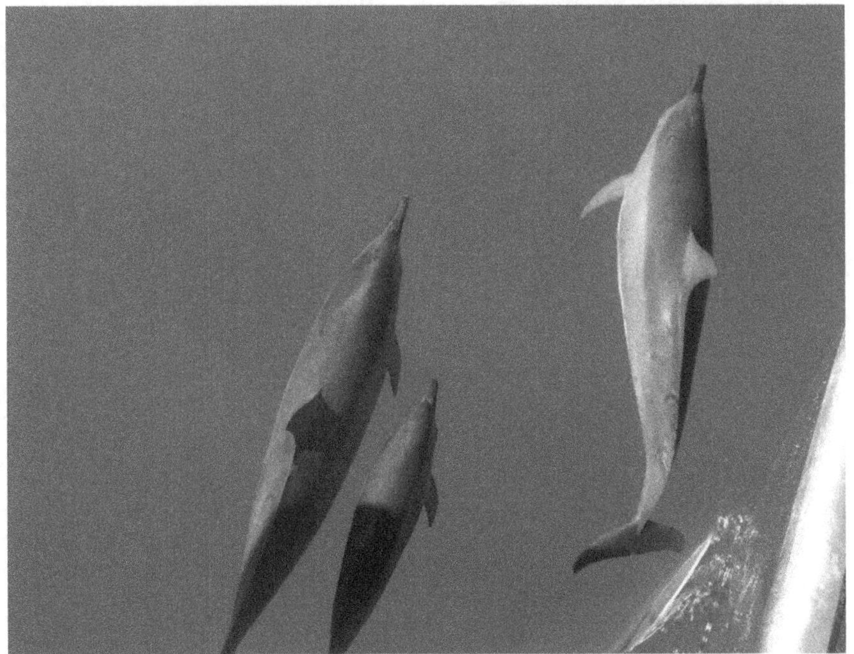

Na Pali Coast, Kaua'i

Rumi said: "How many paths are there to God? There are as many paths to God as there are souls on earth." Create your own map and follow your own path, and keep working with anything from this book which helps you. Put aside anything which does not work for you right now. You may return later to some sections or concepts that initially caused resistance, only to find out that they contain the message you need to hear. Ultimately you need to be true to your own realizations (not somebody else's) as you walk your path.

The path to your dreams is yours alone. My wish is that the hope, inspiration and love we share as we travel together on this journey of life will be an ever-expanding force within and all around us. I hope you'll keep improving your life and the lives of others. It's my hope that you will find your life's purpose, freeing you to make a unique and powerful contribution toward bridging heaven and earth.

Blessings...and Bon Voyage!

"The purpose of human life is to serve, and to show compassion and the will to help others."

—Albert Schweitzer

AFTERWORD

by Kiara Windrider

We have come to the end of a journey. If you have made your way to the end of this book you have come away with many valuable questions and tools which will provide you with the ability to add purpose and passion to your life.

But useful as these might be, the goal of a journey is never the destination itself. A journey finds its meaning in how deeply it allows you to look into the mirror of your own life in order to find the enduring reflection of your deepest Self.

Eventually we recognize that what we are truly looking for is not a collection of good stories, not even the grand inspirations and peak experiences that touch the soul, but the knowing of who we are as the Self. As long as we base our value on success and achievements there will always be the fear of failure or loss.

But once we come to an understanding of who we truly are, it matters not what successes we achieve or what experiences we gain. If I am not identified with the doer, there is no room for fear, and the infinite winds of life move freely and effortlessly through these vehicles of matter.

Discovering the Self is not difficult. It is not the end of a long, tortuous path but the very beginning. The Self pervades all things and is at the very root of our awareness, thoughts, and feelings. It is the very sense of being that exists before thought arises and remains in the midst of every thought. It is the consciousness that animates our body, the consciousness that inspires our thoughts and feelings, the same consciousness that fills the entire universe. Our journey begins with the self-evident truth that this is who we are.

What if there are not two fixed polarities of matter and spirit but one essential reality appearing as two? What if Creator and Creation are not two distinct things but one holographic entity within the fabric of consciousness? What if who we are is a single vibrational essence that flows equally through the stars and through the trees and through these human bodies and every subatomic string of quantum existence?

In letting go of the illusions of the separate self, we know ourselves as the One Self that moves through all things. Paradoxically, the emptier we become of human identifications and fears, the more fullness we can reflect. This is when we can be truly passionate about life, and fully in service to life.

I have known Yves and Eunjung for many years now, and joined with them in some of their journeys of life. I am touched by their sincerity and their passion, their dedication to service, their love for this Earth. I am touched by their fearlessness, their ability to move as the wind moves them, and to become the wind itself.

Thank you, Yves, for demonstrating the 'passion way,' for holding your candle through all the ups and downs of life, so that each of us might learn to trust the One Light that has always already been shining so brightly even through the darkest of nights.

AUTHOR NOTE:

Kiara Windrider was born in India. He is a psychotherapist, cosmic researcher and author of several books, including *Ilahinoor: Awakening the Divine Human*; *Gaia Luminous: Emergence of the New Earth*; *Homo Luminous: Manual for the Divine Human* and *Issa: Son of the Sun* (*www.kiarawindrider.net*). Kiara's books showcase his extraordinary ability to integrate, summarize and structure a vast range of topics, from deeply spiritual teachings to the latest discoveries in science related to this transitional time we are in, in an easy to understand and eloquent manner. I am honored and grateful to call Kiara a dear friend who has inspired and touched me both personally and professionally through his remarkable work over many years.

POSTSCRIPT

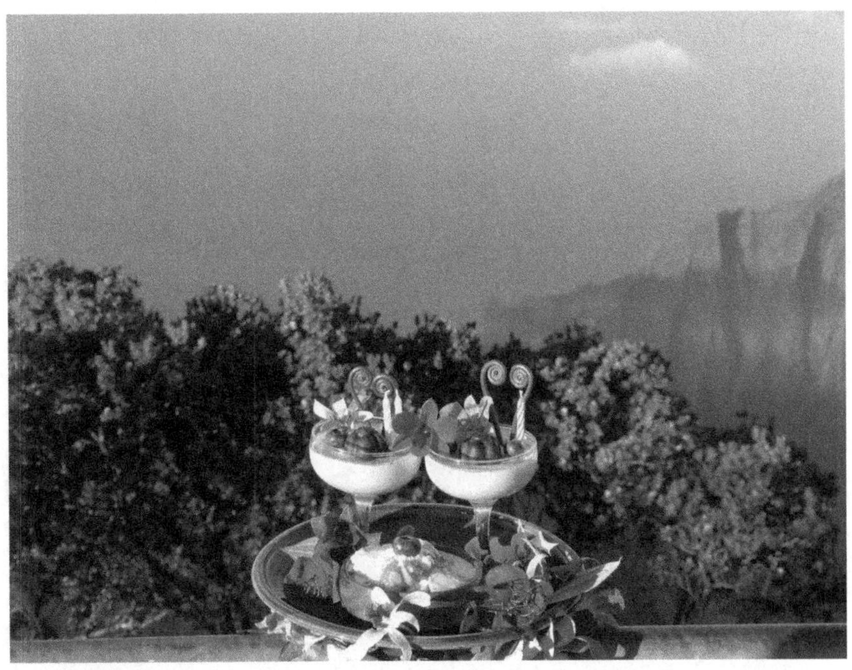

Kalalau Valley, Kaua'i

Are you feeling unsure about how, when and with whom you can take your next steps? It would be my pleasure to be here for you as you learn how to overcome obstacles in your life, discover your gifts, and shine your light. You can find many services and resources on my website. *www.YvesNager.com* Just a decade ago when my journey of realization and awakening started here in Hawaii, I didn't know what possibilities would emerge later in my journey. Through applying the steps and processes I have shared in this book, I was able to realize my life's purpose and transform my life. I'm inspired and delighted to work with you, and to guide you through your own journey of transformation. I want to help you discover the path that helps you to shine your light ever more brightly in the world. Aloha!

GLOSSARY

Abhinivesa	Fear
Advaita	One of the classic Indian paths to spiritual realization
Ahonui	Patience (waiting for the moment)
Akahai	Kindness (grace)
Akh	Luminous body of light
Akua	Source of origin
Asana	Yoga posture
Asmita	Identification
Avidya	Clouded perception
Canang Sari (Sesajen)	Tiny offerings in Bali
Chakra	Wheel (energy center)
Dharma	The path to meaning in your life
Dvesa	Refusing
Galactic Superwave	Cosmic ray bombardment
Ha'aha'a	Humility (empty)
Hala	Contemplation
Hanan Pacha	Upper World. Residence of higher selves
Hatha Yoga	A branch of Yoga
Havaiki	Polynesian name for a homeland

Heiau	Ancient Hawaiian temple
High Self	Super-conscious aspects of the mind
Hihia	Acceptance
Ho'o	Willingness to act differently
Ho'oponopono	Ancient Hawaiian forgiveness ritual
Holographic Merkaba	Vehicle of light
Huna	Hawaiian wisdom
Hypnagogic state	Threshold between sleep and wakefulness
Ida (Pedanda)	Balinese high priest(ess)
Ilahinoor	Divine light
Kahuna	Hawaiian priest or healer
Kay Pacha	Middle World. The world of the human selves
Ke Akua	Supreme Being, divine spirit
Khat	Physical body
Kukui	Light
Kuleana	Taking responsibility
Kupuna	Hawaiian elder
La'au Lapa'au	Curing medicine
Lokahi	Unity (unbroken)
Low Self	Subconscious and unconscious aspects of the mind
Mahalo	Thank you
Mana	Energy
Middle Self	Conscious aspects of the mind
Mihi	Mutual forgiveness
Neteru	Main gods in the Egyptian pantheon
Odalan	Balinese ceremony
Olu'olu	Agreeable (gentle)
Pono	Righteousness
Puka	Doorway
Pule	Prayer

Pura	Balinese temple
Raga	Desire
Sahu	Body of light (associated with the soul)
Schumann resonance	Base frequency of the earth
Sekhem	Power (might)
Shavasana	Relaxation pose in a yoga practice
Sufism	Mystical Islamic tradition
Supra-mental field	Consciousness higher than the human rational mind
Turiya	Pure consciousness
Ukhu Pacha	Lower World. World of subconscious instinct
Veda Lila	Play of Life
Vipassana	Insight into the true nature of reality
Vortex	A place in nature where natural energies are exceptionally alive
Yoga Nidra	Ancient practice of deep conscious relaxation

ABOUT THE AUTHOR

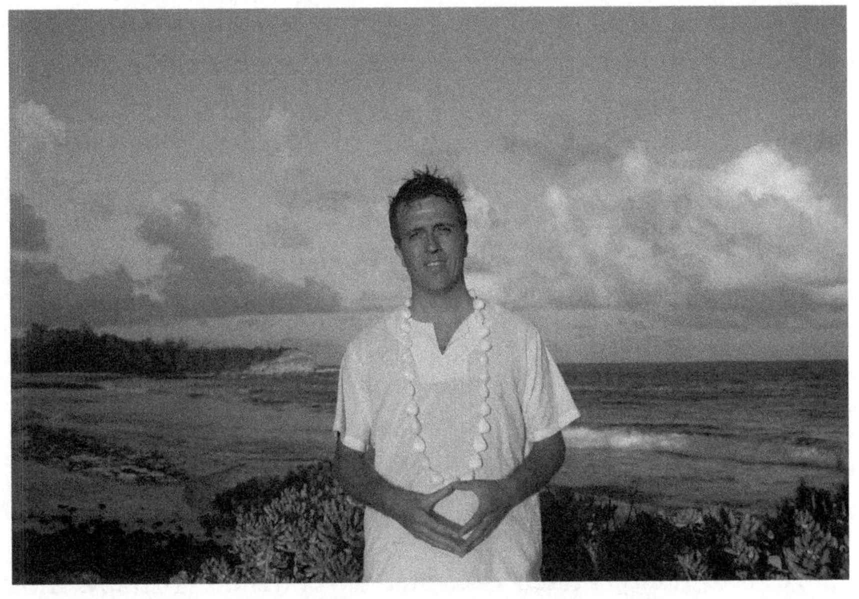

Shipwreck Beach, Kaua'i

Yves Nager is author of *Hawaiian Rebirth: Questions, Stories and Strategies to Guide You to Your Life's Purpose* and a co-author of the Amazon bestseller, *Inspired by the Passion Test*. He also contributed a chapter to the book *Ilahinoor – Awakening the Divine Human* by Kiara Windrider.

Yves is passionate about supporting people in transcending their limitations, creating new possibilities and transforming their challenges into freedom. Having overcome many life obstacles himself, he truly understands the power of forgiveness and gratitude. He believes that when we focus on the heart's desires and intentions, we can create miracles. Yves is dedicated to helping people discover their unique gifts and live a purposeful life with clarity, vitality, joy, love and abundance.

Yves, a Swiss native, grew up in the picturesque town of Spiez, Switzerland. After a decade-long career in the fields of human resources management, business consultancy, social work and insurance, he had a miraculous healing experience during his first visit to Hawaii in 2008. This healing miracle redirected the course of his life by propelling him to embark on a powerful journey of transformation.

After his return from Hawaii in 2008, Yves delved into spiritual practices such as meditation, yoga and self-inquiry and studied energy work. After realizing his life's purpose was to be in service to the evolution of humanity and the planet, he was guided to augment his offerings by studying life coaching at the holistic institute "Living Sense" in Switzerland. Utilizing his background as a Human Resources professional, he first focused on integral and business coaching and then continued with additional training and practice in the field of mental, emotional and spiritual coaching.

Through divine guidance, Yves was back in Kaua'i, Hawaii in 2011 to study Presence Centered Awareness Therapy. This awareness practice became an important pillar of his work. Right after completing this course, Yves had a destined encounter with his future wife, Eunjung, whom he married in South Korea in 2013.

While serving others through sessions and workshops with Eunjung, Yves continued to pursue teachings and training to strengthen his ability to serve others on their transformational paths. This passion led him to become a certified facilitator for the Passion Test and the Passion Test for Business, a certified Dream Coach, a global ambassador and lead trainer of the Discover the Gift program, as well as a Yoga Nidra teacher.

Inspired by a mission to assist with the global shift in consciousness, in April 2012, Yves and Eunjung embarked on a world-wide, five-year trip that took them to sacred power sites in thirty-five countries. Throughout their travels, Yves and Eunjung offered more than 150 workshops, webinars and sacred journeys for groups and individuals. During this time, they also learned wisdom from indigenous wisdom keepers, shamans, priestesses, monks and healers of various ancient traditions and assimilated this wisdom into their teachings.

Having settled on his favorite island on earth, Kaua'i, Hawaii, with Eunjung in 2017, Yves offers his services in healing and life coaching sessions to individuals and groups. He integrates energy work, hypnosis, elements of Hatha Yoga and Yoga Nidra as well as Presence Centered Awareness therapy into his work. He is passionate about taking care of animal friends and lends his healing gifts to beloved pets as part of his healing offerings.

In his coaching and mentoring, Yves utilizes tools and techniques he learned from his formal training in life coaching, The Passion Test and The Passion Test for Business as well as from other transformation-based programs. His personal spiritual practices and working with his clients has brought him deep spiritual insight and he incorporates this wisdom into his work.

Yves' offerings are highly unique. Due to his background in a corporate environment, he understands the business world. Because of his dedication to spiritual practices, he is well-versed in the spiritual aspects of healing and self-development. By helping you develop deeper awareness and appreciation of your core values and passions as well as guiding you to tap into your spiritual nature, Yves can empower you to follow a path with a heart.

Yves strives to continue his own learning and practice to provide you with maximum value and to be the best guide possible to help you live a life of purpose, joy and abundance. Through his keen awareness of the human energy field and his sensitivity to human emotions, he has learned to hold space in a way that makes his clients feel safe, loved and nurtured. Those who have experienced Yves' sessions or workshops have reported deep healing and transformation.

Are you ready to clear the barriers to your own greatness? Are you ready to follow your heart and live a life in which your dreams are aligned with your true calling? Yves is here to guide you on what can be the most meaningful adventure of your life—the discovery of your gifts and passions and discovering how to live your highest destiny. If you say "Yes!" to this invitation, please send Yves an email or call to find out how he can best serve you on your personal journey of transformation. *www.YvesNager.com*

RECOMMENDED READING

Please note that links provided may change over time.

Article about Emotions: *https://www.psychologytoday.com/articles/201501/beyond-happiness-the-upside-feeling-down*

Article about Forest Bathing: *http://qz.com/804022/health-benefits-japanese-forest-bathing/*

Changeology: 5 Steps to Realizing Your Goals and Resolutions - John C. Norcross (Simon & Schuster / ISBN 978-1-4516-5762-3)

Discover the Gift: It's Why We're Here – Shajen Joy Aziz and Demian Lichtenstein (Balboa Press / ISBN 978-1-5043-6444-7)

Dream: Clarify and Create What You Want – Marcia Wieder (Next Century Publishing / ISBN 978-1-68102-062-4)

Earth Chakras – Robert Coon (Coon Robert / ISBN 978-098056-294-1)

Gaia Luminous: Emergence of the New Earth – Kiara Windrider (Kima Global Publishers / ISBN 978-1-928234-21-0)

Hawaii Kauai Dining in Paradise 2016-2017, Tree of Life. https://issuu.com/morrismedianetwork/docs/hawaii_kauaidip_2016_12

Ho'oponopono: The Hawaiian Forgiveness Ritual as the Key to Your Life's Fulfillment – Emil Dupreé (Schirner Verlag / ISBN 978-1844095971)

Ilahinoor: Awakening the Divine Human – Kiara Windrider (Notion Press / ISBN 978-1-947137-87-5)

Inspired by The Passion Test: The #1 Tool for Discovering Your Passion and Purpose – Janet Bray Attwood and Geoff Affleck and fourteen other authors (Persona Publishing / ISBN 978-0-99858-231-3)

Life's Golden Ticket: A Story About Second Chances – Brendon Burchard (Harper Collins / ISBN 978-0-06245-647-2)

Loving What Is: Four Questions That Can Change Your Life – Byron Katie (Harmony Books / ISBN 978-1-40004-546-4)

Nazmy: *Love is my Religion – Egypt, Travel and A Quest for Peace* – Sharlyn Hidalgo (Phoenix Rising Publishing / ISBN 978-0-9911898-0-9)

Supreme Influence: Change Your Life with the Power of the Language You Use – Niurka (Harmony Books / ISBN 978-0-30795-687-3)

The Alchemist – Paulo Coelho (Harper Collins / ISBN 978-0-06-231500-7)

The I Ching: The Book of Answers – New Revised Edition – Wu Wei (Power Press / ISBN 0-943015-41-3)

The Five Love Languages: The Secret to Love that Lasts – Gary Chapman (Northfield Publishing / ISBN 978-0-8024-1270-6)

The Four Agreements: A Practical Guide to Personal Freedom – Don Miguel Ruiz (Amber-Allen Publishing / ISBN 978-1-878424-31-0)

The Four Desires: Creating a Life of Purpose, Happiness, Prosperity, and Freedom – Rod Stryker (Delacorte Press / ISBN 978-0-440-42328-7)

The Grace Factor: Opening the Door to Infinite Love – Alan Cohen (Alan Cohen Publications / ISBN 978-0-910367-03-5)

The Heart of Yoga: Developing a Personal Practice – T.K.V. Desikachar (Inner Traditions International / ISBN 978-1-59477-892-6)

The Lost Continent of Mu – James Churchward (Brotherhood of Life / ISBN 978-0-91473-219-8)

The Mastery of Love: A Practical Guide to the Art of Relationship – Don Miguel Ruiz (Amber-Allen Publishing / ISBN 978-1-934408-03-2)

The Passion Test: The Effortless Path to Discovering Your Life Purpose – Janet Attwood and Chris Attwood (Hudson Street Press / ISBN 978-1-1012-1382-7)

The Power of Now: A Guide to Spiritual Enlightenment – Eckhart Tolle (Namaste Publishing / ISBN 1-57731-480-8)

Your Hidden Riches: Unleashing the Power of Ritual to Create a Life of Meaning and Purpose – Janet Bray Attwood and Chris Attwood with Sylva Dvorak (Harmony Books / ISBN 978-0-385-34855-3)

Zero Limits: The Secret Hawaiian System for Wealth, Health, Peace, and More – Joe Vitale and Ihaleakala Hew Len (John Wiley & Sons / ISBN 978-0-470-4-0256-6)

RECOMMENDED LISTENING AND WATCHING

"Connection" – Miten – *https://www.youtube.com/watch?v=QMgGXzupuv8*

Discover the Gift (Movie) – *https://discoverthegift.com/the-movie/*

Inside Out – https://www.youtube.com/watch?v=seMwpP0yeu4

Rutherford, Mike. *https://en.wikipedia.org/wiki/The_Living_Years*

"The Living Years" – Mike + The Mechanics – *https://www.youtube.com/watch?v5hr64MxYpgk*

The Secret Life of Dogs – https://www.youtube.com/watch?v=CaWZEfx34Cg

RECOMMENDED WEBSITES

Canfield, Jack. *www.JackCanfield.com*

Cohen, Alan. *www.AlanCohen.com*

Dyer, Wayne. *www.WayneDyer.com*

Krishnamurti, Jiddu. *www.JKrishnamurti.org*

Marston, Ralph. *www.GreatDay.com*

Nager, Yves. *www.YvesNager.com*

Niurka. *www.NiurkaInc.com*

Pagnol, Marcel. *www.marcel-pagnol.com*

Robinson, Ken. *Ted Talk 2010. www.SirKenRobinson.com*

Rocky Mountain Orienteering Club. *www.rmoc.org*

Ryder, Lei'ohu. *https://www.LeiohuRyder.com*

Schuller, Robert. *https://www.brainyquote.com/quotes/robert_h_schuller_107582*

Schweitzer, Albert. *https://en.wikiquote.org/wiki/Talk:Albert_Schweitzer*

Solatorio, Pilipo. *http://HalawaVallyMolokai.com*

Stryker, Rod. *www.ParaYoga.com*

Wieder, Marcia. *https://DreamUniversity.com*

Wills, Howard. *www.HowardWills.com*

Windrider, Kiara. *www.KiaraWindrider.net*

www.AlohainAction.com

www.AsapEngagement.com

www.BeyulClub.com

www.brendon.com

www.ChangeologyBook.com

www.CrazyLoveStories.com

www.DiscoverTheGift.com

www.InspiredByThePassionTest.com

www.LanaiCatSanctuary.org

www.LifestyleEntrepreneursPress.com

www.PacsThailand.com

www.PsychologyToday.com

www.rmoc.org

www.SacredEarthVentures.com

www.ThePassionTest.com

www.TheWork.com

WORKS CITED LIST

Bray Attwood, Janet and Chris Attwood. *The Passion Test: The Effortless Path to Discovering Your Life Purpose*. New York: Penguin Group, 2008. Print.

Bray Attwood, Janet and Chris Attwood. *Your Hidden Riches: Unleashing the Power of Ritual to Create a Life of Meaning and Purpose*. New York: Crown Publishing, 2014. Print.

Hutchinson, Alaric. *Living Peace*. Queen Creek: Earth Spirit Publishing, 2014. Print.

Levinson, Steve. *Following Through: A Revolutionary New Model for Finishing Whatever You Start*. Nashville: Unlimited Publishing, 2007. Print.

Lichtenstein, Demian and Joy Aziz Shajen. *Discover the Gift: It's Why We're Here*. London: Ebury Publishing, 2011. Print.

Murphy, Joseph. *Think Yourself to Health, Wealth & Happiness: The Best of Dr. Joseph Murphy's Cosmic Wisdom*. New York: Reward Books, 2002. Print.

Rūmī, Jalāl ad-Dīn Muhammad. *The Rumi Collection*. Boston: Shambhala Publications, 1998. Print.

Ryder, Lei'ohu. *Wisdom Magazine,* 2009. *http://wisdom-magazine.com/Article.aspx/1167/*

Stryker, Rod. *The Four Desires: Creating a Life of Purpose, Happiness, Prosperity, and Freedom*. New York: Delacorte Press, 2011. Print.

Voltaire. *Philosophical Dictionary by Voltaire.* London: Penguin Group, 1979. Print.

Williamson, Marianne. *A Return to Love.* New York: Harper Collins Publishers, 1992. Print.

Windrider, Kiara. *Gaia Luminous: Emergence of the New Earth.* Clovelly: Kima Global Publishers, 2017. Print.

NOTES

❀ NOTES ❀

NOTES

NOTES

NOTES

CPSIA information can be obtained
at www.ICGtesting.com
Printed in the USA
LVHW05s1429220918
590862LV00003B/3/P

9 781946 697936